19w

Advocating Archives

An Introduction to Public Relations for Archivists

Elsie Freeman Finch, Editor

The Society of American Archivists
and
The Scarecrow Press, Inc.
Lanham, Md., & London

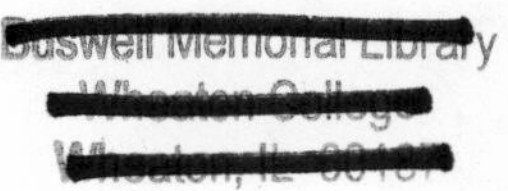

British Library Cataloguing-in-Publication data available

Library of Congress Cataloging-in-Publication Data

Advocating archives : an introduction to public relations for archivists / edited by Elsie Freeman Finch.
p. cm.
Includes bibliographical references and index.
ISBN 0-8108-2935-5
1. Public relations—Archives. I. Finch, Elsie Freeman.
CD971.A3 1994 94-3797
021.7—dc20

Manufactured in the United States of America

Printed on acid-free paper

Contents

Introduction

For many years I stumped the archival hustings to promote public outreach programs, talking with archivists individually and in groups wherever they were found about how to let the public know what their holdings were and how they might be used. A large part of my own career had consisted of managing public programs, and I saw their public appeal and their rewards. But during this time I sensed a lack of context expressed most clearly when archivists were unable to fit what we interchangeably called outreach, public programs, and educational programs into so-called core programs in any systematic way. They didn't have time, they said, they didn't have money, they didn't have skills, the backlog was always there, they didn't really understand why the public didn't know what was there. "Besides," I often heard, "I can't handle more users; I don't have enough staff, enough resources." But always there was a constant, contradictory threnody: "Where are they? Why don't they come in?"

That context became clear to me with the establishment in the 1980s of the Society of American Archivists' Task Force on Archives and Society, first led by David B. Gracy II and later James E. Fogerty. TFAS was established in part as a response to funding cuts, which were, still are and will continue to affect archives nationally. As I served on the task force I saw that outreach programs did not stand alone. Instead, they were part of a series of activities capable of being integrated into an entire program, activities that included fund raising, working with volunteers, establishing working relations with the media, marketing programs, and planning based on an awareness of how archives are seen by the public and how archival policy and practice can best be interpreted to the public—in other words, public relations.

Certainly engaging—or not engaging—in those activities affected funding, but in the longer and more important run, they affected use. The principle remains today: To the extent that the public understands that archives exist to be used for reasons that affect their lives, property, civic well-being, and political influence, the public will be disposed to support and encourage archives. Use, it became clear, was the heart of the matter. Use is our reason for being. And, if archives are properly explained and made reasonably accessible, they will be used and likely be funded.

But the assumption I had made, that archives were established to be used, was seldom clearly articulated. Today a few archivists, understanding that the structure of the words we use governs our actions, say it intentionally: We acquire, preserve, and maintain archives *so that they will be used* by anyone who seeks to use them, for whatever reason.

Using archives is not an easy task for actual or potential clients. Use must be intentionally and actively encouraged. That encouragement, based largely on our relations with our publics, is not an add-on to so-called core functions. If archives exist to be used, then all of the activities that encourage use comprise a core function that permeates everything we do, from the moment that we begin to cultivate a donor, contact an agency, or acquire a collection. How well it is done defines the archivist as clearly as do his/her descriptive systems, the size and quality of the collections, or the amount of funding the archives receives. That use is our fundamental purpose requiring intentional and active encouragement is the premise of this book.

Advocating Archives: An Introduction to Public Relations for Archivists is not intended to be a textbook on public relations, though we urge that it be used in the classroom. Many excellent textbooks on public relations are available and should be part of the archival curriculum. One of the best for our purposes is G. Donald Adams, *Museum Public Relations,* published in 1983 by the American Association for State and Local History, which provides, in addition to practical advice, an intellectual basis for the existence of public relations in cultural institutions. It, too, should be part of the library of every archivist. *Advocating Archives* is an archivist's guide to public relations, comprising a series of chapters, each discussing a function of public relations, written by experienced archivists for archivists. Several of the authors have special skills, including backgrounds in journalism, fund raising, public relations, program marketing, and advertising. Others are self-taught program developers. Together, their skills are probably typical of those found in any medium to large archival staff, if you, the archivist, take the time to investigate them.

You may want to read this book from beginning to end or read its chapters selectively, as you need them. To that end, we have supplied a list of readings at the end of each chapter that is germane to that chapter; titles overlap throughout the book. We have also supplied three studies in public relations that are intended to show how archivists, working in their daily bureaucracies, manage their public relations—warts and all. Not case studies in the formal sense, they are based on actual situations as interpreted by the participants. Instructors may want to develop case study methodology to apply to these interpretations, asking students to identify any management problems inherent in them and propose solutions, to draw public relations management principles from them, or otherwise use them in ways that will encourage proactive analysis and problem solving.

The concepts and policy recommendations in this book will apply to most archives and manuscript collections, whether housed in universities, museums, corporate, or governmental institutions. They are aimed at the archivist who is not a public relations professional, who will probably be self-taught in its skills, and who will in many instances be responsible for the organization's public relations. It should also be helpful to you, the archivist, even if your institution already has a public relations staff, since you must learn to focus that staff's attention on your public relations needs. At the least, the public relations staff is a public of the archives and must be taught about it. At best, public relations staff will work closely with archives personnel to develop programs. In either case, you must see how public relations professionals view their universe and know much of what they know so you can either direct or do your own public relations. A word on point of view: *Advocating Archives* emphasizes the public, daily uses of records, suggesting that archivists be more imaginative about how records can be used and more open to wide public use. This is not to disregard Andrea Hinding when she tells us that the work of archivists serves "a universal human need to connect among people and across time through acts of memory," nor James M. O'Toole when he discusses the "symbolic" aspects of making and keeping archives. Any archivist who has seen a crowd of children standing unexpectedly silent and absorbed in front of the Emancipation Proclamation, or lines of ordinary citizens stretching twice around the National Archives at 2 A.M. to see the Declaration of Independence knows that records have an evocative quality hard to identify but almost palpable. More than any lecture or essay on recreating the past, records reanimate it, allowing us to enter it, to see, hear, almost touch or smell a distant place or event. This capacity of records to connect, enlarge, and move us, to release the imagination, is perhaps the archivist's greatest ally in reaching for the public, but it is one that must be carefully and intentionally used. Too much emphasis on the historical treasure, the documentary heritage, the priceless past smacks of preciosity. Too little overlooks the power of documents to transform the moment.

This book has been funded by the Society of American Archivists, and any profits from it will be returned to the society. It began as a project of the SAA Committee on Public Information, an outgrowth of the Task Force on Archives and Society. James Fogerty was its first chair; subsequently I cochaired it with Karen Benedict, then Kathy Marquis. I am grateful to that committee for its encouragement, particularly to Fogerty, Marquis, and Julie Bressor. Bruce H. Bruemmer joined the committee, asking questions that first startled, then amused, then stimulated me. Susan Grigg, chair of the SAA Publications Committee, encouraged me to present a proposal, gave me practical advice, and was ever cheerful; Nancy Sahli guided the proposal through the committee. Anne Diffendal, then Executive Director of SAA, was both patient and encouraging, as was Anne Kenney, 1992-1993 president of SAA, whose energy, good humor, and intelligence helped me when mine flagged. Timothy Ericson, one of the contributors, also read Paul Conway's and my chapter, sparing me the indignities I had visited upon him as a writer. Teresa Brinati, SAA staff person, cheerfully and ably engineered it to publication.

I am particularly grateful to the writers themselves. With grace and good spirit, they allowed me to treat them like students in English 101, writing and rewriting and writing again on their own time. They were a pleasure to work with, and I thank them for their professionalism and their collegiality.

Finally, I thank Herbert Finch, whose skill, imagination, and leadership as archivist and colleague I observed and learned from for 30 years. When we were married in 1992, he provided a comfortable and happy home, complete with computer, in which to finish this manuscript, which has proved to be equally important.

Elsie Freeman Finch
Ithaca, New York

1

Talking to the Angel

Beginning Your Public Relations Program

Elsie Freeman Finch
Paul Conway

Archivists, together with all professionals who work with several publics, establish their public relations daily. Whether those relations are useful or harmful, sound or unsound, good or bad depends on how well the archivist understands the nature, purpose, and pervasiveness of public relations in an archival program. Let us begin with a statement of what constitutes good public relations, then examine some of the elements in a program that contribute to, or detract from, their quality. Good public relations requires that you assess public attitudes toward your institution, keeping them in mind as you make policy decisions; that you know how those decisions will affect public opinion; and that you choose the channels of communication that will make those decisions acceptable to your publics.

But there is a larger premise of public relations, one that supersedes all others: The public relations of an institution is no better than the quality of its management decisions and its service to the public. The decline and current regeneration of the American automotive industry is a tribute to this proposition, as well as to the adaptive capacities—learned painfully and at high cost to both management and employees over many years—of the industry itself. What do archivists learn from this? As a member of a profession that works directly with the public, providing information that public needs, the quality of service you provide affects not only the people you meet daily, but determines the nature of your relations—your public relations—with communities well beyond that circle. How does this happen?

Your archives has many publics. They include not only those who do research in your institution or seek substantive information from you or your holdings, but staff of the archives, volunteers, donors, resource allocators, members of the community in which your archives is located, and your own colleagues. These publics have at least two characteristics that are important to remember: They are interlocking and they are interchangeable. Among those who do research in your institution or get information from it are a number of publics that are constantly shifting. Think of these publics as forming concentric circles, beginning in the center with those patrons who actually use the records for research and those who write or call for information directly from the records. In the next larger circle are patrons who come to see the exhibit, attend the workshop, lecture, or film series, or who seek information from you, the archivist, based on your professional skills. These might include the man called on to be his church's volunteer archivist or the woman charged with setting up an historical society. In the next circle are those patrons who use the products of the archives, including, for example, the teacher who uses the learning package you have created or in whose classroom you present a document-based program, or the patron several counties away who reads the illustrated book you have produced that is based on a particularly compelling collection. In another circle are the cohorts of those who search the records, professional colleagues or friends unknown to you personally but representing potential users of the records. In a still larger circle are the donors of papers or staff of agencies from whom you acquire records. Next are your resource allocators. In another circle, hard to locate but influential, are your own colleagues in other institutions, whose view of you and your commitment to service affects you and the publics who use your resources in subtle and pervasive ways. In the largest circle are members of the community in which the archives is situated, who are aware of it but have not used it in any way. At best, this group views you as a cultural resource; at worst, they wonder why you are there.

What the public relations minded archivist knows is that at any instant, these publics can change roles. The donor of papers can become the researcher, as can the resource allocator, who may be a board member, the university comptroller, or a state or federal legislator. The exhibit viewer or film series attendee can see a clue to an unanswered family or hobby-related question and become the researcher. The researcher often becomes a donor and is a key to his/her own professional cohort, who comprise potential researchers. Each of these publics must be kept in mind as you serve any one of them, and each has high expectations relating to your probity, your education and professional training, and the quality of your service. Of these, the quality of service is the most tangible and visible, and that service, wherever any public finds it, either meets or fails to meet those expectations.

This chapter will focus on those patrons who actually use the records for research, but the message of service—good, indifferent, or bad—reaches all of our publics. It reaches them because word of mouth is the principal source of information about cultural institutions, including archives. It reaches them because our publics interchange roles regularly. When we were children, many of us were told that we would never know when we were talking to an angel. Today that whimsical instruction has metaphoric overtones for us as professionals. Today's researcher is tomorrow's board member; yesterday's exhibit viewer is today's donor. We send messages to all when we send them to one. The researcher in front of you may be your angel, for good or bad, depending on you and the policies of your institution.

We will discuss five elements of service: the archivist's professional stance, the physical and psychological environments archivists provide the researcher, the nature of records as the public views them, and what research tells us about the users of records. We draw on a small but significant group of studies of patrons carried out by archivists since the mid-1980s. Each study had a different purpose, but together they tell us much about our patrons that defies certain traditional views. They can inform our relations with our publics, helping us assess attitudes to be kept in mind as we develop policy and procedures and discover ways to let our publics know what those policies are.

A caveat: Understanding your publics—in this case, your research public—is only important if you plan to change policy and procedures with that information in mind or are willing to lobby for such change. The archivist who has a public relations orientation is also politically astute. He or she understands that information about users must be used to formulate—or change—policy. Without changes in policy and procedures, information about users—knowing their intent, their research habits, their expectations of our institutions—remains a curiosity. It is for this reason that public relations professionals opt either to be part of upper management or, at the very least, privy to management deliberations. Sensitivity to the needs of your publics—in this case, researchers—must reach all levels of your organization, beginning with your mission statement, legislation, or other terms of governance. The policy and procedures that result should pervade every function of the archives and each staff level. These are management functions either in your control or that of others. If you cannot mandate change, you must prepare to influence change. What you learn about users must be stitched into the managerial fabric of your archives; otherwise it serves no useful purpose. When it becomes policy, it conduces to good service and good public relations.

What are the five elements of service that are fundamental to good public relations?

You and Your Profession

Whatever your rank in your organization, your salary, or your level of experience, you are the linchpin upon which good service turns. Your job as an archivist is to acquire and care for records so that they will be used. Once you have accepted this responsibility, you join the ranks of a profession with a long tradition of responsible stewardship and service. Only in the past 50 years have archivists in the United States seen themselves as professionals separate from historians and librarians and, more recently, other information specialists; but the importance of keeping records of administrative, legal, financial, or historical significance spans centuries.

Since at least the fifth millennia B.C., kings, priests, and bankers have had records offices overseen by records keepers of high rank and social privilege. Biblical stories recount the use of Babylonian archives to authorize the building of the central temple in Jerusalem and the saving of important deeds of purchase in earthen jars. The concept of "recorded history," implying the preservation of physical evidence of human activity across generations, defines the boundaries of reliable human memory.

As a result of the French Revolution, archives became public in character rather than remaining, as they had in earlier centuries, the tool of the government. Records created prior to the revolution were opened for consultation, while current, active records remained in offices, for office use only. Thus began the separation between archivists, the keepers of historical records who worked with papers available to the public, and the keepers of current records, usually their creators.

This view prevailed in the United States, but it was adapted to a new social context. For more than 100 years after the founding of the new nation, the job of collecting, caring for, and interpreting the historical record was found at the local, rather than the national, level. Historians, many of them not formally trained, used local records to write accounts glorifying the past, justifying the present, and certifying an indisputably splendid future.

The debut in the late 19th century of the professional historian seeking a more objective, "scientific" assessment of the past exacerbated the distinction between those who cared for the historical record and those who interpreted it. As they came to view themselves as a profession, historians claimed the status of interpreters, relegating custodians of the records to the position of handmaidens who carried all of the responsibility of the revered local historian and none of the status. Archivists in the United States prolonged this painful separation by remaining within the shelter of the American Historical Association for more than three decades.

For archivists in the United States, their definition of themselves as professionals emerged largely because of three intersecting events in the mid-1930s. J. Franklin Jameson, an energetic, politically able historian who for much of his career worked outside the academy, lobbied vigorously for a national archives. He was successful, and the construction of the National Archives in 1935 was the visible symbol of public commitment to the professionalization of history, now including American history, and preservation of the records from which to write it. The second defining event was the establishment of the Historical Documents Survey, carried out from 1935 to 1940 under the

Works Progress Administration, which dramatized the need for governments at all levels to identify, preserve, and encourage the use of the country's documentary resources. Finally, the formation of the Society of American Archivists in 1936 gave members of this emerging profession a forum to develop a set of unique strategies and procedures for creating full-scale acquisition and preservation programs. Together these three events pushed a small group of self-styled archivists toward a professional course separate from that of historians and librarians. Although archivists debated for many years the quality of that professionalism, today there is little doubt that the historically important role of the archivist lives on in the 20th century. Today, several elements define your professional stance.

Training

Effective public relations is linked closely to the public's sense of the range and quality of the archivist's education and professional training. Significant to our growing sense of the archivist as professional have been questions about the proper academic education and professional training of the archivist, focusing both on where it should take place and what it should include. Still a question of intense argument, personal interchange, and shifting standards, the undergraduate education of the archivist causes less debate than does graduate or professional training. Both formal and market requirements have changed, and will continue to do so. As an archivist today, you may well find graduate academic work in fields other than history useful to you, depending on the nature of your work, the requirements of a given institution, the state of the market, or your career expectations. Over the past ten years, job placement advertisements have increasingly required advanced degrees that include archives management training, programs now found in history and library degree programs.

Whatever questions there are among archivists about preappointment education and training, one fact is indisputable: To provide the best service to your clientele, you must continue your training, wherever you find it. Among the sources of this training are venues provided by national, regional, and local professional organizations, not only in archives but in the library and information fields. In addition to programs offered by the Society of American Archivists, do not overlook programs offered by the American Association for State and Local History, the American Museum Association, the American Library Association, records managers associations, and, in particular, programs offered by information specialists serving all information fields, including archives. As your skills mature and you develop specialties, you will produce papers, give workshops, and publish for the profession, which are good learning tools for you as well as your colleagues.

But because you are a manager of an archives as well as a professional, you must also seek out management training. You will want to consider not only work in personnel management, planning, and budgeting, offered in occasional programs and workshops by the Society of American Archivists and regional associations, but also in broader fields, such as communications, organizational behavior, and training in leadership and strategic planning. Consider, for example, courses offered by any of the highly skilled private management training services that come to your area once or twice a year, or those offered by local universities or businesses. Depending on their needs, some archivists also take very practical training in publication design, exhibit planning, or community relations. Together, this kind of learning helps you reach beyond the bounds of traditional archival work, honing your planning, judgmental, and interpersonal skills.

But you don't carry public relations alone. The technical and support staff of the archives is often on the front line, meeting and serving the public. Indeed, no archives is large enough to ignore the public function of staff; everyone reaches the public, whether directly or through other staff. Unfortunately, the bureaucracies in which we operate often create a them-and-us attitude between support staff and professionals or between all staff and management, an attitude that is invariably harmful not only to the productivity of the people involved but, inevitably, good public relations. Studies of U.S. companies that excel repeatedly make clear that staff must be trained, then brought into the planning and implementation of procedures in ways in which they can invest. Experiments based on Scandinavian factory methods, which organize workers into small production units or task forces responsible for their own governance and work product, are equally persuasive. This means that staff must be part of what is going on in the archives, whether this includes new initiatives, new procedures, or new or changed policies that affect the public. The factory mentality typical of many archives—and many other business and cultural institutions—is dangerous to both personal and public health. As a manager, you are responsible for staff training, whether on a one-to-one basis, in small group sessions, or through outside trainers. However you choose to train and engage staff, remember you are doing it to serve better the publics on whom you all depend.

Your Relations with Researchers

Studies suggest that researchers have high expectations of our service, even when they are unclear about our status as professionals. It is difficult to trace the roots of this ambiguity, but we can assume that not only the way we deliver service but also the messages we send in our appearance and demeanor are part of it. These messages do more than condition the researcher's view of you. They tell the researcher what you expect of him or her. You have control over these messages, beginning with visual and behavioral clues.

Your Appearance

Although the "dress for success" vogue of the 1980s was both overzealous and misdirected, it made clear the critical role of appearance in establishing rules of behavior between people. Consider, for example, what a laboratory coat tells you about how you will behave toward the conservator or chemist, or how a uniform instructs your behavior toward authority, even when that uniform is a pinstripe. In general, dress like the person with whom you most want to be a colleague, not a servant or a superior. Peers attract peers. If you want a collegial relation with users—a partnership, not a superior-inferior relation, either way—dress like the best of them. If you are dealing with upper management, a resource allocator, or a donor, dress accordingly. Nothing is prescriptive; circumstance is everything. Just remember that the way you dress tells your client a great deal about you and what you expect from the client.

One of the simplest, cheapest, and most frequently overlooked techniques for establishing a professional presence in the workplace, one that also welcomes the public, is to wear a name tag. The name tag identifies you as a representative of your institution, a provider of service. Careful use of your name and title, if it is instructive, or your function, strongly influences how patrons perceive you. Technical and support staff should also be supplied with name tags indicating their organizational connection.

You also control your behavior, which sends even stronger messages.

Eye Contact

Establishing and keeping eye contact with the person with whom you are speaking or working is one of the most effective ways to control the situation. Consistent eye contact sends a message of confidence and self-control. It sets the tone for the transaction. It also tells the researcher what you expect of him or her: confidence and professionalism, a sharing of information, and combined effort toward solving a problem. We are equals, it says, and we are both working on solving a problem. There is work to be done, and we are both going to do it.

Listening

Many archivists are a great deal better at giving information than listening to it. To learn about user needs and perceptions, you must listen actively. You must be aware not only of words but also of the situation, attitudes, and feelings behind the words that govern the user's perception of you and his or her own research competence.

A researcher's question is not simply a matter of fact; it is the sum of fact plus expectation and self-confidence. It reveals confusion and embarrassment as often as focus and strength of purpose. Once you learn to listen to these unexpressed elements, you learn the real questions. Any sentient adult is capable of hearing these unexpressed elements. Archivists hear them all the time, but may not acknowledge them. The basic rule is: Don't begin to formulate a response until you are sure the user has finished speaking. Hear the speaker out, evaluate, then respond. In the end, you will save a great deal of time and contribute to your institution's public relations.

Your Speaking Style

How you speak to a user is part and parcel of how you hear him or her. Ask many more questions and give fewer answers. Speak directly to the patron and repeat the inquiry if you have the slightest question about what is meant. Repeat the question or ask it in reworded fashion, even if you think you know what is needed. You will find that the response is never yes or no; it almost always expands the inquiry. Finally, when you have supplied information, ask this simple question: "Does this answer your question completely?" Studies have shown that these simple no-cost techniques improve accuracy of service and patron satisfaction.

Personal Space

Students of communication tell us that 18 inches is the recommended distance in our society between client and professional. If you are unpersuaded by this, consider the use of *overbearing,* a word with clear metaphoric overtones. The closer you come to a person, the more you are seeking to control the situation, either positively or adversely. In a professional situation, keep your distance and require that the patron keep his or hers. Thus you indicate mutual responsibility for the research problem, not a superior-inferior relation. At best, understand that space—close or distant—defines relationships and can be used to change the archivist-user relation.

We have talked about user-archivist relationships. Let's consider three models and the messages delivered by each of these styles.

Model 1: Archivist as Servant

Researcher Jones walks in the door, approaching you in a state of mild anxiety. She pleads a shortage of time and ignorance of your procedures, though her question is of the why and how variety, not simply what or when. Rather than requiring her to learn what she should know about your institution and holdings, your demeanor says "I'll do the work for you." Through her dance of demands and desires, she comes to expect that you will work quickly to produce the information she needs at no intellectual cost to her. You have put yourself in a subservient role masquerading as one of good service.

We see this historic view of the archivist as handmaiden to history in many guises. For example, an article in a local newspaper recently marveled at the ease with which an archivist was able to serve up sophisticated documents on a political campaign with no effort on the reporter's part. It is quite possible that in this case, the role of handmaiden was well chosen. In general, however, it is a disservice to researchers and detrimental to your professional stance to provide information on demand rather than teaching the user how to find it. At the outset, teaching takes more time than serving up; over time, it is the best choice.

Model 2: Archivist as Gatekeeper

Researcher Smith explains his research topic to you during an orientation interview. You do not explain the research process; you tell Smith how complicated it is. You probe and reformulate Smith's question for him so that the records you have appear to address the topic. You tell him where to start and offer continuing assistance as his research unfolds, keeping him and his access to "your" records on the shortest possible string. By making yourself indispensable to Smith, you deny him the independence he might want, putting yourself in a superior role that pretends to be good service.

In the gatekeeper role, the archivist either opens doors or keeps them firmly shut. From the aspect of good public relations, this stance tells the user that he/she is a dependent, even a penitent, at the door of knowledge. Given the assumption of Americans that they have a right to information, the gatekeeper role is unacceptable, except in very limited situations. Occasionally it is the archivist's role to be gatekeeper, as, for example, when protecting national security information or matters of personal privacy. But typically it is the archivist's job to make material as readily accessible to users as its contents and condition allow. To be gatekeeper indefinitely not only distorts the function and tires the archivist but denies the researcher the opportunity to learn. Your job as a professional is to maintain balance, to decide when the contents of records requires the gatekeeper and when it does not. Keep in mind that from the aspect of good service and good public relations, the gatekeeper is a throwback to a time when information was limited to the elite and knowledge was seen as the property of a few. In the twentieth century, when information is available from multiple sources, gatekeeping is anachronistic, and the archivist who consistently practices it is an anachronism.

Model 3: Archivist as Partner

Researcher Johnson has done occasional work in the records. She seems to know what information she needs but is not always familiar with the complex arrangement of large record groups. She comes to you for advice, and you interpret her request to mean that she wants strategies for making efficient use of the time she has available. You explain the organization of the records, suggesting related record groups in which she might work, points of intersection in the records of which you are aware, and related records in other institutions. You suggest several starting points, depending on her specific interests, and talk with her occasionally about changes in the strategy. You let her seek you out, but you are open to her questions.

In this role, the archivist seeks to give the user a sense of self-sufficiency, emphasizing separate but mutually useful skills. That is, the archivist understands the organization, relation, and location of records; the user understands the nature of the problem. The archivist is partner in research, seeking to tailor the level of service to the user's needs while empowering the user to solve the historical problem.

In reality, your interactions with users should be a rich combination of these roles, favoring the latter role but fitting the occasion. The archivist who views his or her central responsibility to be teaching the patron to function as efficiently and independently as possible leaves that patron with an impression of quality that reaches well beyond the door of the archives. A study of librarians and patrons done by anthropologists in 1976 concluded that when patrons expressed dissatisfaction with the quality of the help they received, both librarians and patrons agreed that no instruction in research skills had taken place. Extending this conclusion to the world of archival research argues strongly that you help patrons more effectively when you consciously cultivate the role of teacher as opposed to that of a passive, impersonal information source. It suggests the teacher as partner, not as a source of information or censor.

Understanding that you have control over the visual and behavioral messages you send the user—through your appearance, eye contact, listening skills, space, and style of speaking—is knowledge that can be put to immediate use. Doing so enables you to enhance the quality of your relationship with the user; it is not only an invaluable reference skill, but a sign of your professionalism and capacity to provide good service. Using this information ethically and effectively is also a necessary element in developing good public relations.

Physical Environment

Researchers who spend time in an archives have a right to an environment that is physically comfortable, aesthetically pleasant and conducive to good work. From a public relations view, the built environment and the way it is maintained is rich in sensory clues that tell visitors about the nature of the place they are in. Admittedly, as an archivist you do not always have control over the architecture or maintenance of the building in which your patrons work, but if you are aware of the messages that the environment sends to patrons and its impact on public relations, you begin to plan changes. Let's look at four hypothetical physical environments and the messages they carry, understanding that they represent a combination of archives we have all seen.

1. A major university archives is situated in a building separate from the library, on the outskirts of the campus. Entry to the building is through a dark, poorly lit hallway with casually handwritten directional signs. Inside the archives, tables are covered with stacks of unboxed records; work areas are intermingled. Service, however, is sophisticated, attentive, and personalized. The message is: Here is a competent but managerially ineffective staff, unable to control their physical environment or influence the administration; archaism, virtue without strength, the kind of physical environment that encourages the media in such words as *musty*, *jumbled*, and *buried*.

2. A large county historical society loses its lease and moves into a commercial building that is undistinguished architecturally and historically. All resources—exhibit areas, archives, museum shop—are on the main floor, with loading, processing, and other nonpublic functions in the lower level. Initial signage is simple but clear, including those indicating restrooms and other public facilities. Historic pictures are hastily mounted with captions nearby, saying "We start here." The museum shop immediately mounts a sale, and an open house includes unpacked boxes. The message is: It isn't beautiful, but it's a start. We are here to help you; come and help us.

3. The corporate founder of a large and successful chain of pizza restaurants is a devotee of Frank Lloyd Wright architecture, classic sports cars, and baseball. Corporate headquarters reflects these historical interests, as does the archives. Located inside the main entrance to the building, the archives displays an eclectic mix of baseball memorabilia, historic pizza boxes and rare Deusenburg models. The message is: The archives is central to the corporate culture, both because of its physical location and its reflection of the interests of the founder. It also reflects the public stance of the companies under the corporate umbrella. It will be a pleasure to work here.

4. A state archives builds a large, imposing building on the campus of a major university. Its facade rises several stories above the campus, with an imposing surface of brilliantly covered archives boxes greeting the visitor at the entrance. Inside the door, the user crosses a marble space half the size of a football field before reaching a staff person. The message is: Elitism, exclusivity, the need for power. This is a place that barely tolerates the genealogist or other avocational researcher, for example.

Although you seldom completely control your own space, within your physical limitations, you the archivist can send an intentional, conscious message to users that your archives is accessible, comfortable, and current. More importantly, you can persuade upper management that physical environment counts; it sends a message about your archives, how you welcome users, and how you want to be perceived.

Here is a suggested checklist to be used as you plan changes.

Location

Remember the three important elements of real estate sales: location, location, and location. Ideally, a research room is located near the main entrance to the building or adjacent to other vital information sources. This location tells the visitor that the archives is central to management and to the institution. On the other hand, a research room in the basement, near the mechanical room, can send the message that the archives is peripheral to the organization.

There are alternatives. The writer once ran an archives located on the third floor of a major university library, somewhat remote from library activity. Though the location was not prime, the space was open and naturally lit. We created signs that clearly marked the path to the department, then put researchers in bright, open spaces that were pleasantly and comfortably arranged. The principle is a simple one: Do what you can to overcome disadvantages in location or space, and emphasize advantages.

Directional Signs

The most frequently asked question in any public institution is not "How do I conduct research?" but "Where is the restroom?" Public facilities should be clearly marked and directional signs frequent. All signage should be uniformly designed and, if possible, professionally made. Where it is needed, the master building directory should show the location of the archives, as should elevator directories and building maps. Good signage can be a temporary antidote to poor location.

Name

Don't assume that visitors know what an archives is. Consider other terms such as "historical collections," "records repository," or "research collections."

Entry

Glass doors suggest accessibility; solid doors suggest secrecy, mystery, or security. Prefer the former, or an architectural illusion that conveys a message of openness.

Appearance

An orderly, clean research room is a happy room. It promotes security because material has its place and is unlikely to be lost, and conduces to serious work.

Records Security

If your institution requires a security checkpoint, place guards so that they appear to be monitors, not barriers. Consider carefully whether guards with firearms are necessary in an institution where theft or damage to archival material almost never leads to violence. Ask yourself whether guards dressed in blue blazers and grey skirts or trousers, for example, are not just as efficient as those in police serge. At the least, give careful thought to the level and obtrusiveness of security measures.

Patron Security

Users also need security for their possessions and their persons. If you do not allow bags, large purses, or briefcases in the research room, provide lockers or other safe places for them. See that comfort facilities—restrooms and cafeterias—are accessible through well-lit corridors and open passages. Although the safety of elevators is regulated by local government, be alert to complaints of disorder or sudden change. Have an emergency evacuation plan and a plan in the event that a patron behaves improperly, and be sure that staff knows how to implement each. Be sure that your medical unit is open to users as well as staff. Consider security from the user's point of view: Is the patron, as well as the records, safe in my archives?

Furniture and Study Facilities

Some patrons are content to work at open tables; others want carrels. Study styles differ; if you can, accommodate these. Sit in any chair you plan to order for users for several minutes, to decide whether you would like to sit in it for several hours; work for an hour or so at any table.

Equipment and Maintenance

Assume that the number of patrons using their own computers will increase geometrically within the next few years; provide adequate space and facilities for them. Similarly, plan for public terminals and computers to access data bases, printers, typewriters, telephones, audiovisual equipment, and maintenance of all of these. This means staff to replenish toner, supply ink and paper, for example.

Finding Aids and Bibliographic Tools

The independent researcher moves continually back and forth between the records and the finding aids or the records and library tools. Be sure these are conveniently located and that assistance is available from a trained staff. As a step toward this, some institutions are now training archivists, librarians, and museum curators to provide comprehensive reference service at the outset, discussing with the user all formats in the institution's holdings that may contain suitable information. This avoids the fragmentation inherent in discussing library formats, followed by record formats, followed by artifactual holdings, or moving the researcher from station to station to repeat his/her story to each new reference person. And in an era of digitization, format is an increasingly obsolete system both for storing and retrieving information.

Lighting

The light level of the archives, beginning at the doorway and proceeding to the research room, is one of the most telling clues to an archives' accessibility. The low light levels recommended for records storage areas are wrong for entrances, reading rooms, and other public spaces. If the architectural aesthetics of your research room calls for dim, discreet lighting, equip each worktable with individual reading lamps. In short, do not extend preservation lighting levels to public places. Public places should be well and cheerfully lit.

Temperature

Heat and humidity levels that are good for records are not necessarily good for people. Keep the records cool; keep the patrons comfortable. Ideally, research room temperatures should be in the very low 70s, with 50 percent relative humidity.

Sound Levels

Researchers vary in their need for quiet as they work. Some object to any disturbance; others thrive in an environment where they can discuss their discoveries and meet users with similar interests. Generally, a vibrant, busy research room is more inviting than one wrapped in monastic silence. If you can, place researchers with different needs for quiet in separate parts of the research room, even if this complicates service and security requirements. At its best, your research room will be large enough to accommodate users who want quiet as well as those who want to talk discretely with their colleagues and staff.

Physical Access

We are all handicapped in some way: You wear glasses, another wears a hearing aid, one is too tall to fit the chairs, another too short to touch the floor. Physical access is more than wheelchair ramps. It includes—for all of us—nearby parking, wide and easily opened doors, elevators for operations on several floors, uncluttered lobbies and corridors, and, if possible, signers and self-help equipment.

In making the case to administrators for improvements in physical space, think of the archives as a learning laboratory worth the space and equipment of a science laboratory. In a university environment or corporate research and development unit, research scientists require equipment and resources to support creative inquiry, otherwise a comprehensive and product-oriented program would not grow. Similarly, medical schools are judged on their capacity to provide a well-equipped physical environment conducive to learning the practice of medicine. Archives need parallel amenities, because their products will adorn not only general knowledge but the institution in which it takes place.

Psychological Environment

Few archivists would disagree that use of an archives should be free of economic, sociological, or ideologically biased prejudices, but any of us would also admit that in too many archives, some users are seen as more equal than others. Let's consider three categories of users and the public relations implications of their treatment.

Typically, genealogists have been seen as the meat and potatoes of archives and academics—"scholars"—as the pâté. Certainly archivists identify more readily with academics than with avocational users, who include many more than genealogists. Later in this chapter we will discuss the misinformation inherent in classifying users solely by what we will call occupational category, such as "genealogist." For the moment, we can remember that in a democracy, access to information is not only a right but a necessity. For the genealogist, the answer to the question we all ask, "Who am I?" is answered by tracing one's family through public records, and my family is, by virtue of having survived, equal to yours, whatever its origin.

Numerous, well-organized, accessible, and forceful, genealogists can be quickly reached when advocacy is needed. Often comfortably situated, with a background of professional and community commitment and often with leisure time, they comprise a potentially influential group that an institution may seek to enlist in its support. The National Archives, for example, traces much of the success of its independence movement to the lobbying of genealogical organizations. Archivists who acknowledge genealogists' right to information and understand their enthusiasm for their research and their loyalty to archives have correctly sought to make their work easier. Popular means include providing orientation films, workshops, and seminars to guide them through the records and connect them with other researchers, and other public programs in which they can share their findings and discover new sources. In return, genealogists have been outspoken, active, and effective supporters of archives. With respect to public relations, there can hardly be a fairer exchange.

A second group likely to be treated less equally is what we will call the "general researcher": the private citizen who wants a set of photographs to adorn a historic building, the representative of the neighborhood business association seeking photographs for a calendar, or the club person seeking information for an informal history. The astute archivist knows that these users carry the message of service—or lack of it—to a public difficult to reach, made up of members of the patron's own cohort and the patron's public, who use the product.

Serving general researchers well is the most economical form of public relations. It requires only good reference and consultative service to reach a public too large for the archivist to reach independently. Studies over the past 20 years tell us that this kind of user makes up as much as 50 percent of our research public, though he/she is seldom well identified. It follows that one incident of poor or condescending service gets wider publicity than many instances of good service. Thus the consequences of bad service can seriously damage a large potential for use.

A third category of user, whose numbers and influence will increase dramatically in the next several years, comprises those who use computers and computer networks. These researchers do far more than bring laptops instead of typewriters to your research room. No longer working in isolation encumbered by tedium, they are part of research and communication networks, both informal and organized, that speed the search for information dramatically and are changing the form, nature, and breadth of research inquiries. Archivists who plan to stay in touch with these changes need not only current equipment but also inquiring minds, since good relations with technologically alert users depends on our knowledge of how their research inquiries and methods will change. Conversely, archivists will spend increasing amounts of time teaching researchers who are not computer literate to use the systems we are now installing and adapting those systems to researchers' requirements. Indeed, the teaching function of archivists that now requires us to show researchers how to use our manual systems will enlarge to include the archivist and the researcher learning from each other about research technology.

The Records

Archivists have control over certain characteristics of records that can limit or advance access to them.

Physical Condition

Preservation of the records is a good illustration of a basic archival practice that affects public relations. Nothing limits access so much as fragile, unrepaired, or disorganized records that affect not only the researcher's work but also his/her impression of the archivist's skills and the archives' dedication to the record. There is no archives so small or understaffed that time cannot be spent on basic preservation techniques: flattening, refoldering, labeling, boxing, and maintaining order. Probably no other basic archival function converges so visibly with good or bad public relations.

Just as important is a long-range preservation plan and an archivist willing to explain to patrons that, for example, processing is a progression and that the collection he or she may need is in the early stages of conservation. Without a basic preservation plan, the concept of archives public relations becomes moot, since the holdings are unusable or about to become so.

Description

Studies from the 1980s show us that traditional descriptions, even those we distribute to other libraries and archives, seldom bring users into the archives. They are useful to us in many ways, but they seldom enlarge the numbers or kinds of users. But *description* is an expandable term. It can include, for example, printed brochures that group apparently unrelated collections for transportation enthusiasts or other avocationists, newspaper and newsletter articles, or exhibits. If you have both use and good public relations in mind as you plan your descriptive program, you will develop a range of these less classic, very useful "descriptions" for every collection or group of collections in your holdings, ranging from broad-based popular articles to more specialized pieces for specific publics, depending on your analysis of the potential uses and users of the collections. Perhaps a good archival rule of thumb is to ask yourself the question, "When I describe it traditionally, how can I describe it popularly?" In this way, another traditional archival function becomes a public relations function.

Studies also suggest that users of records want to work as independently as possible. Although there is little if any research on just how researchers use descriptions once they have come to the archives, we know from library literature that convenience counts. We can therefore assume that the goal of all description should be ease of use by the researcher, requiring minimal intervention by the archivist. Traditional archival description still comes in many forms, ranging from local card catalogs to regionally accessed databases, from calendars and checklists to sophisticated computer-accessed inventories or registers. Whatever their form, you should have descriptions readily available to the researcher, physically situated where he/she can find and use them interchangeably, and intellectually constructed so that they suggest research strategies to the researcher, not simply provide a numbered list of boxes.

Restrictions

Restrictions are by definition a limitation on access, and although necessary, they have public relations implications as well. Problems can arise if restrictions are capricious or not well explained to users. Archivists who work with governmental or institutional records restrict records for privacy, security, or other legitimate reasons. Archivists who work with personal papers must also understand the impact of donor and third-party needs for privacy. Archivists seek to open records and limit restrictions as much as possible. The nature of your archives' restrictions on records should be part of a written policy that can be seen by the user upon request. Similarly, you must be able to show and explain to the user his/her recourses, doing so with an attitude of helpfulness, not obstruction, as a colleague seeking a balance between the interest of the creators of the records and the researcher, not as a gatekeeper.

Uses of Records

Traditionally we categorize the users of records in terms of the purpose of their research, i.e., genealogical research, historical research, and the like, a custom we will hereafter refer to as definition by "occupational" categories. From a public relations view (and possibly also from the aspect of managing records), this tradition does not serve us well. First, defining use by occupational categories tells us almost nothing specific about the results of research, which may bear little relation to the occupational category itself and therefore misleads about why and even how that research is being done. Secondly, in explaining the function of an archives to the public, be aware that your listeners are seldom interested in possibilities; they are interested in results. One is reminded of the story of the successful storekeeper who was asked why his customers bought quarter-inch drill bits. "They don't buy quarter-inch bits," he replied. "They buy quarter-inch holes." The public relations minded archivist understands that people in our market-oriented culture are far less interested in knowing what an archives contains—and even less what archivists do—than they are in learning about the products created by research and how these products help them.

In thinking of our users as primarily historians or administrators or genealogists, rather than thinking of the products of their work, we have created categories that conceal products and therefore deny us public relations opportunities. In a section following, we will expand on this proposition. Just now, let's consider some of the general uses of archives, exclusive of the names we give to those who use them. None has ever said this as well as the staff of the New York State Archives, whose 1984 publication, *Toward a Usable Past,* was published as a report to the governor and citizens of the state. In addition to the more abstract uses of records related to the documentary heritage and the advancement of scholarly knowledge, the writers list nine practical uses of records that help expand our sense of the significance of records and the service to which they are put—the products created from them—in our society. These practical uses—and the publics who benefit from these uses—are worth remembering. We have paraphrased them here.

To individual citizens, organizations and institutions—Records are used to document agreements and obligations, to substantiate claims, and to back up contentions. Government records on the formulation of legislation, for example, are essential for understanding legislative intent....Court records...are useful to attorneys and judges dealing with similar cases and to legal scholars charting long-term judicial trends. "Vital records"...are often crucial to establishing individual rights....

To institutions and organizations, including governments in conducting their affairs—Archives are used to study the origins of policy and program decisions...and to ensure the continuity of administration. Through ready access to their own past, such organizations achieve perspective on their progress and partially compensate for the rapid turnover in personnel that often leads to repeated changes in program direction and to policy discontinuities.

To the schools—Records enable students to understand their community's past, and to relate that past to the present. Use of historical records also develops reading and cognitive skills...[Students] analyze evidence...reach their own conclusions from evidence that may be inconclusive and contradictory.

Environmental issues—Engineers and investigators have used land use permits, maps, photographs and other archival records...to determine the location and nature of...toxic dump sites....

For repairing and maintaining the physical infrastructure.

To illustrate and entertain—Businesses use historical records in advertising campaigns, newspaper writers draw on them for background for stories, and movie makers and television producers seek them out....Writers of fiction draw on them for portrayals of past conditions and lifestyles.

Historic preservation— ... Records are used, for example, to determine the original appearance of the buildings and the location and type of their framework, electrical wiring, and plumbing.

To document land ownership—Land grants, maps, deeds, and other records are used by public authorities, corporations and individual citizens to determine property boundaries and ownership.

To improve health care—Medical researchers study patient records to understand genetic and familial diseases...transmitted from generation, and to trace the spread of contagious diseases within geographical regions....

Seen thus, these products become a rich source of public relations material, interesting to the public and essential to the well-being of society, providing the specificity that no simple listing of occupational categories could achieve.

The Users of Records

Since the mid-1980s, a series of studies have told us a great deal about our users. Almost none of these studies relates this information to public relations, yet we know that understanding who our publics are, how they perceive our services, and how they use our resources is a precondition of good public relations, provided that knowledge is turned into policy. Perhaps the most extensive study of users was done at the National Archives from 1990 to late 1991 by Paul Conway, who interviewed more than 800 persons using the records. Much of what that study tells us about the habits and point of view of the largest number of researchers studied to date can be generalized to our own institutions, particularly because large portions of it are supported by other research on archives, libraries, and museums.

A patron's use of the records moves, generally, through four stages: *discovering* potential sources of information; *orienting* oneself to the procedures at a particular archives; *searching* groups of records in several media to retrieve specific chunks of information, or having someone else do it; and *applying* this information to solve at least partially the research problem. Researchers tend to repeat this cycle until their information needs are satisfied or they quit. Let's consider each of these stages from a public relations aspect.

Discovery

On the surface, this process is user-driven, though archivists can influence it. Confirming studies in archives and its related fields, Conway suggests that the user knows about the archives and its likely relevance to his or her research by word of mouth or the force of logic. Fewer than one in five researchers learns about the institution from specific written sources (including institutional pamphlets) or from courses, tours, or lectures. Those researchers who come do so because archival materials are essential to the success of their projects. They are a creative, enterprising group who take the initiative to learn about an institution.

What these findings should suggest is that your patrons are ingenious in finding solutions to their historical questions. That they learn about you primarily by word of mouth in no way diminishes your need for creative outreach programs, since information from these programs undoubtedly becomes part of the general consciousness, from which word of mouth often derives. It suggests that successful outreach is not merely intended to give information but to demonstrate to the user the relevance of the institution's resources to specific problems and the researcher's need for those resources. The impact of word of mouth is overwhelming, and the message to you, the archivist, is clear: Though the user initiates discovery, you can influence it profoundly, since you control the ways in which you present yourself to actual and potential users by your presence and the programs you create to publicize the usefulness of your holdings to solving research problems.

Orientation

Orientation is the means by which researchers learn access rules and regulations, find their way about the building, meet archivists or other researchers who will be helpful to them, learn about the physical and intellectual organization of the holdings, and, most importantly, test their expectations against the reality of a particular archives. Orientation is largely archivist-driven, and its success depends on your willingness to participate in easing the patron's access to the building, the records, and the staff. In interview after interview, National Archives researchers expressed enthusiasm for the hunt but scarce patience with the access barriers placed before them there and in other institutions. Researchers can be oriented by signs, maps, short courses, audiovisual presentations, or by trained volunteers working with individuals or groups. But it is staff of the archives who set the tone for this learning, exhibiting helpfulness and order (or the lack of these) by their demeanor and the quality of their information.

Training the user to work through your holdings is primarily your job. In particular, you cannot assume that the first-time researcher has oriented himself in the ways you might traditionally expect, namely, by reading secondary sources or consulting guides in other repositories. Every archivist knows this from experience, but still we retain the notion that every new researcher should know what the archivist knows about research. When we consider the variety of products created by archival research and the range of experience represented by those who create those products, it is clear that the majority of users will be "untrained" by our standards. Earlier we discussed three reference styles, portraying the archivist as servant, gatekeeper, or partner, suggesting that the archivist as partner should be the most frequent role because it helped the researcher develop strategies for research. The archivist as partner might also be called the archivist as teacher, and its advantage is that in teaching the user how to approach the records, we satisfy the need to learn at the same time that we free ourselves.

Search and Retrieval

Archivists know very little about how patrons search for information, which is startling in view of the centrality of the reference function to the public's perception of our services. Although some institutions have recently sought to develop expert systems, you will find very little in archives literature about reference, suggesting that much reference and description is done without regard to the user's reality.

From recent studies of users, however, two elements seem to be clear. First, we can be reasonably sure that six out of ten users are willing to use sources regardless of their format or storage media and that others would use them if they knew what they were. This suggests that institutions that provide multimedia reference service, rather than reference service organized by record type, are responding correctly to users' needs. That there is a gap between the researcher's needs and the reference staff's mastering of these more comprehensive skills is inevitable, but the concept speaks directly to our present understanding of the creative connections possible among bodies of information disparate in format but linked in content.

More importantly, researchers seem able to provide a clear statement of their research problem in ways that facilitate retrieval, whether they are making inquiries by telephone, mail, or in person. When problems arise, it may be that archivists do not hear the patron out, ask the right question at the right time, or do not have adequate finding aids. Researchers tend to cluster their questions in one or more of three ways.

- Known items (the 1943 final report of the 50th anniversary committee)
- Specific formats or media (photographs of the 50th anniversary celebration)
- Specific subjects (material on the 50th anniversary celebration)

It is from this third cluster—subject searching—that we can learn the most. Researchers almost never approach the archival record with a broad subject in mind. It is possible to categorize our patrons' research topically—for example, women in the military—and researchers themselves will supply topical descriptions of their work that sound rather like book titles. But when they are closely observed or questioned, they prefer to break their information needs into aspects of the broader subject. Researchers writing the National Archives, for example, typically specify four or five aspects of their topic by which information might be searched. We thus waste time on both sides of the desk when we refer the researcher to large bodies of records resembling their general topics, rather than smaller series and subseries within related record groups, i.e., related for their research purposes. If our finding aids do not sufficiently describe these smaller categories, we are not providing useful finding aids; if we spend a great deal of time with the researcher, explaining what we know about a topic rather than referring him or her to smaller, informative series, we have frustrated that person and no learning has occurred. In short, the kind of detail we build into finding aids and give the researcher in person governs our ability to help that person quickly, which in turn affects his or her view of our skills.

This information has several managerial and public relations implications. The first and most obvious is that we don't know enough about how researchers approach our material. We need to observe it more closely and analytically. The second, based on what we now know, is that in many institutions reference service should be reexamined and refocused so that a high priority is placed on putting the expertise of archivists—which is about the format, organization and likely content of records, and the relationship of record groups—into written or automated finding aids that are readily accessible to the researcher. The third is that the methodology of reference service should be taken far more seriously than it now is. Archivists have generally viewed reference as an intuitive process for which training is not necessary, as revealed in the paucity of courses, articles, or studies on the process. Compared to the gallop of the library profession, archivists are barely crawling toward understanding of the interchange of information, ideas, and intuitions we call reference.

A fourth application suggests itself. How users define their information problems and search for information should influence the form and structure of the online and manual descriptive systems we develop to help them. Technology has seduced us all. Irresistibly, archivists, other information specialists, and organization men and women generally pursue technological ends that may have limited relation to market needs. If the technology exists, we use it, often employing, as a colleague puts it, the "lemming approach" to technology investment. We currently invest vast amounts of time and human resources into systems that may or may not serve patrons' needs well, possibly creating rational systems based on incorrect understandings and premises. Archivists are not alone in this tendency; it is probably societal. But it is worth considering, before the next several million scarce dollars are spent, how the automated system we are about to buy relates to what we know about how users work, how willing we are to teach users about it and its limitations, and how we will modify it accordingly.

Finally, we can develop procedures that enhance the self-sufficiency of our patrons. Our best service to them may be to teach them, by any means available to us, how to define research questions in terms that relate to the records and to show them how to move creatively between reference tools and records. We may not understand as well as we should that the efficiency and effectiveness of the researcher is a powerful research tool.

Application

The final step in research is application, or the uses to which the information from records is put. We may never understand the complex variety of uses of archival information, which are questions of epistemology as much as outcome. Information from records may or may not be vitally important to the researcher, or other sources of information may be used in a patchwork fashion to illumine records or address historical questions. But studies provide some insights that can affect our administrative thinking and therefore our public relations.

We have earlier defined our use of the term *occupational* in describing categories of users. The National Archives study, with others since the 1980s, illustrates the deceptiveness of this. Nearly one-quarter of those interviewed at the National Archives who said they were academics also reported that their work was being done under contract to third parties, suggesting constraints of time and money not typical of traditional academic work. Similarly, a number of full-time students, as they were defined occupationally, were actually doing research for other persons, often under contract. Of a group of retirees, over half were engaged in extensive projects aimed at a specific product. One-quarter had been hired to do research, and almost one in four were doing traditional academically oriented studies. Those registered as genealogists were often studying their personal family history for pleasure, but others were doing so to a specific and unexpected end. One "genealogist," for example, was actually seeking to document his family's emigration from Ireland so that his daughter might be eligible for a scholarship at Dublin University. Another was planning a book using nineteenth-century family history as the basis for a study of westward expansion.

The study also revealed the category of government historian, that is, historians hired as full-time employees by government agencies to write the agency's history. Sixty percent of these were doing work-related research; but an astonishing 20 percent were spending personal time on their hobbies, and 20 percent were doing academic research unrelated to their jobs. Thus the accomplishments of 40 percent of this cohort were lost to an occupational definition and therefore to public relations uses.

These studies tell us that finding out what users plan or have produced from their research, rather than asking them what they call themselves based on occupational categories we have defined, yields information that has managerial, professional, and public relations uses.

From the perspective of serving patrons, it is important to know what motivates the researcher to contact an archives and the scope of the archival information he/she seeks. Knowing whether that person is self-motivated or approaches the archives within the context of a group affiliation, such as a law firm or planning agency, for example, gives us important clues about the uses to which archival information will be put. At the very least, we learn that our low-volume, low-speed reference styles do not serve well a research universe in which research is increasingly paid for, time constrained, high volume, and high speed. At a more specific level, knowing whether a patron needs specific or narrowly defined records such as birth certificates or court case files, or whether he or she seeks broad documentation on a topic or event such as environmental damage in Minnesota since 1950 or the trial of the Catonsville Nine should help us identify access tools and personal service appropriate to the user's requirements. These are management as well as professional issues, and how well responses to them are built into policy and procedure affects our public relations.

Conclusion

Our definition of "access" at the beginning of this chapter may be both broader than you had imagined and more comprehensive. We suggest that access is a matter of general program planning and daily implementation; that it is largely cost-free; and that it is intimately related to good public relations. Put otherwise, every day's activities affect public relations. Every day that is seen from the user's point of view is one well spent, without cost, on good public relations. To the extent that this view is built into policy that invariably and overwhelmingly reflects the repository's bureaucratic needs and interests, that repository has improved its public relations position.

In the end, each archivist, whether professional or managerial, must remember that the ultimate purpose of acquiring records is to see that they are used. Reference service and programs that bring records and users together are the hub of archival activity. Making the reference room rather than the loading dock that hub requires acknowledging what we already know about users and learning more about them, then making that information part of institutional policy. We need not wait for perfected automation, professionwide policy statements, or other awakenings, although as professionals we must contribute to their creation and growth. We do this one by one, each by each, in our own archives, in our own community, in our own region. We become user-responsive archivists seeking to effect change.

We operate in bureaucracies whose function is less often to expedite than to control. Understanding our patrons and coming to terms with ways to serve them well increases the tension between the archivist, who seeks to be a neutral but active intermediary between the user and the records, and the institution, which resists change, however essential change might be to its future. Professionals who work in other institutional settings share this quandary. The rich literature on organizational change created since the first quarter of this century has produced a concept that may help us to lessen that tension. If the professional studies and documents his or her program, evaluates it with or without independent advice, enlists supporters within the institution, then enters the political arena as an advocate of change, change results. Archivists have a head start on this process. We know how to do certain kinds of research, and we can learn, without prejudice, the skills required for other kinds of research. What we learn can be used to create change, if we use it to affect policy. When we discuss user studies, for example, the criterion for success is not what we learn about users, but the extent to which we use this information to improve reference and information policies, implementation procedures, staff understanding and action, and subsequent program plans.

Good public relations begins simply with a focus on the user's interests, requirements, comforts, and intended products. Our job as archivists is to mobilize that information, integrate it as well as we can into policy, keeping in mind that our purpose is to maximize the use of the records in our stewardship, and then make those policies clear to the public in their terms. Our professional interest and those of the public coincide: The best management decisions and the best service create the best public relations.

Additional Readings

Conway, Paul. "Partners in Research: Toward Enhanced Access to the Nation's Archives." Unpublished report on a user study at the National Archives, July 1991.

___. "Facts and Frameworks: An Approach to Studying the Users of Archives." *American Archivist* 49 (Fall 1986): 393-407.

___. "Research in Presidential Libraries: A User Study." *Midwestern Archivist* 11 (1986): 35-56.

Dearstyne, Bruce W. "What is the Use of Archives: A Challenge for the Profession." *American Archivist* 50 (Winter 1987): 76-87.

Dowler, Lawrence. "Availability and Use of Records: A Research Agenda." *American Archivist* 51 (Winter/Spring 1988): 74-86.

Freeman, Elsie T. "Buying Quarter Inch Holes: Public Support Through Results." *Midwestern Archivist* 10 (1985): 89-97.

___. "In the Eye of the Beholder: Archives Administration from the User's Point of View." *American Archivist* 47 (Spring 1984): 111-23.

___. "Soap and Education: Archival Training, Public Service, and the Profession—An Essay." *Midwestern Archivist* 16 (1991): 87-94.

Helsley, Alexia Jones. "The User Survey as a Planning Document." Unpublished report on a study at the South Carolina Department of Archives and History, 1988.

Howell, Benita J., Edward B. Reeves, and John Van Willigen. "Fleeting Encounters—A Role Analysis of Reference Librarian-Patron Interaction." *RQ* 15 (Winter 1976): 124-29.

Maher, William J. "The Use of User Studies." *Midwestern Archivist* 11 (1986): 15-26.

___. "User Studies and Information Practices of Archival Researchers: Report of a Literature Review and Survey Pre-Test." Unpublished report prepared at the University of Illinois at Urbana-Champaign, September 1989.

Major Findings, Conclusions and Recommendations of the Researcher and Public Service Component Evaluation Study (Ottawa, Ontario: Public Archives of Canada, 1985).

Mick, Colin, George N. Londsey, and Daniel Callahan. "Toward Usable User Studies." *Journal of the American Society for Information Science* 31 (September 1980): 347-56.

Pugh, Mary Jo. "The Illusion of Omniscience: Subject Access and the Reference Archivist." *American Archivist* 45 (Winter 1982): 33-44.

Turnbaugh, Roy C. "Archival Mission and User Studies." *Midwestern Archivist* 11 (1986): 27-33.

2

Money Talk

An Introduction to Private Sector Fund Raising for Archives

Judy P. Hohmann

Funding support is a continuing problem for many archives, whether it be dodging a budget cut, sustaining current levels of support, or increasing funds to meet increasing needs. This chapter argues that archives that are serious about planning for their financial future should look to the private sector. The primary audience for this chapter is archivists who have never systematically and decisively approached the private sector for funds for their institution. We will present an overview of fund raising principles, dispelling some myths and offering some practical suggestions, covering in a few paragraphs subjects about which entire books have been written. However, the bibliography, listing a variety of sources on many different aspects of fund raising, should be helpful for the reader who is interested in a more in-depth treatment of the subject. "Money Talk" issues a challenge to archives to reexamine their traditional thinking about generating funds and seize the opportunities that abound among private corporations, foundations, and individuals.

In one recent year, Americans gave a record-breaking $122.57 billion to nonprofit organizations. In spite of recent unemployment, business failures, and drops in real weekly earnings not experienced since the 1950's, American individuals, corporations, and foundations continue to contribute to a variety of worthwhile religious, educational, cultural, and social organizations.

Attention archivists! Did you get yours? Is your membership drive, annual appeal, or capital campaign the beneficiary of these gifts? Is yours one of the educational institutions that received a total $12.41 billion in contributions in 1990? Or one of the cultural organizations that benefitted from the $7.89 billion in funds that Americans donated? No, you say? Is it possible that you do not consider the private sector when you think about fund raising? That you did not think about asking?

A recent Gallup Poll revealed that for most of the population, the immediate spur to contributing to every cause other than religion was being asked to give. A 1985 study commissioned by the Rockefeller Brothers Fund confirmed that the most effective fund raising technique is one person asking another to give.

For example, as part of a 1986 project funded by the National Historical Publications and Records Commission, staff of the New York State Archives and Records Administration interviewed several business and philanthropic leaders in the Albany, New York, area to find out if they had ever contributed to an archives. Their overwhelming response was no. When asked why not, they replied that no one had ever asked them to do so. (Interestingly, some of these people did contribute to a local historical organization that has an archival program, but the profile of that archives was so low that it did not exist in the minds of these givers.) As part of the interview, staff discussed the importance of archives and the various ways that archival records could be used, including health, meteorological, business, historical and other scholarly uses. Without exception, these business and philanthropic leaders responded with great interest and enthusiasm. Some of them expressed surprise that archival records had such varied and important uses, indicating that no one had ever told them about archives. Again, without exception, every interview ended with the interviewees' saying that they would seriously consider a contribution to an archives that demonstrated its importance to the community. The consistent patterns of American giving and the information gathered from national polls and regional surveys send a clear message: Institutions that successfully tap the generosity of American foundations, corporations, and individuals are those that carefully identify these organizations, define their purpose, articulate it in a way that is meaningful to the donor, and ask for support, often through personal solicitation.

If you did not claim a piece of the $122 billion private sector pie for your institution, it may be that, like many archivists, you did not consider the private sector to be a source of funds. Instead, you may immediately think of one of the many alphabet federal and state agencies to fund your need to process collections, add climate controls, microfilm records, or establish outreach programs. Archivists are accustomed to seeking funds from public grant-making agencies; but these efforts have drawbacks, whereas private sector fund raising has potential benefits. What are some of these drawbacks and benefits?

Under the best of circumstances, public funds are limited, competition for them is intense, and their use is more restricted than that of private funds. The process of preparing a grant application often involves hundreds of staff hours to produce multiple copies of lengthy narratives, budgets, and appendices that may earn funds for a few years for a specific project. But the strong possibility also exists that the grant will be denied, leaving the institution with little to show for its effort except a tired staff and reams of paper for the circular file. In other words, the institution as a whole has gained little from the grant application process.

In contrast, the funds obtained from the private sector can be continual and less restricted than those from government agencies. Annual appeals, membership drives, and regularly scheduled events can be sources of support year after year. The proceeds from these efforts can be used for specific projects or for more mundane, but essential, general operating expenses. Seldom do individuals or businesses publish guidelines or provide examples of projects they wish to support. This may be disconcerting to the archivist accustomed to the very specific focus of public grant-making agencies. Viewed in a more positive light, it means that the range of interests and giving patterns in the private sector is far less circumscribed than that of the public sector.

More importantly, the *process* of raising money from the private sector is a strengthening experience for the entire institution. Much of the fund raising process is an internal one, requiring that an institution know itself thoroughly, that it be unified in its purpose and direction, and that its fund raising efforts be planned and well organized. This means that both the staff and the board of the archives must do considerable preparatory work before anyone asks for a single dollar. But the value of board and staff working together toward a common goal transcends that of fund raising alone. Even in the unlikely event that the institution decides not to do any fund raising, the experience will be useful for other institutional efforts such as policy making and strategic planning.

A comparison of public sector and private sector fund raising would not be complete without a consideration of external influences on the private sector. There is a common perception that the vagaries of the economy and the ever-changing tax laws have significant impact on private sector contributions. Statistics compiled by the American Association of Fund Raising Counsel confirm that contributions continue to flow to the nonprofit sector despite economic hard times. Such contributions are not immune to economic downturns; 1990 contributions, for example, barely outpaced inflation, and the future is uncertain. But private sector contributions do not dry up because of hard times. The state of the economy is not an excuse for failing to raise money, particularly when other educational and cultural institutions do so. Similarly, changes in the tax code do not have a lasting negative impact on contributions. Americans support institutions in which they believe, regardless of the tax deductions they may or may not receive.

Finally, an archives may consider itself to be unique, thus any venture into private sector fund raising is seen as too problematic to warrant the effort of justifying its existence. Here, it is useful to recognize that an archives has much in common with other nonprofit educational and cultural organizations. It is likely that your institutional structure is very similar to that of others in the nonprofit sector that have received support in the past. Aspects of an archives will be familiar to potential donors: possibly a board of directors that serves without pay, in effect volunteering its services, or a paid staff consisting of an executive director and professionals with such specialized titles as archivist, librarian, or curator. Like other institutions that receive money, the archives may be an independent entity within a small institution, such as the county historical society or the city museum, or part of a larger institution, such as a library or university.

In summary, private sector money is available; private sector fund raising compares favorably with seeking funds from public grantmaking agencies; institutions similar to archives have succeeded in obtaining it; and people give because they are asked. Is the message, then, that an archives has only to ask and it shall receive?

The fundamentals of fund raising are simple and easy to understand. But such a message implies that fund raising is easy, and it is not. It is an undertaking that can reap great benefits, but it requires time and energy. There is no magic formula for raising money. It is an art, not a science.

However, most fund raising professionals agree that there are some fundamental steps that an institution should follow when it decides to raise money in the private sector. These steps will systematize the process and make success more likely. First, an institution should conduct a thorough self-assessment, including writing a mission statement and making an analysis of its strengths and weaknesses. Secondly, it should determine what it will do with the money it will raise, from whom it will raise the money, and how it will raise the money.

Institutional self-assessment is necessary if the archives is to present itself to potential contributors in the most positive and credible way possible. To do this, your archives must frame answers to such basic questions as: Why does it exist? Whom does it serve? What are its strengths? Its needs? On what will it spend donated money? Simple questions, but ones not having obvious or simple answers, especially for an archives unaccustomed to articulating its importance to the public.

Answering these questions is not necessarily the executive director's task alone. Instead, framing these answers is a step to be taken by a group comprising both board members and staff, even though the executive director may be able to provide all the "right" answers. With only a few exceptions, it is the board of directors, the engine of fund raising, that will actually be asking for the money, with the support of the staff's knowledge and expertise. Everyone involved in the institution's fund raising effort must get on board as early as possible, if the effort is to succeed.

It may seem peculiar that the most expert and knowledgeable component of this equation, the staff, should defer to board members. However, in fund raising, board members have a degree of credibility and cachet that staff members do not. A staff person is paid for work done; staff has a personal and pecuniary interest in the success of the program. A typical board member may be the president of a bank, serving on the board because he/she believes in the intrinsic merit of the institution. The board member volunteers his/her services because of that merit, not to make money or acquire a professional reputation. The board member is engaged but more disinterested than the professional. For these reasons, when the board member solicits a contribution from peers, he/she has credibility a staff member may lack. While there are exceptions to the rule that staff provide expertise to volunteers who solicit (as in the case of a well-established annual fund with known constituencies or a position combining development with other professional duties), research shows that the great majority of gifts of $100 or more are raised by volunteers asking peers to give.

The group that tackles these important fundamental questions can be called a Development Committee, Needs and Assessment Committee, or some other name that fits its purpose. Other configurations are possible. If the archives board is small, these fundamental questions can be addressed by the entire board and the executive director. Or a small committee can be established, consisting of some board members and the executive director. Still another configuration is an advisory committee of board members, interested volunteers, and senior staff.

The responsibilities of the Development Committee will require much thought, analysis, and debate. The committee must report regularly to the full board to keep it informed, to gauge the board members' response to its proposals, and to draw the entire board into supporting the committee's work. The full support of the board is vital to a successful fund raising effort. No institution can afford a disgruntled board member who sabotages its fund raising by public and vocal opposition.

The committee must first develop a *written mission statement* answering the questions, "Why do we exist?" and "Whom do we serve?" When the committee is able to answer these questions to everyone's satisfaction, the statement should be written down to make sure everyone understands it and will know in the future what they have agreed to. If the archives already has a mission statement, the committee must review it to make sure that everyone understands it, agrees that it continues to be an accurate reflection of the archives' work, and that it is stated in terms that potential donors will understand.

Providing clear, jargon-free answers to the fundamental questions of why the archives exists, whom it serves, what are its strengths and its needs, is critical to an archives, perhaps more so than to other nonprofit institutions. The public understands why a hospital or school exists and is accustomed to giving money to these institutions for improved health care and better education. An archives' purpose is not so clear. Most people, if asked, would probably describe an archives as a storehouse of documents important to understanding history. They see an archives as nonthreatening and noncontroversial, but may also see it as elitist, irrelevant to their lives, or otherwise not worthy of significant support. That is why, in this very early phase of the fund raising, the archives faces one of its greatest challenges: articulating its mission and its importance in such a way that donors will be persuaded to support it. Invoking the importance of one's documentary heritage will not persuade most potential donors to give. A statement that shows specificity and relevance to the donors' interests will go far to convince potential contributors that archives matter and are worth their support.

An archives would do well to confront the challenge of explaining itself by focusing on some of the uses of its holdings. Scholarly research, genealogy, legal, scientific, medical, and administrative uses of records, described in specific, anecdotal ways, will strike a responsive chord in the potential contributor. Still another way to explain the uses of archives is to remind donors that so much of what we know and understand today comes from the information in records. The monuments and historical sites that dot our landscape would make little sense if we had no record to tell us the story behind them. Documents that tell us how the nation responded to influenza and polio epidemics of the past contribute to our understanding of current epidemics. The records of the construction of our bridges, tunnels, electrical and sewer lines provide vital information for maintenance and renovation. We are able to understand the impact of humans on the environment because of the evidence in historical records. If we want to continue knowing, we must care for our archives. If your archives does not have familiar and popular historical records, you can help donors understand the importance of records by citing the more popular and familiar elsewhere: the Dead Sea scrolls, the logs of Columbus, the diary of Anne Frank, census records in the National Archives, and the records from the Warren Commission.

The Development Committee must also probe beyond a ready, simple answer to the question of whom the archives serves. Who are the archives' researchers? Are they from a particular geographical location? From a particular subject area, such as the natural sciences or colonial history? Do genealogists constitute a sizable percentage of the archives' users? Are they from fields not traditionally served by archives, such as engineering, medicine, or architecture? Do only researchers benefit from your service? Does your archives mount public exhibits or provide services to the schools, for example? Defining whom the archives serves and how it serves them is also a way to articulate the strengths of the institution. To a potential contributor, the archives must establish itself as a viable institution that wants to accomplish more than it now accomplishes through increased financial support. Finally, descriptions of whom the archives serves may also lead the Development Committee to identify potential contributors. For example, not only might the scientist doing research be asked for a contribution, but the scientific community in general may be interested in supporting an archives that provides service to scientists.

After the Development Committee assesses the strengths of an institution, it must then turn to assessing its weaknesses. Talking about weakness, however, implies an ailing entity, possibly one so weak that it can barely survive. Thus, from the outset, the Development Committee must talk about the institution's *needs*—what it needs to accomplish its goals of expanded service, new programs, and the like. Not just semantic subterfuge, this word shift will begin to set the necessary tone for any fund raising effort, one that is positive and confident. Even a small, struggling archives, one that feels overwhelmed by its needs, must adopt a positive, can-do attitude. No one wants to contribute money to a cause that perceives itself as failing. People want to believe that their contribution will make a difference and ensure success.

When the Development Committee addresses the question of what the donated money will be used for, it discovers a plethora of worthy projects and programs that need funding. The committee decides whether the proceeds of the fund raising effort will be dedicated to capital projects, such as a new roof for the building or renovation of the research room; to specific programs, such as an exhibit or development of a document package for schoolchildren; or general operating expenses, such as salaries, utility bills, archival supplies. Individuals are potential contributors to all three fund raising categories, while foundations and corporations are generally more selective, often prohibiting contributions to capital projects or general operating expenses. The Development Committee may decide to seek funds from a variety of private sector sources for all three categories. In this case, when the Development Committee identifies prospects for contributors, it identifies them for each category of need. Three-tiered fund raising is sophisticated and requires experience. Archives that are new to private sector fund raising would do well to be more modest in their first efforts, perhaps beginning with an annual appeal to expand public programs or to process a particular collection.

When the Development Committee has completed the tasks of defining the archives' mission, assessing its strengths and needs, determining where the money will be spent, and creating a positive, confident attitude, it should pause a moment to congratulate itself and take satisfaction in its accomplishments. It has developed what is known in fund raising parlance as *the case.* The case (or *case statement,* as it is sometimes called) says why money is being raised. It is presented to prospective contributors to convince them that they should support the institution.

The members of the committee have probably worked harder and longer than they had expected to when they agreed to serve, and although their work is not done, they have completed a vital piece of it. Some fund raising professionals contend that the process of developing a case statement is at least as important to an institution's fund raising efforts as the case itself. As board members and staff wrangle with the tough, fundamental issues of the archives, they develop the involvement, commitment, and ownership that are essential to success. Both board and staff will be motivated to put out their best efforts to support the archives' fund raising.

Case statements vary in length and design, depending on the institutions' resources and its fund raising goals and objectives. For a large capital campaign, the case statement could be a multipage booklet, similar to the format of a corporate annual report. For a more limited annual campaign, the case statement may be a small brochure or even a one-page letter. Be careful that your desire for attractiveness does not lead you to create such an expensive, slick format that potential contributors wonder if you know how to spend money wisely. Conversely, an amateurish, poorly designed, unattractive format may cause donors to question your financial status and your taste. Appearance counts; be sure your case statement shows you honestly and at your best.

With case statement at hand (or soon to come from the printer), the archives is now poised to ask for money. But exactly which corporations, foundations, and individuals should be asked? Figuring out who to ask and how much to ask for is called *prospect identification and evaluation.*

Staff now lends its expertise by researching likely corporation and foundation prospects for the Development Committee, which in turn identifies and evaluates them. The committee then presents the full board a list of corporations and foundations it proposes to solicit, with suggested dollar amounts and solicitation strategies for each.

Archivists accustomed to seeking grants in the public sector will find comfort and familiarity in the clearly defined research aspect of prospect identification and evaluation. Research to determine which foundations should be approached for funds can be done by staff using the resources of the Foundation Center, whose reference books can usually be found in larger libraries. If such a library is not close to your archives, send a staff person to the nearest major library to access this important information. Thousands of foundations contribute to nonprofit institutions, but the staff researcher can immediately narrow the search by identifying those foundations that have contributed to similar projects or institutions. The initial search should be a broad one. Using *The Foundation Grants Index,* which contains information about the 400 largest U.S. foundations, the researcher can search terms such as "historic preservation—documents," "history-archives," "history, document conservation," and simply "history," which will reveal foundations that have made historical records grants. Then the researcher can expand the search by consulting *The Foundation Directory,* which contains information on over 4,000 foundations with assets of over $1 million or grants totaling $100,000 or more annually. Descriptive entries in this directory will tell the researcher whether or not a foundation will give money in a specific geographic area and whether or not it will provide the type of support the institution needs. For example, some foundations will not give to building campaigns; others will not contribute to endowments.

Source Book Profiles provides more in-depth information on the thousand largest foundations. It also provides a grant analysis and an extensive, though not comprehensive, listing of grant recipients. Names of foundation trustees are also listed. *The Taft Foundation Reporter* should be used for its biographical and career information on the trustees of the various foundations. It provides information ranging from their date and place of birth to colleges they attended and professional affiliations. This information is helpful for determining whether your archives has a connection with a potential funding source. A fund-raiser's dream is to present such information to a board, then have a member respond, "I didn't know Susan was on that foundation. Why, she and I were in school together at..." The connection, and probably the contribution, have been made.

After consulting these and any other local sources that the librarian recommends, the researcher should bring back to the Development Committee a list of those foundations that may have an interest in supporting the archives. The list should include the dollar range of grants given by each foundation and information about its board of trustees. Board members and key staff of the archives should review information about foundation trustees, looking for connections between the archives and the foundation. Does anyone in the archives know anyone in the foundation? Is there any specific connection that can be made between the foundation and the archives? For example, would the foundation, whose chairman was active in World War II commemoration activities, be interested in supporting your archives, which includes significant holdings related to the war? Whether or not a connection is made, the next step remains the same: Call the foundation and ask for a copy of its most recent annual report, which should detail the kinds of grants it has given in the past year and give a more complete picture of what the foundation does and what its interests are.

If, after reviewing the most recent information about the foundation, you still think it may be interested in supporting your archives, call and ask to speak with a program officer. Briefly outline your project to see if the response is encouraging or indifferent. If the program officer wants to know more about the archives, request information about application procedures and deadlines. Some foundations will have specific forms to fill out; others will not, requiring only a letter. Deadlines will vary, as will suggestions about the length of proposals, the desirability of personal visits, or the time needed by the foundation to make a decision. As you develop your application proposal, keep in touch with the program officer and seek guidance on any troublesome parts. Don't ask unnecessary questions, but try to maintain enough contact with the program officer that he/she is familiar with your proposal even before receiving it.

The archives researcher who goes to the library for information about foundations should also seek information about possible sources of corporate support. The librarian can be very helpful in guiding the researcher to several useful volumes: *Guide to Corporate Giving,* the *Corporate Giving Directory, Standard & Poor's Directory of Corporations,* the *Taft Corporate Giving Directory,* and the *Directory of Corporate Philanthropy.* These directories will provide such information as who runs the company, who the officers are, and what kinds and amounts of grants have recently been awarded.

It is important to remember that while foundations exist to give away money, corporations exist to make money. Although corporations are allowed to deduct charitable contributions, most corporations do not give, and those that do so like to give in their own backyard. Therefore, one of the first places to look for corporate support is to those companies doing business in your own community.

Perhaps your library research has told you that a major national insurance company contributes to history-related projects and the regional branch of that company is located in your community. Call the regional branch and find out how the corporate giving program is handled. You may find that it is very centralized, with all requests going to headquarters, or that the branch has a discretionary charitable fund of its own. Then find out from your board if there are any connections to be made between the archives and that company. Beyond personal connections, could your archives interest a paper manufacturing company in supporting preservation activities? Does the insurance company's restoration of a historic building for its offices indicate an interest in history, possibly in your archives' historical architectural holdings? If you do not find these connections, don't give up. Call the company to find out who is in charge of corporate giving. Write to that person to find out the company's criteria, deadlines, and such other requirements as special forms. Although the senior archivist or archives director writes a corporation for money, a few words of caution are in order. Do not write a "Dear Friend" letter to a corporation for money. Many corporations assume that if you do not have the time or skill to find out where to direct a request, you are not worth their support. Be sure to follow up any request for a contribution with a phone call, to make sure the request was received and offer to answer any questions the company may have about it. You may also want to arrange a meeting to discuss your request in more detail. Some companies have strict rules about such meetings; others do not. The fact that you are denied a meeting does not necessarily mean that a company is not interested in supporting your archives.

Before submitting your request for support to any company, find out whether that firm links its corporate giving to marketing. A company that wants recognition for its good works will respond more positively to funding proposals that offer opportunities for it to get its name before the public. It may be interested in supporting an exhibit of archival documents, as long as all the written materials about the exhibit boldly proclaim that it was made possible by the generous support of that firm. The company will also want to know about the kinds and extent of publicity the archives plans for the exhibit.

Another area of corporate support that should not be overlooked is contributions of goods and services. Perhaps a local printing company would be willing to produce your case statement. A company that is moving to new offices might be willing to donate its old but perfectly usable file cabinets or office furniture. Although these may not be the cash contributions you were hoping for, they will help the archives save money and, more importantly, will establish a relationship between the archives and the corporation that may produce even more significant contributions at a later time.

The path to identifying and evaluating foundation and corporate prospects is clearly defined and relatively easy to follow: Do library research, use directories of information, obtain and submit application forms, following institutional guidelines. However, this path should not be the only one the archives travels.

Let's recall the $122.57 billion given by donors, referred to earlier in this chapter. You may be surprised to learn that corporations with instant name recognition and huge foundations with enormous assets did not contribute most of this money; in fact, foundations and corporations accounted for one-tenth of it. The remaining nine-tenths was contributed by individuals, by millions of people with a vast range of interests, predilections, resources, quirks, and eccentricities, who do not show up in a directory and for whom there are no specific guidelines or application forms. In recent years, that percentage of total giving has remained fairly constant. These givers are the people who support such causes as sheltering the homeless, protecting the rain forest, advancing AIDS research, saving whales, buying new uniforms for the school football team, and underwriting the local symphony orchestra. No archives serious about raising money from the private sector can afford to ignore this tremendous source of support. Although the path to individual prospects is not as straight as that to corporations and foundations, ways can be found to organize your efforts.

The Development Committee should convene specifically for the purpose of identifying and evaluating individual prospects. Of the many places from which the archives can establish a pool of potential supporters, it should first look to those people who know it best. These include current and former members, vendors, people who have used the archives or have made inquiries about it, and people who have attended programs at the institution. If you are among the archivists who have no idea who attended a particular program, or if you threw out the names and addresses of people who did not renew their membership, adopt the mind-set that everyone is a potential contributor. The next time the archives holds a lecture, opens an exhibit, or offers any program, provide a "guest book" for names and addresses. Hang on to the names of your nonrenewal members. These people supported the archives once; their interest can be developed again.

Secondly, supporters of other institutions similar to yours may be a source of support for your archives. For example, members of a friends group of the library or contributors to the local history museum can also be made interested in your archives. Write or call those organizations and suggest an exchange of membership lists. Some organizations guard these lists as if they were state secrets; others are very willing to share them. If the archives holdings or its programs relate to business, religion, education, or any other subject that is linked to a specific organization, write or call that organization and request an exchange of membership lists. If the answer is no, maintain contact with the leadership of those organizations to educate them about the archives holdings, programs, and fund raising efforts.

In addition to using membership lists, your general knowledge of the community will contribute most to the identification process. Pursue any obvious connections between the archives and the community. Would members of your local chamber of commerce be interested to know that your archives has thousands of photographs and documents that tell the story of the industrial development of the waterfront area? Would the members of the PTA be interested to know that you are planning an exhibit and curriculum package based on the one-room schoolhouses once common to the region? Having explored these connections, the Development Committee must use its imagination. Information that a prominent individual has recently purchased an old building with the intention of restoring it suggests that person's appreciation of history. Perhaps such an interest translates into an appreciation of your archives, too!

Simultaneous with identifying prospective donors, the Development Committee should be *evaluating the prospects,* that is, determining what amount of money each donor can reasonably be expected to contribute. A history of an individual's support of the archives, philanthropic activities in other organizations, and professional and business activities all serve as indicators of his/her giving potential. Evaluation is important because, first, 90 percent of the money in a typical fund drive comes from 10 percent of the donors; second, generally people do not give more than they are asked for; and finally, evaluation applied to individuals, corporations, and foundations can help the archives establish realistic goals for its fund raising efforts.

Once a pool of prospective individual supporters has been established, divide it between those who will be solicited personally and those who will be solicited as part of a general mailing. Those selected for personal solicitation should be major donor prospects, a classification that will mean different things to different institutions. In general, major donors are those who can reasonably be expected to give the most money. For some archives, that amount may be $250 and above; for others, it may be more than $1,000. The key word here is "reasonably." Just because a prominent individual regularly contributes $5,000 a year to the library does not mean that he/she can automatically be expected to contribute the same amount to your archives. If a prospect knows nothing about the archives, you must "cultivate" that prospect before expecting a contribution of any significant sum.

Cultivation is the term fund-raisers use to describe giving prospective donors the opportunity to become better acquainted with an institution. It is an educational effort intended to convince donors that the institution is worth their support. The archives that is serious about fund raising in the private sector should view everyone as a prospective donor, establishing or expanding its public programs so that increasing numbers of people learn about the archives. The archives should pay careful attention to maintaining and increasing its mailing list. Those who sign the guest book at the opening of an exhibit should be placed on the mailing list for future programs and asked to contribute to an annual appeal or future membership campaigns. This is cultivation in the broadest sense.

More specifically, the archives should focus on those people whom the Development Committee has identified as potential major contributors, seeking to inform them about and involve them in archives activities. A member of the archives board or the executive director should be responsible for cultivating major donor prospects. As a necessary first step, the donor should be placed on the archives mailing list. The board member or executive director should then write a letter to the prospect, using the name of a mutual acquaintance, offering an invitation to a lecture or dinner, or asking for assistance on a specific issue affecting the archives. If a prospect has no interest in the archives, he or she will make this known early by declining these overtures. If the prospect responds positively and appears willing to have future contacts with the archives, the chances are good that he or she will respond positively to a request for a contribution. The first contribution may not be as large as you might have hoped, but by continuing to cultivate the donor, you will improve your chances of later being among his/her most significant contributions.

One way of looking at cultivation is that it is a way for an institution to make new and closer friends. To foster these relationships, the archives must pay attention to the impression it creates. It should constantly evaluate the face it presents to the public, because that face contributes to making an impression on someone. The physical state of the research room, the lighting, the amenities, the friendliness of the person answering the phone, and the helpfulness of the reference archivist all have an impact on how people perceive the institution, whether casual users or prospective major donors. For most archives, developing this outward orientation is as challenging as writing a case statement that is understandable and meaningful to a broad audience. This kind of institutional mind-set—one that continually assesses the kind of image it projects—is essential to an archives that expects to generate broad-based support in the private sector.

To this point, we have discussed preparing to raise money. Everything from the case statement to prospect identification, evaluation, and cultivation has been directed to the task of actually asking for money. Now is the time to *solicit funds*.

For most prospects (the 90 percent that will provide 10 percent of your funds), it is enough to send a solicitation letter signed by the Chairperson of the Board, accompanied by a response card and envelope. But for the 10 percent of contributors who are major donor prospects, personal solicitation is required.

When the archives turns its attention to the personal solicitation of major prospects, committee members are likely to become uncomfortable. Very few people like to ask others for money, and the best way to deal with this reluctance is to talk about it and present effective, positive counter arguments to resolve discomfort. Otherwise, the discomfort will remain an obstacle to effective fund raising. Before solicitation assignments are made, the Chairperson of the Development Committee or the Chairperson of the Board should lead a discussion that acknowledges the general unease people often feel about asking for money. Board members should be encouraged to analyze the reasons for their reluctance. For example, a board member might suggest that a staff person call Joyce, a major donor prospect, and use the board member's name as an endorsement of the fund raising effort. This is a poor approach; it is important that the consequences of following it be addressed immediately. Peers approach peers. If Joyce is worth calling on, she should be called on by her peer. What impression will Joyce have if staff, and not Joyce's friend the board member, calls her? Perhaps Joyce may think the fund raising effort is not really worth her friend's time. She will probably feel that only a token contribution is necessary. Board members may also try to excuse themselves from fund raising by claiming that they are simply not good at it. A discussion of this excuse may reveal that the board member is really expressing a fear of being refused. It would be useful here to remind the board that a donor's no is neither a personal rejection nor an irreversible decision. Board members are not asking for money for themselves, but for an archives whose work they believe in, work for which outside funds are crucial. Remind the board member that careful research has indicated that the prospect has the ability to give and the chances of a successful solicitation are always enhanced by a personal solicitation. Another way to address board members' reluctance to make personal solicitations is to create pairs of board members for personal solicitations. Each board member can then bolster the other's resolve and confidence. A frank discussion about these matters will not immediately eliminate board members' reluctance to ask for money, but it can diminish it, foster solidarity among the board, and build a confident, positive attitude that is critical for successful solicitation.

Finally, a solicitation is more likely to be successful if the person asking for funds combines the attributes of volunteer, contributor, and peer. (See Appendix 2a-e for solicitation guidelines.)

Volunteer. Unlike a member of the archives staff who has a vested interest in seeing funds raised because his or her job depends on it, a volunteer's interest in fund raising is perceived by a donor as pure, motivated only by a desire to help the archives. The volunteer, who is often a board member but who can also be a friend or member of another archives committee, is untainted by any suggestion of self-interest. Although a member of the archives staff might accompany the volunteer, ready to supply facts and details if asked, it is the volunteer who is best suited to ask for a contribution.

Contributor. All board members should make financial contributions to the archives. The board that is serious about raising funds from the community must show that it, too, thinks the program is worthwhile enough to command its financial support, and an archives should be able to tell a prospect that all board members have made a financial commitment. Such board support indicates that the archives has the internal commitment to make its program work. Serving on the board of trustees of any organization is a responsibility that should not be taken lightly. Agreeing to serve on that board should be a public declaration that the organization and its work are among the board member's highest priorities and that his or her level of financial commitment reflects that importance. The level of financial commitment will, of course, depend on the board member's ability to give, but that contribution should be among the highest of his or her contributions to nonprofit organizations, whether "highest" for that individual is $50 or $50,000.

Before board members or any other solicitors ask for money, they should make their own contribution. Prospective donors may ask solicitors about their commitment, and the response may affect the success of the solicitation visit. The solicitor may offer information about his or her level of contribution to demonstrate how committed he/she is to the organization. Other early fund raising successes, such as foundation, corporation, and individual contributions that have already been received, should be mentioned to the prospective donor as evidence of your institution's level of effort.

Peer. The person who asks should not only have made a contribution to the archives but should also be assigned to prospects who can be asked for a similar level of support. In other words, the solicitation should be peer to peer. A board member who has given $250 can be matched with prospects at the $100 or $250 level but should not be assigned to donor prospects at the $500 or $1,000 level. Understandably, this is not always possible, but it is preferable.

When the board is prepared to solicit, the archives should supply solicitors with a packet of materials to review before each call. These packets should contain the following: a one-page fact sheet on the archives and its programs; the most recent annual report, case statement, brochures that convey a favorable impression of the archives, and significant statistics about the program and its services. Solicitors may refer to these materials during the call or carry them, knowing they have information at their fingertips. The archives should also provide a staff person to accompany the board member, preferably the executive director. The presence of a knowledgeable person capable of providing assistance should allay any nervousness or apprehension the board member might feel. The focus of the conversation with the prospect should be on what the contribution will help accomplish, and the solicitor should suggest a *specific amount* the prospect might contribute. A request for the prospect "to do what you can" rarely results in a significant contribution.

After the donor contributes to the archives, an *acknowledgment* is necessary. Often overlooked and undervalued, the acknowledgment is the final step in the solicitation process. It represents not only good manners and a good record-keeping tool, but it also builds a feeling of goodwill that enables future solicitations. Every contribution should be acknowledged as soon as possible with thanks and a specification of the amount of the contribution. For most contributors, the thanks can be a form letter or a combination receipt and thank-you form.

Because major donors have contributed in a special way, they should be thanked in a special way. A personalized letter signed by the chairperson of the board of the archives is the minimum acknowledgment for a major donor. Beyond that, it is up to the archives to decide what is appropriate: an open house or recognition dinner, publication of contributors' names in the annual report, or media publicity (if approved by the contributor) are possibilities.

After major donors have been properly thanked, they should continue to receive information about the archives and be invited to become more active in the institution. *The cultivation that preceded the solicitation is ongoing.*

Another group of people who should not be forgotten are those prospective donors who said no. Their refusal to contribute should be viewed as temporary, and they should be asked again in six months or a year. Unless a prospect appears totally uninterested in the archives or tells the solicitor not to bother coming back, a refusal to contribute may only indicate a need to know more about the archives or that other financial commitments preclude a gift at the time. Once again, the archives should continue to cultivate the prospect.

Until now, we have talked about fund raising that uses mailings and personal solicitations. Where, you might ask, are the gala balls, the sold-out lecture series, the bowl-a-thons, bake sales, and other events that most of us associate with raising money? *Special events* do have an important place in fund raising. However, they should not be central to the institutions's fund raising because, generally speaking, events are an inefficient way to raise money. Staging an event that raises only $10,000 often requires as much effort as one that raises $100,000. Many times, the individual who purchases a $50 ticket should have been asked to contribute $1,000 to the archives. Events also consume staff time and energy.

In spite of these drawbacks, an archives intent upon raising money from the private sector should hold special events. But understand clearly that the purpose of holding these special events is to raise the profile of the archives in the community, to attract new friends and supporters by educating them to the importance of historical records, to serve as a means of cultivating prospective donors, and to provide a way to say thank you to supporters and volunteers. As a way to raise large amounts of money, special events are not cost efficient.

An archives should bear in mind several constraints when it mounts special events. First, it should develop special events that are either consistent with its public image or with the image it is trying to establish. The ideal event should bear some relation to the archives holdings, so that participants leave the event having learned something more about the institution. Secondly, the archives should carefully evaluate its ability to organize and successfully carry out an event. An archives on a tight budget should not commit substantial resources in the hope that the event will make money. Special events are labor intensive; when an organization calculates how much money it has made on a particular event, it often ignores the considerable staff and volunteer time spent to it. Thirdly, the public nature of the event increases the pressure to make sure it is successful. No one enjoys a public failure. The sight of a handful of people in a room that accommodates hundreds, lingering over tables laden with food, does not bolster either the archives' image or staff morale. An archives should recognize that few events draw capacity crowds, sell out all tickets, or command long lines at the door. Fourth, numbers of people attending an event are not the only criterion for gauging its success. Was the event well publicized? Did many people know about it? Did planning and organizing the event unify board members or promote collegiality among staff? Did a debriefing reveal the possible causes of low attendance or a way to improve attendance? What were the objectives of the event? Did it meet those objectives? Did it succeed in helping people recognize that there is an archives in their community that is available for their use? If the results of the event met your objectives for it, whatever they were, the archives can declare truthfully that the event was a success.

Because fund raising will cost an archives money before it is able to raise the first dollar—whether for printing a new brochure, providing the postage for the appeal letter, the fees for the speakers, or the food for the reception—it should also consider hiring a fund raising consultant. We emphasize the word *consultant.* From the beginning, the archives must understand that the consultant does not solicit money for the archives. Consultants are not fund raisers; they only advise and train. The fund raising consultant will bring to the archives experience in fund raising, proven research methods, sound management theory, strategic planning skills, and an adeptness at training and motivating volunteers. They do not approach donors for funds.

Good fund raising consultants are objective and dispassionate. They will bring to the archives an outsider's often beneficial and eye-opening perspective, which helps the institution see itself as others do. A fund raising consultant views the archives through the very special prism of fund raising, seeing the composition of the governing board, its commitment and enthusiasm for fund raising, and the level of existing support from gifts. The institution may have a national reputation for excellence among scholars and archivists but be viewed very differently by a consultant whose task it is to advise and guide a client through a successful fund raising campaign.

Some members of the archives board will protest that hiring a fund raising consultant is expensive and unnecessary. This objection can be countered by pointing out that most consultants will discuss their services with representatives of an institution at no cost or obligation to the institution. Although this meeting will cost an archives time and energy, it will cost no money. Second, the cost to raise funds might be less than imagined, depending on the circumstances of the institution. A new campaign for annual support might cost 30 percent or more in its formative years; a $3 million capital campaign, as low as 3 to 6 percent.

Finding a consultant to interview need not be difficult. Begin with institutions similar to your own that have had successful fund raising campaigns: the library in the next city, the museum across town. Call them, asking for the name of their fund raising consultant and whether they were satisfied with his/her work. You may also want to call the National Society of Fund Raising Executives or the American Association of Fund Raising Counsel (see additional readings at end of chapter), groups with clearly defined codes of ethics, for the names of consultants who are members. Development officers at institutions with which board and staff of your archives are associated, e.g., colleges, schools, other educational or cultural institutions, also might be able to suggest consulting firms.

A small group representing the archives should meet with two or more consultants before it decides whether it wants to hire any. This group should consist of one or two board members and the executive director of the archives. If this small group has no fund raising experience among its members, recruit someone from outside the archives who has such experience: a board member's friend who was involved in his college's capital campaign or the executive director of an institution that has worked with a fund raising consultant.

The meeting between this small group and the fund raising consultant is appropriately called a *mutual assessment meeting,* with each party evaluating the possibility of a successful relationship. Information must be freely exchanged. Representatives of the archives will explain why the institution wants to raise money and describe its basic structure, its financial health, and its current programs. The consultant will outline his/her services and discuss how he/she can help. The consultant, who is as interested in success as the archives, may decide that the archives is not ready to hire him/her until it has reached a consensus about its goals, or built a stronger, more active board. Or the consultant may decide that the archives can benefit from his/her services and suggest ways that the archives can find the money for the consultancy.

The final decision may reflect the board's earlier opposition, or it may not. In either case, the board will probably have learned a good deal that is useful about fund raising from these meetings, and will not have had to pay for it.

Conclusion

Fund raising is not a mysterious process. Much of it combines an understanding of human needs with good management practice. For example, people must feel that their contribution matters. They will want to be thanked appropriately. A successful institution will define and set down in writing its mission and will set budget priorities. Fund raising is challenging because its requires a constant focus on the donor: this year's donor, last year's donor, and all those potential donors who might be persuaded to contribute, once they understand the institution and its needs. That focus is unceasing. Every successful fund raising effort concludes with an acknowledgment that is essentially the beginning of the next year's fund raising effort. For many archives, fund raising requires a commitment to reach out beyond the scholar, the historian, and the traditional user to new constituencies who may not at first understand why an archives is important.

Year after year, statistics demonstrate that the private sector in America is notably generous to nonprofit institutions.

Year after year, archives complain that they lack appropriate funding support for their programs. Our solution has typically been to search the latest grant application guidelines to see if our programs can be bent to fit the most recent requirements of the grant-making agencies. But in focusing all our efforts on grant-making agencies, archives overlook not only the magnitude of private sector support available to us but its nonpecuniary advantages as well. Private sector fund raising may not be a path that every archives will care to follow, but it should be one that every archives carefully considers.

Additional Readings

Books

American Association of Fund Raising Counsel. *Giving U.S.A.* (New York: American Association of Fund Raising Counsel, 1991). Standard source of statistics and information about charitable contributions for any given year. American Association of Fund Raising Counsel, 25 West 43rd Street, Suite 1519, New York, NY 10036.

Lant, Jeffrey. *Development Today, A Fund Raising Guide for Non Profit Organizations.* rev. 4th ed. (Cambridge, MA: JLA Publications, 1990). Comprehensive, how-to-do-it book including chapters on time lines, special events, and direct mail.

O'Connell, Brian. *The Board Member's Book, Making a Difference in Voluntary Organizations* (New York: The Foundation Center, 1985). Outlines the responsibilities of a board member, including a discussion of the relationship between staff and board.

Raybin, Arthur D. *How To Hire the Right Fund Raising Consultant* (Washington, DC: Taft Group, 1985). Practical advice on what an organization should look for in a good fund raising consultant, including interview questions to ask prospective consultants.

Schneiter, Paul H. *The Art of Asking, How To Solicit Philanthropic Gifts* (Ambler, PA: Fund Raising Institute, 1985). Conversational, practical guide to how to ask for money.

Smith, William J. *The Art of Raising Money* (New York: American Management Association, 1985). Basic fund raising management, with examples of specific fund raising situations.

Trenbeth, Richard P. *The Membership Mystique, How To Create Income and Influence with Membership Programs* (Ambler, PA: Fund Raising Institute, 1986). Basics of membership development, with an emphasis on cultural organizations. Fund Raising Institute, Box 365, Ambler, PA 19002.

Periodicals

Chronicle of Philanthropy. Published 24 times a year, this newspaper of the nonprofit world keeps you informed of the latest developments in fund raising, grants, tax and court rulings, and the role of boards and volunteers. *Chronicle of Philanthropy*, P.O. Box 1989, Marion, Ohio 43305.

Corporate Giving Watch. Provides detailed information on where corporations are giving their money, and how much. Taft Group, 5031 MacArthur Boulevard, N.W., Washington, DC 20016.

Foundation News. Published 6 times yearly, this is the official publication of the Council on Foundations, to which many foundations belong. Council on Foundations, 1828 L Street N.W., Suite 1200, Washington, DC 20036.

Fund Raising Management. Monthly magazine dealing with general topics in fund raising. Hoke Communications, 224 Seventh Street, Garden City, Long Island, NY 10530.

3

In Print, On Air

Working with the Media

Megan Sniffin-Marinoff

"Every cause that tries to enlist the interest and support of the public may be thought of as an iceberg. The public is interested in and supports only what it sees, even though the portion that lies below the surface of its vision may be much greater and more important."

Edward L. Bernays
Public Relations

Archivists spend a great deal of time talking to each other; they are absorbed with day-to-day activities, immersed in the substance and detail of the profession. Yet despite all their hard work, many archivists do not understand why few people clamor to use a newly opened collection or attend an archives' special event. Archivists express frustration with a public that does not understand what archives are or why they are needed, a failure that for some institutions translates into poor facilities and lack of funding.

In the past decade, much has been said and written on the need to promote better public understanding of archives and archivists. To act upon this charge, archivists must rethink the priorities of daily activity and designate time to publicize their own or their institution's activities in both print and broadcast media outlets. Basic publicity activities must be considered core activities in any archives program, as important as processing a collection or appointing new personnel. Once basic publicity activities become routine, additional media campaigns such as informational tours or press conferences become easier to visualize and mount.

There is no quick way for an archives to obtain regular and successful media coverage. Relations with the media are like relations with friends and relatives: They require work, time, and understanding. But as with human relations, the hard work of developing media relations is worth the effort.

Basic Publicity Activities

What Are The Goals?

The goals of any regular, basic publicity activity in an archives are to heighten awareness of the archives' activities and increase public support in all its forms. Improved visibility, combined with attention to quality service and ease of access should eventually lead to increased use of the collections, more varied use of them, better attendance at special events, or new sources for collections or funding, depending on the archives' objectives.

Just as all politics is local, often all news is, too. While you may occasionally aim your sights toward national coverage of an event, getting local coverage for your archives must be a high priority, because it will yield measurable results.

The most publicized activities in an archives should be announcements of

- **The receipt of new accessions.** *Example:* The Hampstead Collection announces the acquisition of a famous or well-known artist's personal papers.
- **The opening or availability of collections.** *Example:* The North Utah State Archives announces the opening of a group of records long withheld, such as census records. (See Appendix 1 a, c, e for examples.)

These are perhaps the most important types of activities to publicize, for they emphasize the basic purpose of most archives: collecting and access. However, don't stop here. Other activities are of interest to the public as well. Some examples include

- **New or changing personnel.** *Example:* The Cascade Corporate Archives announces the appointment of a new director.
- **A grant award.** *Example:* The Truman College Archives announces the receipt of a grant of $50,000 from the Newhart Foundation to study the appraisal of college and university records.
- **An exhibit opening.** *Example:* The Charlotte Perkins Gilman National Historic Site announces the opening of a permanent exhibit of archival materials found on the site.
- **Scheduling of educational programs.** *Example:* The Omaha Municipal Archives announces the availability of new instructional programs for conducting research on family history.
- **Plans for special events.** *Example:* The Forest University Literary Collection announces the scheduling of a new theater production based upon letters from the collection.
- **Significant or nontraditional uses of records.** *Example:* The Southern Maine State Archives announces the successful use of highway department records in assisting urban archaeologists to locate colonial dumping grounds for excavation before new building projects begin.
- **Improved access to collections.** *Example:* The California Nineteenth Century Photograph Collection announces the availability of its collections on videodisc.
- **Significant developments within the field.** *Example:* The Lincoln County Archives announces changes in its collecting policies due to changes in the law.

Coordinating with Public Relations Staff

Coordinating publicity with public relations staff is a must for archives in large institutional archives. Before beginning a publicity campaign, be certain that other departments in the institution are not already releasing this news. Where inter-institutional coordination is imperative, cultivate a working relationship between the staff of the archives and public relations staff.

What Are The Necessary Materials?

Learning to work with the media means speaking their language and using formats for the presentation of information that conform to industry standards. The basic formats for issuing information to the print and broadcast media are news releases and broadcast media releases.

News Releases

The primary tool for communication with the media is the news release, also referred to as a media release or press release. The release is usually a one-page document laid out so that it provides the reader with progressively more information. The media expect that certain types of information will always be provided and style books such as those of the New York *Times* or Associated Press should be consulted. Remember, just as archivists provide information in standard formats in inventories and registers, the media also has requirements that help get news into print or on the air in a timely fashion.

The information in a news release answers six basic questions: Who? What? When?

Where? Why? and How? Journalists refer to these questions as the "five W's and the H." An example might be:

> A new publication, *The City's Historical Parks* [what], is available free from the Grove City Historical Society [where] beginning June 10 [when]. The publication highlights many of the city's forgotten and neglected historic parks [why] with photographs recently restored [how] by staff at the Society [who].

Archivists must learn that although a news release is used to educate, it cannot be a heavy-handed education. By answering as many of these questions as possible, the essential information necessary to sell your story is provided. See Figure 3.1 for a sample release format.

Editors shorten releases by cutting paragraphs or lines from the bottom of the story up. This is particularly true in newspapers, where late-arriving advertisements, the bread-and-butter of a paper, are of unexpected size and stories must be changed quickly to get the newspaper pages to the presses on time. Whether the editor cuts by hand or on a computer, he/she will—literally—cut a story starting from the last paragraphs.

For this reason, releases can be written using the "inverted pyramid" method. The most important information should appear in the first paragraphs with subsequent paragraphs used for expanding the story. For example:

National Archives Presents Encore Performances of "In the Mood."

> Due to an overwhelming popular response, the National Archives will present three encore performances of the World War II musical program, "In the Mood," in commemoration of Veteran's Day. "In the Mood" played to full houses at the National Archives in July.
>
> The performances feature the female vocal trio "String of Pearls" and male vocalist and dancer Brian Donnelly. "In the Mood" is a production of Bud Forrest Entertainment and includes members of Forrest's Washington Swing Orchestra.
>
> "In the Mood" will be performed on Monday, Tuesday, and Wednesday, November 4, 5, and 6, at 7:30 P.M. in the National Archives Theater. There is no charge for these performances, but seating is limited.
>
> Passes will be issued on a first-come, first-served basis beginning at 5:00 P.M. on the day of the performance, until all passes are distributed. The theater will open at 7:00 P.M.

These paragraphs contain the essence of the story and could stand alone.

The final lines or paragraphs should be used for minor details or details not critical to the story, such as an indication of how to get further information, who is available for an interview on the subject, or (if not essential to the story) who funded the project. For example:

> "In the Mood" is written and directed by James Morris and features many wartime favorites, including a selection of lively swing music. "String of Pearls" members Cindy Hutchins, Ann Johnson, and Brenda Brody will perform selections by the Andrews Sisters, including "Boogie Woogie Bugle Boy" and "Rum and Coca-Cola."
>
> "In the Mood" is part of the National Archives continuing commemoration of the 50th anniversary of U.S. participation in World War II. For further information on other commemorative events, please call the Public Programs Office at 202-501-5200.
>
> Please use the Pennsylvania Avenue entrance, between 7th and 9th streets, NW. For updated information, please call 202-724-0454, or the Public Events line at 202-501-5000.

Generally speaking, a news release meant to provide *filler*, i.e., a short story to be used when there is extra space on a page or empty air-time—is kept to 250 words or one double-spaced, typed page. If a second page is included, indicate so by adding the word "more" to the bottom of the page.

Multiple-page releases are usually used when a longer or feature piece is sought. They are most successful when sent to journals or other sources that have a direct interest in the

Figure 3.1. Elements of a Sample News Release Format

For Immediate Release

This phrase appears in the upper left hand corner of a release. If you are printing a release on letterhead whose design does not allow for such placement, use the upper right hand corner. If information is not for immediate release, suggest a future release date, that is, the date at which the copy can be used.

For More Information or Contact

The name and phone number of the person who will handle calls for further information or clarification should be listed immediately beneath the release line. Never send out a release without identifying a contact.

Headline

Provide a short, descriptive summary of the story beginning about one-third of the way down the page. This headline probably will not be the one that appears in print. However, just as editors use headlines to catch readers' attention, you will write a headline to catch the editor's attention.

Body of the Release

Paragraph 1 begins with a statement summarizing the story. The paragraph should be succinct but lively, written to grab the readers' attention. The basic elements of the *five W's and the H* should be mentioned here. Occasionally this paragraph begins with a dateline, or statement of the city of origin of the story, and the date of transmission. This is a rare inclusion, usually only noted when news will be sent to large media operations or the news wires.
Paragraphs 2 through the last paragraph expand upon the first paragraph. Each paragraph explains, with progressively more detail, the important or interesting facts of the story.

or End or 30

One of these symbols is centered under the last paragraph to indicate the end of the story.

institution's news and few reporters to cover stories. Scholarly journals tend to feature an entire piece or will add news to an "Announcements" or "News Accessions" section. For an example of such releases, see Appendix 1e.

The News Release Versus the Feature Story

The print or air media use most news releases without seeking additional information. However, you or a reporter or editor may have ideas for fuller *soft news* or feature stories that require conducting interviews or other research. Feature stories are usually appropriate for only one or two media outlets. For example, you may prepare a general news release announcing the opening of the records of social service agencies or charities. One of the institutions featured in the collection is a local charity still in existence. By writing a query letter to a local editor suggesting a feature piece on the charity and its history, you could tell your story in a larger and perhaps more interesting context. The simple act of suggesting topics for feature stories to the media outlets you contact most often, particularly local outlets, may also have the effect of encouraging editors and reporters to seek you out regularly for ideas and information.

Photograph Releases

A good photograph attracts attention to your news or feature story. If you can, include one. In fact, a photo release, in which the text of the release or caption focuses solely on the image itself, is very effective.

When choosing these photographs, consider several rules of thumb. Always favor photos with people in them. However, shots of large crowds do not reproduce well; choose images with three or four people at most. Make sure images of people show none with their eyes cast down or shut. Try to focus attention on the central object in the photograph, but avoid a posed look. Avoid sending the same image to media in the same geographic area.

Most newspapers prefer photographs that are black and white, 8 by 10 inches in size, with a glossy finish, free of scratches, graininess, or other flaws. Magazines, on the other hand, use better printing processes and can accept larger photographs with a matte finish. Magazines also willingly accept color photographs, even though there is no guarantee the image will appear in color. For easier handling, print all photos with borders.

Whether sent separately or with a release, each photograph should have an attached caption. The caption should be a brief identification of the event and contain appropriate credit for the photographer or the institution. Since the photograph can easily become separated from the written release, use the caption to include much of the same information found in the basic news release: release date, contact, and the basics of the story.

Once the caption is written, it should be typed or printed on the bottom half of a full sheet of 8-1/2 x 11 paper. If the photograph image is vertical, type the caption on the bottom half of the sheet held vertically; type on the horizontal for a horizontal image. Tape the paper halfway up, onto the back of the photograph, so the caption appears under the photograph. Fold the caption over the photo, enabling it to fit into an envelope and offering protection to the photograph, which will surely be handled by several people. When you mail a photograph, put a sturdy piece of cardboard the same size against the front and back of the photo.

Photographs are not the only images that can accompany news releases. Engravings, line drawings, or maps can also be used. Fig. 3.2 is an example of a captioned image designed to accompany a news release announcing the opening of a collection of digitized images.

Photograph releases are often successful when aimed at the wire services (such as the Associated Press) that circulate news nationally and internationally. The wire services distribute photographs that are visually interesting and can tell stories with only the addition of a caption. One caution: Since wire services require exclusive use of a photograph, do not circulate the same photograph to various services simultaneously.

Figure 3.2. Sample Photograph Caption

For Immediate Release

Contact: John Jones, 617-555-1414
The Simmons College Archives announces the availability of online access to its photograph collections containing 50,000 digitized images of twentieth-century women at work. Shown here is a digitized version of a 1944 photograph of nurses organizing a stockroom. The completion of a two-year project to create complete online access to the images and the index to the collection was made possible by a grant from the Friends Foundation. For further information, contact the Archives at 555-1414.
Photo credit: John Whipple, photographer. The Whipple Collection, Simmons College Archives.

Community Calendar Announcements

Many newspapers and magazines provide free space to not-for-profit organizations in a special section often called a community calendar. Community calendar announcements sent to calendar editors are often shortened, more tightly edited versions of news releases. Listings range from exhibit openings to not-for-profit fund raising events, to club meetings. In many places, daily newspapers print a weekly calendar of local cultural events in weekend issues. Many magazines list items based upon readers' geographic or subject interests.

In urban or tourist areas, separate calendars are often published by local tourist boards and distributed in hotels, restaurants, and other public places and used by tour guides. All these calendars are excellent ways to reach a general audience. Find out which are available in your area.

When preparing community calendar announcements, list the Who, What, When, Where, Why, and How of an event. For example:

> **For Immediate Release**
> Contact: Martha Baskin, 515-555-1313
> The Manuscript Department of Northern University will exhibit its collection of letters and photographs of American playwright Eugene O'Neill in the New Art Gallery of Northern University, December 1-31, 9:00 A.M. to 5:00 P.M., 12 Rocky Road, Nord City, 555-1313. Free admission and parking.

If the listing provides sufficient space, squeeze in an additional line to read:

> Northern University's collection documents the personal life of the playwright and his family when they lived in Bermuda in the 1920s. During this time O'Neill began writing his play *Lazarus Laughed*.

Calendars often require six to eight weeks lead time, so be aware of these deadlines. To avoid missing deadlines when mailing calendar listings, be sure to indicate on the release and its envelope that the enclosure is "dated material."

Radio and Television Media Releases

Radio and television stations are often required to provide free airtime to not-for-profit organizations. Broadcast media releases or public service announcements should be provided to the broadcast media as scripts. For television, provide a script and suggested still or moving artwork, or an air-quality, finished product such as an audiotape, film, or videotape. Speak to staff at your local station to find out what they need from you.

Figure 3.3. Sample Broadcast Media Release

Date: October 15, 1993
Children's History Collection
23 Canal Street, New York, NY, 10005
Contact: Sandy Hook
212-555-1515

Speaker: Ann Peters
AIR DATES: November 25 to December 31

10-SECOND ANNOUNCEMENT (25 words)
For television with graphic: slide

SLIDE IDENTIFICATION
Slide is a color close-up shot of antique toys.

WHISTLES, TOPS, JACKS, AND TIN FIRE ENGINES.
RELIVE YOUR CHILDHOOD.
VISIT NEW YORK'S CHILDREN'S HISTORY COLLECTION.
PLAY BEGINS DECEMBER FIRST.
CALL 555-1515 FOR TICKET INFORMATION.

A script should be more informal and livelier than a news release. Allow approximately twenty-five words per ten seconds of radio time and twenty words per ten seconds of television time when you write a script. Sentences are shorter. There are fewer facts. For example, see Figure 3.3.

Some radio and television stations allow free access to studio space and even assistance with the production of a message. This free service is important, because a series of professionally produced color videotapes could otherwise cost you thousands of dollars. In-house productions can cost much less, but this assumes the presence of knowledgeable staff and access to equipment.

Public service announcements are traditionally provided in ten- , twenty- , thirty- , or sixty-second taped segments. When you send a broadcaster a tape in a finished format, accompany it with a copy of the script, usually triple-spaced in capital letters with wide margins. Indicate clearly the contact person and phone number, number of words, tape length, and the release date (see Figure 3.3) in the heading of the script. Be aware of two constraints: First, broadcasters cannot tell you when—date or time—an announcement will appear. Second, unless you arrange to collect the materials once they are no longer current, the station will discard them. If you want material returned, get it yourself.

If a tape is to be recorded with the voice of an in-house staff member, have the reader practice recording the message on a tape recorder, perfecting timing, sound, and clarity before making the final recording. If at all possible, try to use a professional studio. A poorly presented piece can do damage to the image of an institution. Read one of the many good books available in public libraries on audio or videotaping. Because the technology changes rapidly, look for current literature in the field.

Most local radio and television stations publish booklets or fact sheets that will guide you in preparing public service announcements.

Since station requirements may vary and the preparation of tapes is time-consuming and often costly, obtain copies of these booklets early. Among other topics, these booklets give information on film, video, or slide specifications, shipping tips, multiple copying, tagging or identification, cover letters, proof of not-for-profit status, and script writing.

Press Kits

For the reporters who always arrive unexpectedly, as well as those you schedule, have available an ample supply of information packets or press kits, which are also useful for other visitors. These kits should provide information about what the institution does, who uses it, and what is currently happening in it. They need not be elaborate or slick, but they should convey visually and by their written content the image the repository seeks to foster.

Most press kits consist of a sturdy paper portfolio with inside pockets to hold loose materials. The name of the institution and a logo, if one is used, appear on the cover. Include in the packet:

- **Brochures.** The archives should use its own information brochures. If it is an institutional archives, information about the parent institution or company can also be included.
- **Sample clippings.** When you have been successful in getting the institution into print, choose a few of the better pieces written about the collection or its activities, photocopy them, and put them together to form a "clip pack" in the kit. If major journal articles about the archives or the collections have been published, consider their inclusion as well.
- **Fact sheet.** If basic facts about the archives, such as collection areas, size of holdings, bulk dates of holdings, founding date, usership, and products of use are not in the brochure, create a one-page information sheet.
- **Schedule of upcoming events.** Such schedules are useful for prepublicity, but staff must keep packets up-to-date.
- **Photographs.** Images of key items from the collection or of the facility—those that may have universal application for almost any story published about the archives—should be included. The images should be black and white, glossy, and 8 x 10 inches.
- **Business card.** If a particular staff member is appointed the press contact, include that person's business card. These cards can be mounted easily onto the outside of a paper pocket by simply cutting slits in the pocket, angled as for a photograph in an album. Place the card inside the openings.

Occasionally the reporter who visits is from the broadcast media. Consider keeping on hand several copies of video broadcast announcements produced as general publicity statements about the institution. If the collections contain good film or video footage, make note of the exact location, format, and length (number of seconds) of such pieces. If it is within the organization's budget, have duplicate copies of excerpts from these materials reproduced, too. These tapes can help the reporter looking for quick filler put the organization on that evening's news.

Getting Ready to Approach the Media

At the same time that you produce news releases, broadcast media releases, and press kits, begin directing information to the appropriate media outlet. Using the journalist's *five W's and the H* as a guide, plan a long-range strategy to attract media attention. (See Appendix 1k and following for a media plan.)

Where Should I Aim?

Archivists recommend regularly that researchers avoid disappointment by "doing their homework," particularly checking tools such as the *National Union Catalog of Manuscript Collections*, online databases, and guides to local and special collections. Heed this advice yourself and plan time to do research on the various media markets. Just as the archival world is composed of many kinds of repositories, so also is the media world. The print media consists primarily of newspapers and magazine operations in several categories.

- **Internationally circulated**. *Examples:* Reuters, Associated Press, the *International Herald Tribune*
- **Nationally circulated**. *Examples: USA Today, New York Times, Newsweek*

- **Regionally or locally circulated.** *Examples: Boston Magazine, San Francisco Chronicle, Quincy Patriot Ledger, Southern Living, MidAtlantic*
- **Technical trade publications and scholarly journals.** *Examples: Analytical Chemistry, American Historical Review, American Archivist, Foreign Affairs*
- **Specialty magazines.** *Examples: Architectural Digest, Arts & Antiques, Gourmet Magazine, Road and Track, Woman's Day*

The broadcast media consists of local and national radio and television stations, both commercial and public, with an increasing amount of local programming found on cable networks.

A media release should be written for a specific audience. So that information will reach a targeted audience, understand which populations a newspaper or television program aims to reach. Using a card file or one of the many software packages available for the creation of lists, begin to create profiles of those print and broadcast sources whose printed space or airtime will most benefit the institution. Whichever method you choose, make sure that it allows you to change or update information frequently.

Media directories provide a rich resource for deciphering the demographics, i.e., size, density, education, age, gender, and income, of the readers or viewers of a particular medium. Many of these directories are available in public or corporate libraries and are nearly always found in public and private academic libraries whose institutions house communications departments. Generally speaking, multivolume media directories are expensive, falling in the $75 to $350 range. Many are published annually. Take the time to look at several of the leading directories before deciding to purchase any of them on a regular basis. A few of the more useful works include:

For General Reference

Eleanor S. Brock and James K. Bracken. *Communication and the Mass Media: A Guide to the Reference Literature* (Englewood, CO: Libraries Unlimited, 1991). An excellent book to examine before searching for directories. An annotated guide to basic English-language sources in communication. In particular, see Chapter 6, "Directories and Yearbooks," an annotated list of media directories, with full citations.

For the Press in General

Working Press of the Nation (Burlington, IA: National Research Bureau). Published annually. A basic five-volume work (vol. 1, Newspaper Directory; vol. 2, Magazine Directory; vol. 3, Radio and Television Directory; vol. 4, Feature Writer and Photographer Directory; vol. 5, Internal Publications Directory) with various indexes to subject specializations.

For National Newspapers

Editor & Publisher International Yearbook (New York: Editor & Publisher Co.). The classic in the field, published annually. Comprehensive information on U.S. and Canadian daily and weekly papers, foreign newspapers, and news services, including addresses, telephone numbers, editors and other personnel, political orientation, and circulation statistics.

For Television and Radio

Broadcasting Yearbook (Washington, DC: Broadcasting Publications). Published annually. Basic geographically arranged guide to radio, television, and cable television stations in the U.S. and Canada, with profiles featuring demographic analysis, news services, maps of markets, and media rankings.

Bacon's Radio/TV Directory (Chicago: Bacon's PR and Media Information Systems, 1987-). A geographically arranged guide to over 10,000 commercial and noncommercial U.S. broadcasters, with call numbers, telephone numbers, national affiliations, and contacts for type of program (news, features, interviews, and so forth).

International Television & Video Almanac (New York: Quigley Publishing). Published annually. A superb source of general information on U.S. and foreign broadcasters.

Don't be afraid to start big! If the opening of a collection, a new exhibit, or any special event is truly newsworthy, contact the source that will offer the widest and best exposure first. If at first you have little success, work down the list. When you appear in print regularly, those at the top of the list will begin to pay attention to you.

Whom Should I Contact?

Once you decide to contact particular print or broadcast outlets, decide whom to contact. Many of the directories mentioned here, particularly those published annually, can provide names. While it is not necessary to address all of your releases to a specific person, if a name is available, use it.

The general rule of thumb for both print and broadcast sources is that most media releases are directed to the news editor (print) or news director (broadcast). (Note that most large media operations have separate weekend news operations and weekend news or assignment editors.) The news editor determines how much or how little space or time a story will receive and assigns other editors and reporters to work on stories. You may develop rapport with an editor. You may even find that a particular reporter is assigned regularly to cover your institution or stories about it. However, the editor or reporter you know personally may not be the best person to contact for results. Find out who the editors or reporters are for each section and direct your material accordingly.

If a media release is sent to a specific reporter, be sure to send a copy to the news editor as well, indicating to each that this has been done. For small or local print and broadcast outlets, send one copy of a release to the editor only. If the target is several specific reporters or departments in a large operation (arts editor, features editor, business editor, columnist) be sure to let each party know who else received a copy. An archives will not endear itself to an operation that suddenly finds itself assigning several people to cover the same story.

Editors will occasionally ask whether the information you supply is an *exclusive.* Some print or broadcast outlets run only those stories that will not appear elsewhere, or before they publish them. While an organization may be anxious to gain publicity, staff should tell editors if other releases were sent out. In this case, use the opportunity to explore the editor's policies. If this is an important outlet, you might arrange to provide information exclusively with a time deadline; that is, to offer first refusal. Another option is to supply the same release with a different angle.

When Should I Begin?

Timing is everything. It wastes staff energy to prepare releases or hold special events when a chosen media outlet's deadlines have passed. Also watch deadlines if you want to piggyback a story onto an event outside of the archives. For example, planning to send announcements of a new accession of Irish manuscripts near St. Patrick's Day will be useless if the deadline for the St. Patrick's Day issue of a newspaper is two weeks before the holiday. Information about deadlines will be at a your fingertips, however, if you take time to do your research.

News editors must receive releases and other materials well in advance of the event an organization hopes to publicize. Most news coming from archives falls into the *soft news* or "feature" category, which means that stories are printed when there is space or in special feature sections, or they are aired when more important stories do not take precedence. Of course, if an organization decides to contact either print or broadcast sources with quick-breaking hard news—a disaster such as a theft or a fire, or a sudden visit from a well-known dignitary—it should be done immediately.

In most cases, plan to mail releases to newspapers at least fifteen days in advance of papers' deadlines. Magazines and journals may require releases anywhere from fifteen days to nine months in advance of their deadlines. Periodicals that appear monthly or quarterly of necessity have early deadlines. Check media directories carefully for deadline information.

If you have an exciting story, consider sending a media advisory, media alert, or teaser twenty-five days in advance to pique curiosity. For example, if an important local or national personality is planning a visit to your archives to make a donation of papers or records, consider first announcing the impending visit without providing details of the donation. Follow up with a full release closer to the date of the event, but within the time necessary to meet media deadlines.

In the broadcast media, *talk or community-service shows* need approximately six weeks of lead time. In major cities, feature pieces on news shows may require three to six months of advance work. In smaller cities, a week's notice may serve. Try to understand media time pressure. If you are following up a release with a phone call, do not call near airtime or at similarly inopportune times. Find out who to call and when to call, then call back at a suitable time. When you plan a mailing date, remember that Sunday newspapers or news shows often feature soft news or society items. Late summer, holiday weekends, and late December are all times when the media, like every other organization, is short-staffed and therefore unable to fill its allotted print space or airtime adequately. News releases timed for these periods are often most welcome.

What Will Attract Attention?

When you undertake research on where to direct news releases, begin by deciding what it is the archives wants to promote about itself. Are you trying to promote your uniqueness or a generally friendly image? Do you have a new facility or new equipment allowing better access to your collections? Are you planning a conference on a controversial subject? When you have made this decision, first gather information from the media directories on the subject content of the various media outlets. Then make a point of reading the local newspapers or special-subject magazines. Listen to or watch different radio, local news, or community service shows. This will give you a much better sense of what angles to try for each medium.

As you read and listen, think as a news editor thinks. Ask the questions the editor will ask.

- Is the story interesting?
- Does the story hold my attention?
- Is there relevance to a specific group of readers/viewers?
- Is there any potential for interesting visual backup?
- Is this story worth a feature or only a few paragraphs?

What you, the archivist, find interesting may not be what an editor considers the engaging part of a story. For example, while your archives may be interested in announcing the opening of an exhibit including formerly restricted portions of President Gerald Ford's papers, the press may be more interested in highlighting the bear made from beer cans given to the former president. Consider items that will attract popular attention; these are often the links the press needs to convey your story to the public.

With thought and imagination, you can find several natural local outlets for information. For example, you hope to promote the activities of the Acme Corporation Archives. The Acme Corporation, founded in 1892, employs much of the population of Acme, Pennsylvania. With a release that is professionally presented and interesting, the local or regional newspaper is likely to publish—for the benefit of residents interested in family history—an announcement of the availability of newly microfilmed company newsletters containing detailed human-interest information about the many townspeople who have worked for the company over the past one hundred years.

Or, if a local newspaper is supplied with print or photograph release announcing the opening of an exhibit of images of the buildings that housed the company for the past century, it will not only be likely to list the exhibit in a calendar of local events, but also consider featuring the exhibit, using either supplied artwork or that of the paper's own photographers. With patience, you will find that your organization can find a niche in the news if it supplies targeted, publicly interesting information.

The local media will be more interested in your archives than will national outlets and will also provide the best coverage. After all, local people, local places, and local events are local media territory. This kind of coverage often produces the best results. For example, if you are announcing the opening of a modest exhibit, local people who read about your exhibit will likely attend. But there are exceptions. A large exhibit of local history materials or a large grant for outreach on local records may command national exposure.

How do you decide how much time and effort you will expend to promote ideas outside of natural geographic or subject interests? For example, a repository has a fine collection of letters of U.S. Senator X, many of which are to be put on display. History magazines, Senator X's alumni publications, Senator X's hometown print and broadcast media, and the organization's local print and broadcast outlets may make an announcement or cover the story. Will the national media be interested? To ensure that they are, find a *hook*, an angle to attract interest. Perhaps the fact that this large exhibit is funded by an organization of national prominence may be that hook. Characters in the story may have reached national prominence. A nationally known person may have written the catalog. If the exhibit is timed to open on a date important in the person's life, such as an anniversary of a birth or death, it may provide a sidebar, a story that can be tied into a larger story. Consider both the local and national connections of the exhibit as you plan publicity.

In addition to gaining an understanding of what types of stories the media outlets cover, be aware that you face competition for media space from other archives, special collections, and historical societies in your geographic or subject areas. You should therefore ask yourself what is different about your organization's work. What makes your institution unique? The staff undoubtedly knows the policies of neighboring archives or those archives collecting in subject areas similar to yours; consider this information when you choose what to promote. If you share collecting interests with other institutions, promote what is unique, interesting, or different about your organization.

How Can I Do All This?

First, consider how you pace your activity, then, view every part of your operation—collection development, processing, reference, public programs, use—as public relations potential. Successful publicity requires time, but everything need not be done at once. This is particularly true for the archivist who works alone or has only volunteer help. In fact, whether staff is volunteer or paid, their enthusiasm will wane if the work is not carefully paced or mounted over time. Build up a regular and streamlined operation slowly.

Second, make public relations part of your program. To be taken seriously, public relations efforts must be part of job descriptions and the long-range plans or goals for a repository. Only then can staff integrate the work into their regular responsibilities, making it routine.

One excellent approach to public relations is to make one staff member the coordinator of activity and liaison with the media, while all staff participates in activities. Instead of asking one person to do the drudge work of mass mailings, for example, encourage other staff to help out during tense deadline periods to keep morale high. If announcements of the availability of newly processed collections are to be issued routinely, make it the responsibility of a collection processor to provide the coordinator with interesting images or other materials in the collection that can accompany news releases. Before considering the processing of a collection complete, ask the processor about items in the collection that may not surface in the inventory. In all cases, make sure that you get appropriate in-house approval for all releases or other press material before giving it to the media.

Send thank-you notes to the appropriate editor or reporter when a piece appears. If you decide to make a follow-up phone call after sending an important release, make sure to check media directories to find out the best times to call. Keep records of phone conversations to make sure that you do not call the same person twice and to remind yourself of what was said. Keep track of successes by subscribing to a clipping service, which for a fee searches, cuts out, and sends newspaper or magazine articles about an institution's activities to the institution. Or assign staff to watch for news about the archives as it appears.

Beyond The Basics: Additional Media Campaigns

Issuing Press Kits

Aside from having press kits on hand for the occasional visitor, regularly consider initiating or updating long-term relationships with the press, particularly the local press. An archives' circumstances, particularly those relating to collection policies, holdings, and staffing, can change frequently. This type of general news, intended for education purposes, can be shared by sending news editors or directors, reporters, or even columnists updated press kits. Each press kit should be accompanied by a brief cover letter explaining the reason for the mailing and urging the recipient to call with further questions. Media staff may file this information at the outset, but when they need updated information, they will know whom to call with questions about the repository or the subjects of the staff's expertise.

Writing a Regular Column for a Local Paper

If you have staff and time for a long-term commitment, offer to write a regular column in a local paper. This is a wonderful opportunity to discuss your archives in detail and work with an editor. At the least, you will bring the work and collections of your archives to his/her attention. In a college or university setting, for example, try writing columns on various aspects of the history of your school for alumni or student publications. Religious archivists often write regular historical pieces for diocesan newsletters or newspapers. The archivist of the Boston Archdiocese launched such a column in the archdiocesan publication, *The Pilot*, to good effect (see Chapter 8). Corporate archivists can often publish company history in in-house organs or industry trade publications. College and university archivists can seek space in alumni publications.

After examining a publication and understanding its purpose and readership, approach an editor with ideas for a series of stories or a regular column. Be open to suggestions of format, style, deadline, and space requirements. Again, do not promise what you cannot deliver; make sure your institution is able to make a commitment. If you do not follow through on your offer, you may harm your relations with a publication's staff.

Meeting the Press

By urging staff to keep up with what is happening in the news, an institution can often claim air or viewing time. Staff members who become known as local experts or spokespersons on a topic may be called upon to appear on radio or television shows. For example, during the yearlong media fascination with the Civil War, in part created by public broadcasting's airing of Ken Burnses' *Civil War* series, archives that provided a local angle to the war or planned exhibits or accessions of Civil War-related materials would most probably have had success in getting their staff on television and their message to the public. Since this was primarily a broadcast media event, archivists who sought airtime during the peak of this interest would probably have been successful.

With a little advance preparation, meeting the press or being interviewed can be a stimulating, though often unpredictable experience. Be prepared for an appearance to be moved forward, backward, or canceled altogether. Keep your interview conversational and be prepared for the unexpected. You may be asked questions for which you do not have a quick or popular answer. For example, if a public figure under investigation placed his or her personal papers in your archives under terms of restricted or limited access, your inability or unwillingness (for ethical reasons) to provide answers to all the questions about the public figure may prove frustrating both to you and the interviewer. But the experience can be useful.

A few tips:

- **Assume that no one knows what an archives is.** Prepare a few simple advance statements explaining what the institution or the profession does, if this seems appropriate to the topic. Avoid jargon or technical language. Talk about the *products of archival research*, not about archival techniques or processes.

- **Expect to have less time than you wanted**. Because the announcer will make introductory remarks about you or your topic, you will have less time to discuss substance than you would have expected. Make a short list of the important points for discussion and try to stick to them.
- **Be yourself**. Answer questions honestly and positively. Do not pretend to be an expert in an unfamiliar area. Do not be afraid to admit not knowing an answer to a question.
- **Wear comfortable clothing**. Even if the other guest on a television show is an award-winning fashion photographer, dress comfortably and naturally. Broadcast personnel may suggest what to wear, including colors that will look best on television. (Generally, single, primary colors work best. Avoid plaids or prints in dresses and ties.)
- **Request a tour**. Arrive at the station early. Familiarize yourself with the equipment. At a radio station, ask to test out the microphones. Most television stations will assign a contact person to guests. Ask for information about set-up of the studio and the cameras and where to look when you are on camera.
- **Know the format**. Find out if this is a solo interview or a panel discussion. Ask who the other guests will be. Be prepared for discussion with those whose viewpoint differs from yours. Request information on the amount of time set aside for the interview.
- **Take a friend**. If possible, ask a colleague along for company and moral support. If transportation arrangements are not made by the broadcaster, suggest that the other person drive.

If you are on television, do not hesitate to ask whether visual accompaniments would be appropriate. Take along a few mounted photographs to illustrate a point. If you are taking film or video, find out the format used by the station (16mm, 2-inch tape, cassette) and conform to it.

Press Conferences

When used judiciously and appropriately, press conferences can attract immediate attention to an archives. Calling a press conference suggests that the institution has news of tremendous importance: a rare or unusual find in a collection, a very large or important bequest, or ground breaking for a new building. The information must be for a broad public, not specialists or antiquarians. If the press conference is called because of a mishap, such as a theft or a loss, be prepared to answer tough questions about organizational procedures and responsibility (see Chapter 7).

Since press conferences are held at the archives or at the parent institution's facilities, choose a site in advance that will provide for crowds, electronic equipment, and a backdrop that will appear favorably in print or on the air. Be sure you have electrical backup. If you have a podium with an organizational logo or a background image appropriate to the organization, set these up in advance. Think about the idea you want to convey. If you are making a plea for assistance following a theft, for example, an appropriate backdrop might be the space in a partially empty box or the empty space on the wall.

When you send invitations for the press conference, present a *briefing sheet* or a short piece of information on the story, but not the whole story. Only provide enough information to entice an editor to assign the story and encourage reporters to come prepared with questions.

One spokesperson should be prepared to make a brief, initial statement and to anticipate specific questions. He/she should either answer questions or direct them to the appropriate speaker. If the media sends a photographer or cameraman in advance, the staff should be prepared to suggest items or people to be photographed and have space cleared for that purpose. Staff should know where outlets and light switches are. If powerful lights or a great deal of equipment are to be used, you may have to rent special electrical equipment.

When a repository's rules and regulations about access are followed, handling and filming of materials for a press conference can be extremely difficult. Staff must prepare for this in advance. If you know which items are to be photographed, prepare them for ease of use and handling, keeping in mind not only archival considerations but also media needs. For example, photographs can be placed in individual sleeves and handed quickly to a photographer one at a time, returned safely to a carton, and set aside securely when filming is completed.

If a press conference is called but no one comes, find out why. If important news occurs elsewhere that cannot be anticipated, send out or FAX news releases and chalk the experience up to unanticipated timing. Otherwise, calmly call a few editors to find out why the story was not covered and learn from the experience.

Summary

The most important step in any publicity campaign is the first one: Understand that publicity about an archives' activities, encouraging use of collections and participation in the archives' events should be part of the basic management functions and long-range plans of any archives. Success, to be sure, may be slow, but to be successful, you must approach publicity activities with commitment, professionalism, and a research mentality. The needs of the media must be understood, researched, learned, applied, and respected. Public relations master Edward L. Bernays' maxim about the iceberg (quoted at the beginning of this chapter) needs to be taken to heart by archives managers. Archives will remain that hidden mass beneath the surface, however precious, unless archivists become advocates for their work and their institutions.

Additional Readings

Adams, G. Donald. *Museum Public Relations.* AASLH Management Series, vol. 2 (Nashville, TN: American Association for State and Local History, 1983).

Beals, Melba. *Expose Yourself: Using the Powers of the Public Relations to Promote Your Business and Yourself.* (San Francisco: Chronicle Books, 1990).

Bernays, Edward L. *Public Relations.* (Norman: University of Oklahoma Press, 1952).

Block, Eleanor S., and James K. Bracken. *Communication and the Mass Media: A Guide to the Reference Literature.* (Englewood, CO.: Libraries Unlimited, 1991).

[Freivogel], Elsie Freeman. "Education Programs: Outreach as an Administrative Function." *American Archivist* 41 (April 1978): 147-153.

Gracy, David B., II. "Archivists, You Are What People Think You Keep." *American Archivist* 52 (Winter 1989): 72-78.

Gracy, David B., II. "What's Your Totem? Archival Images in the Public Mind." *Midwestern Archivist* 10, no. 1 (1985): 17-23.

Jones, Robert D. "Don't 'Sell' Records Management—Give It Away." *Records Management Quarterly* 23, no. 1 (January 1989): 3-10.

Lanzendorf, Peter. *The Videotaping Handbook: The Newest Systems, Cameras, and Techniques.* (New York: Harmony Books, 1983).

Pederson, Anne E., and Gail Farr Casterline. *Archives and Manuscripts: Public Programs.* SAA Basic Manual Series (Chicago: Society of American Archivists, 1982).

Weiner, Richard. *Professional's Guide to Publicity.* (New York: Public Relations Publishing Co., 1982).

4

Modest Proposals

Marketing Ideas for the Expansionist Archives

Philip F. Mooney

Large numbers of researchers have effectively mined the treasures in archival repositories by accessing the traditional finding aids that serve as guideposts to collections. With the explosion of information systems and shared data bases, archivists have subsequently succeeded in opening their holdings to an even more diverse audience with broad research agendas. Still, much work remains to be done if archival programs are to develop the strong constituencies required for preservation and growth. Managing collections and publicizing their availability with either standard or electronic reference tools represent only two aspects of a progressive archival philosophy. Disseminating information *about* collection content to external clientele requires using a multifaceted public relations strategy focusing on the relevance of archival material to contemporary society. While the scholarly and institutional user will always be an essential element for most programs, it is equally important for archivists to cultivate the wider community. Rather than serving as custodians of a documentary heritage alone, archivists should seek to open their institution's doors to new audiences and educate a general population about the varied uses of primary source materials.

Viewing their collections in the same light that marketing executives view their commercial products may be a helpful exercise for information professionals who have little experience in advertising or promoting their collections. If we make the very healthy assumption that consumers know little about our product and that they must be persuaded to use it, we will be more open to considering a wide range of programs that achieve public recognition and acceptance. Just as most marketing managers recognize that they must differentiate their products and services from those of their competitors, so too must archivists devote time and energy to planning and executing effective publicity campaigns that use a menu board of techniques. Regardless of the size or financial status of your institution, there are numerous ways to broaden your user base and create a distinct institutional identity. The key element in any successful publicity program about your holdings and services is your knowledge and understanding of your potential audiences. Marketers use such terms as "segmented" or "targeted" marketing to identify and solicit likely consumers of their products in order to achieve sales and volume growth. Similarly, archivists should explore new options to expand their consumer base and expose wider audiences to their products. No single educational technique appeals equally to the various publics you may wish to reach, but a broad range of offerings will help establish a wider constituency.

Commercial products can and do succeed by appealing to a small, well-defined clientele, but the most successful products enjoy widespread acceptability. Considering your collections in a similar framework may be useful in suggesting archival marketing applications.

Marketing techniques for archives fall into four major categories: publications, exhibitions, audiovisual productions, and public relations activities. Each of these groupings includes several subsets with strong interrelationships between segments, but it is useful to analyze them independently in order to discover the full range of possibilities. Any one category could and should include elements from the others.

Publications

Almost every archives produces both formal and informal publications as part of its regular outreach effort. These printed pieces inform the institution's public about its holdings and stimulate use of its collections, and should simultaneously generate fiscal, moral, and political support for its programs. A well-designed publication distributed to appropriate audiences can attract patrons that can be captured in no other way.

The most common publication form, and arguably the most important, is the institutional brochure or flyer that every archives should produce and distribute both to its internal and external constituents. The beauty of this form is that the brochure is a flexible and economical medium, allowing the creator to employ varying design techniques to convey a sense of the institution. From a simple three-fold, single-sheet handout to a multipage, lavishly illustrated presentation piece, the brochure serves a basic function: to convey a sense of the institution, to let people know what the collection contains and how they can access it, and to demonstrate that the repository performs very important scholarly work. An attractive, well-designed brochure printed on quality paper stock will appeal to the visual senses and encourage the reader to pay attention to the message it delivers. Once those essentials are established, publication content and presentation are only limited by the creativity of the author and designer.

A basic brochure emphasizes the mission of the institution and describes in broad outline the jewels of the collection. It might also include information relating to available finding aids, conditions of access, and research services. Highlight hours of operation, address, phone numbers, and other pertinent data.

In developing any brochure, stay focused on your objectives. Do not try to mention every collection you hold. Keep the information succinct and enticing. If possible, include interesting photographs and colorful graphics to break up the text and add visual excitement to the piece. Remember, you are selling a product. Consumers often make purchasing decisions based on packaging. The more appealing your presentation and design, the more likely you are to attract new patrons.

In addition to providing general information for the research community that helps stimulate use, the brochure format serves other archival needs. For developmental purposes, you can produce separate brochures that feature institutional subject strengths: literary or political holdings, ethnic or labor collections, transportation or religious records. For a relatively low investment, you not only publicize the availability of collections, but you have an opportunity to solicit new materials. For instance, if your collections include the records of regional social welfare organizations, you can develop a targeted mailing for agencies providing similar services that educate a potential user about your holdings and also subtly deliver the message that their records might be appropriate additions to these holdings. Many brochures of this type will include a direct invitation to the recipient to participate in collection development by donating relevant items. Even institutionally associated archival programs can benefit from producing brochures. Governmental, religious, cultural, and business archives must inform their internal audiences of their services while they actively promote the preservation of historic records. A graphically exciting, informative pamphlet reinforces the institutional commitment to the archives and its services and positively influences decision makers when budget and personnel allocations are being made.

Linking repositories in a small, single publication is another approach that can broaden the general public's awareness of archival holdings. A good example is the *Guide to Philadelphia Special Collections Libraries* that provides thumbnail sketches of eighteen regional repositories. A joint effort, this publication received much wider distribution than any of the repositories represented could have individually achieved, and the costs were absorbed by a sympathetic local foundation. Similar cooperative projects, organized by geography or subject areas, have enjoyed comparable successes.

Another relatively inexpensive publication is the periodic newsletter that doubles both as an information piece and as a tool for resource enhancement. Using a simple four-page, two-color format allows the archives to produce an information vehicle that helps keep patrons informed about new developments while it exposes potential clients to institutional holdings and programs. The advent of affordable desktop publishing and word processing software puts this vehicle within the reach of almost every archives. Quarterly production schedules seem realistic for most institutions, though more ambitious programs prepare monthly reports. Regardless of frequency or size, a newsletter provides regular communication with many audiences.

A typical newsletter issue features stories about use of collections, taken in the broadest context. Lead stories often relate to collection use and the products of research, and researchers working in your facility will frequently be willing to contribute brief essays on their work for this purpose. Other features focus on exhibition programs, media use of resources, institutional awards and honors, and general news items. The newsletter also provides a formal means of recognizing those who donate time, money, or material to your program. A simple honor roll of contributors and volunteers spotlights their individual gifts and encourages others to consider making similar contributions. Such periodicals convey a sense of programmatic energy and vitality that often persuades recipients to support your developmental effort. *Image File,* a journal of the Curt Teich Postcard Archives of the Lake County Museum in Illinois, *New Dimensions* from the Balch Institute for Ethnic Studies in Philadelphia, and the *Business History Bulletin* issued by the Center for the Study of Business, Technology and Society at the Hagley Museum and Library in Wilmington, Delaware, are three fine examples of the newsletter form.

A regularly issued newsletter signals an active, growing program that produces meaningful work. The newsletter allows archives managers to monitor progress and measure accomplishments, while donors, researchers, and community members receive positive reinforcement that their efforts are appreciated. Most archivists loathe the preparation of statistical reports that quantify their program's importance, yet most institutional officers view these reports as significant evaluative instruments. The newsletter offers a creative alternative that satisfies the managerial mandate for regular updates, and also provides an attractive means to cultivate a wider following. Similarly, archivists should consider issuing an annual report of progress and achievements to donors, patrons, resource allocators, and key community contacts. The report should certainly contain the expected data on research inquiries and numbers of collections processed, but it should also emphasize results as expressed by collection use and products and contain a strategic initiative that maps out an action plan for the future.

In addition to the enumerations of books, articles, and scholarly papers that have been produced, the report should note other research applications, particularly those by such nontraditional users as journalists, audiovisual producers, educators, community leaders, and others. When annual reports fail to document such diversity, archivists and institutional managers may need to review the repository's outreach objectives.

While many archivists have successfully identified segments of the general public sympathetic to their programs, other links should be established with groups that distribute information to the general public. Universities, corporations, governmental agencies, churches, museums, and similar institutions maintain press offices to generate stories about the parent body. The job of these offices is to find new ways to promote and advance their organization's missions. Archivists should share that goal and work to forge alliances that meet joint objectives.

Make sure that your press office is totally familiar with your holdings. Invite press officers and staff to your archives to show them those materials that have the greatest news value. Develop a press photography file that is immediately accessible to the news bureau staff. Reporters are always on deadline, cannot always anticipate their needs in advance, and need useful material on hand. Be aware of upcoming anniversaries and key historical dates, and be prepared to assemble pertinent documentation to publicize these events. Draft an outline of possible feature stories at the beginning of each year and circulate it to the press office. Follow up on at least a quarterly basis with reminders and addenda to that list. In a very short time, you will develop a mutual support system that will benefit your program and reinforce the perception of your archives as a viable contemporary resource. Depending upon your ingenuity and the network of contacts you have cultivated, archival links to breaking news stories offer unlimited possibilities for increased exposure.

Though you offer strong support services for institutional publicity, do not neglect your own agenda. Use the press office to promote your collections and raise community awareness of your holdings. Employ press releases to announce the acquisition and opening of collections, commemorative events, birthdays, firsts, and other historic milestones. As you work with collections, look for opportunities to link past historical events with contemporary news stories. There are few developments in the 1990s that do not have parallels in other eras. The alert archivist will recognize such opportunities and exploit the publicity potential.

In some cases, the archives may be unable to access internal public relations support and may need to explore other avenues of professional help. Consider hiring an outside public relations firm to help develop a long-range publicity plan and generate media contacts for your program. Consider also creating internships with a local collegiate journalism school or investigating the possibility of *pro bono* services from local public relations firms. Many newspapers and magazines publish an historical column as part of their community coverage. Archivists can seize this opportunity to introduce heritage as part of the contemporary landscape. Question-and-answer columns, anecdotal pieces, trivia quizzes, feature articles, and photographic essays are but a handful of techniques that can be applied to this medium. In most cases, staff members can prepare material as they handle the normal flow of reference requests or complete research reports. Junior staff members and even student interns can hone their writing skills here and enjoy the satisfaction of seeing their work published.

Archivists at regional history centers and universities can seize upon additional opportunities to promote their collections to a public audience that might not be familiar with institutional resources. They can, for instance, approach regional newspapers and magazines to consider the inclusion of an occasional column of local history as an extra benefit to their readers. In turn, the archives gets additional coverage that leads directly to soliciting donors for materials. The possibility is certainly worth exploring with regional print and television media.

Exhibitions

Exhibitions offer extraordinary potential for outreach in a society attuned to receiving messages in short visual bursts. Many archives do not fully exploit either the opportunities inherent in their collections or the habits of television viewers. We often concentrate only on the preservation aspect of our craft, failing to show the general population the intellectual and evocative excitement of primary source materials. Although questions of cost and scale may impact the use of this methodology, any archival agency can effectively use exhibition techniques in a very practical manner.

First explore the home front. Public spaces abound in archival facilities that invite exhibits of the letters, documents, photographs, printed material, and ephemera that characterize our collections. Theme shows organized by staff, students, or volunteers are simple, inexpensive productions that can introduce visitors, researchers, and associates to the wonders of documentary materials. Displays add color, texture, and vitality to a research room, front entrance, or hallway and reinforce the role of the archivist as the custodian of the historical record. Exhibits also send the clear message that the materials are there to be used and that their display is an invitation to research. Such frequently changing programs reveal the kaleidoscopic dimensions of your collection and gather more converts to its use than a few elaborately produced shows.

Marketers tell consumers about their product and services through advertising messages that speak to them where they work and play. Employing similar tactics, archivists should consider the most appropriate sites for them. Both the public and private sectors want to use their physical plants fully and welcome overtures from the nonprofit arena to create interpretive educational displays. Schools, libraries, and government buildings view such programs as natural extensions of their charter to the community; shopping malls, banks, and businesses position the use of their public spaces as part of their obligation to be good corporate citizens. In cities such as Atlanta and New York, large companies devote full time use of parts of their facilities to cultural presentations, while others offer free space on an occasional basis. Archivists should seek out and seize these promotional opportunities as they cultivate new audiences for their products.

Temporary exhibits expand the concept of outreach to the community and make archival materials accessible to audiences that may never have visited a research center. Some archivists may resist the notion of traveling shows because they are concerned about the security and preservation of the original documents, but they forget that the general public does not require the presence of original items for a valid educational or emotional experience. Quality reproductions or audiovisual presentations make strong statements about collection content without jeopardizing the original materials. While nothing can replace the impact of seeing original materials, reproductions can convey a powerful message to general audiences. If your message can reach people on their home turf, in whatever form seems reasonable, you have shown potential clients a world that otherwise would have been unavailable to them.

Archivists need to think outside their box, considering interrelationships with organizations that share their mission to enrich the community's cultural life. Networking is a concept that has found widespread acceptance within the human resources community for advancing through personal contacts. But networking is also essential to expanding archival circles of influence. By cultivating associates in the arts, historical, and other cultural communities, you will uncover new opportunities for publicizing your archives. Advocating loans from your collection, for example, will stimulate curators of art and artifact collections to think creatively about documents as critical elements for exhibition that reveal new ideas to the general public. Once an institution has established a reputation as a willing partner for joint programming efforts, other associations will develop naturally.

The museum and art world have long recognized the value of public interface and use such events as festivals, craft shows, and fine-arts competitions to sell their organizations. Membership booths, attractive displays, enthusiastic volunteers, and live demonstrations convey vitality and relevance. The emergence of "archives week" in several communities represents one of the more progressive trends among archival agencies intended to capture public attention, but such initiatives are more episodic than substantive. Archivists need to seek additional opportunities for direct public interface and establish ongoing formal links with the wider cultural community.

Ideas for increasing public awareness of archival resources are limitless, but two very popular themes on which to build programs are family genealogy and the preservation of personal documents. Whether or not your institution holds extensive genealogical files, you can direct neophyte researchers to sources that are unfamiliar to them. A booth in a mall that provides a road map for personal historical inquiries, for example, establishes a lasting bond between the archivist and the researcher. Similarly, a large segment of the population uses do-it-yourself methodologies for the preservation of family records, often inflicting serious damage to the very items they think of as priceless. Public demonstrations or workshops on basic home preservation techniques to prevent the deterioration of family records always attract an audience and enhance the image of archivists as professionals possessing valuable technical skills.

Audiovisual Productions

Current and future generations of archival users come from an environment where most selling messages are conveyed electronically. To compete for attention in our visually oriented society, archivists should include slide presentations, video productions, and sound recordings as standard elements in their communications repertoire. For ease of production and return on investment, a good slide presentation is hard to beat. It is a portable and flexible medium that requires no sophisticated equipment. It can be altered easily without additional costs and can be adapted to the time constraints of the audience. It can work with or without a narrator and usually has a very long shelf life.

As a presentation instrument, the slide show can convey detailed financial data and statistical reporting in a streamlined, visually appealing format. It allows decision makers to digest complicated information without working through volumes of written opinion. Collections development and fund raising can be enhanced by the use of customized reports aimed at targeted audiences.

Videotape and film productions can achieve the same objectives, but the costs of development are much higher, and editing new material into an existing tape or adapting it can become very expensive. Videotape is user friendly and it enables the viewer to see its contents in a leisurely fashion. It is also a very powerful medium that brings its messages directly to the viewer at work or play. However, unless a videotaped presentation can be totally developed in-house with many of the associated costs borne by the host institution, the slide show offers more bang for the buck.

In addition to self-generated audiovisual programs, archivists should identify other publicity opportunities that exist within the broadcast industry. The collections themselves will often suggest marketing possibilities for use in local media. Local television stations often use slides featuring regional images to highlight their channel position and call letters. Archives with collections of photography have a unique opportunity to provide a wonderful backdrop for such messages while promoting their own objectives. A regional music archives may contain selections that radio stations can adapt to establish their links to the community. In addition, all media outlets will usually carry public-service announcements as a regular part of their programming. Be sure to furnish stations with regular updates of happenings and special events. A brief mention on a television station can reach thousands of families in a few seconds and create an interest that you could never generate with your own resources.

If the timing is correct, you can occasionally find a positive reception to the concept of supporting a series of short historical vignettes. Radio stations using a total news programming concept offer the best possibilities for such series, but you should not overlook the community affairs programs that all stations must carry. The success of the *Civil War* television series has convinced program directors that

Americans will watch history if it is presented in an enticing package. Archivists should not only advocate more programming time for their materials, but they should also stand ready to actively participate in developing these programs.

Institutional anniversaries and milestone events demand retrospectives of some kind. Whether an "historical minute" treatment, a detailed documentary, or a lighthearted collage of random clips, the retrospective is one of the new opportunities for archival institutions to garner center-stage treatment. The impact you make in developing this kind of programming enhances public perception of your archives when the event itself has passed.

Finally, use your general telephone number as an information center. You can supply information on all of the basics with a simple recorded message that saves innumerable hours spent on individual general inquiries. A voice message also allows you to update listeners on special events, exhibit openings, and other institutional news. Callers should have access to your system twenty-four hours a day, making it convenient for them to learn about your programs.

Public Relations Activities

In the three marketing categories above, we have examined specific marketing techniques in some detail. Public relations activities encompass a broad range of programs that are directed toward the cultivation and expansion of your resource base. By looking creatively at your operations and their possible use to other people, you will begin to think more creatively about your market and your mandate.

A natural bond exists between archivists and the press, because both groups are interested in the dissemination of information. Reporters rely on a cadre of experts to flesh out stories and provide a local perspective on the news. As key information professionals, archivists can provide an historical framework in which to measure the impact of breaking stories and supplement print coverage with photographs and films. Archivists have subject specialties in historical themes that claim strong public interest, while the news media has the mechanism for mass distribution. The archivist's challenge is to marry the two components into a partnership with mutual benefits.

The lifeblood of any news organization is its access to timely, accurate, and concise information. Any source that can consistently deliver this information gets rewards not easily achieved in daily reference work. Just as the traditional researcher respects and relies on reference staff for guidance and direction in exploring large collections, so the media perceives the archivist as a resource who brings credibility and depth to their reporting. The return on investment for the archivist comes from the high visibility of such exposure. In addition to free advertising, media inclusions bring archival agendas into thousands of households that might never be exposed to historical documentation.

Cultivating media attention should become as much a part of the archival program as promoting collection availability through academic channels or developing long-range strategies for donor relations. The techniques are similar, but the focus shifts and requires some adaptation. As we have noted, many institutions maintain news bureaus or press offices to generate media coverage, but archival themes may not be among their primary publicity objectives. While the archivist must coordinate public relations activities with public relations personnel, you should also develop your their own list of press contacts and make sure that sympathetic reporters and editors receive periodic updates on archival programs or issues. Over the long term, such contacts reveal an institution that seeks to broaden its constituency and is prepared to respond to community needs.

Formal communications vehicles establish valuable organizational links, but personal contacts make things happen. To the outsider, the archives is an impersonal entity until a staff person intervenes to personalize it, capturing the excitement and potential of the historical record. This is best achieved at the individual level, where archivists speak one on one with leaders, media representatives, and other influential decision makers at public events and private social gatherings. By stimulating interest in their programs, archivists lay the foundation for an informal information network that members can access at will. The press will have discovered a source that can comfortably be used, while the archivist has claimed enthusiastic converts who will be open to suggestions for future stories.

Finally, when dealing with the media, be an unabashed promoter of your collections, institution, and staff. Establish your programs as a bellwether in the public application of history and stand ready to serve as a spokesperson on archival issues. In an age of global communication, news gathering must react quickly to breaking stories. With solidly organized collections and sophisticated information-retrieval systems, archivists can enhance the quality of media coverage and, at the same time, strengthen their own position.

In addition to the media, service organizations such as the Lions, Optimists, Kiwanis, and others provide a natural forum for promoting your archives. These groups meet regularly and always seek educational programs as part of their meeting agenda. Harried program coordinators want speakers who can deliver a ten- to fifteen-minute presentation of general interest to their members, whose ranks include professionals, managers, and independent businessmen, all of whom are potential supporters and donors. Church and youth groups, garden clubs, and other social organizations have similar needs and welcome an introduction to the mysteries of historical research. A general mailing or personal telephone call announcing that your staff can deliver a well-organized, anecdotal talk advances the charters of all organizations.

Once considered the sacred domain of the academically credentialed, many archives have opened their collections to other educational levels by crafting programs designed to introduce students from the elementary through undergraduate levels to primary source materials and initiate them in the process of historical analysis. Teacher workshops, directed student seminars, school tours, packets of historical documents, traveling exhibits, and specialized audiovisual presentations are some of the more popular techniques that link archival and educational organizations in joint programming efforts. Responding directly to the requirements of state or local curricula, creative archivists present a range of exciting options to schools which add value to the educational experience and stimulate a new generation of users to look beyond their textbooks to primary documentation for answers to both historical and contemporary issues. One way archivists can insure programmatic relevance to the community is by creating a representative citizens' advisory board that provides regular feedback to the institution on its outreach performance. Comprised of business leaders, educators, politicians, and community activists, such groups can suggest innovative ways to take the archives to the people and can serve as good barometers of public opinion. The synergy that results from healthy interchanges of views benefits all the participants. The community begins to recognize the potential of the archival record, while professional staff expand their vision of institutional mandates and services.

In some cases, your collection may contain images that have direct commercial appeal. Viewing your collections from an entrepreneurial perspective helps you identify nostalgic items and suggests methods to create consumer demand for them. While some administrators view such initiatives as fund raising ventures only, their long-term benefit lies in the permanent messages they communicate to purchasers. Merchandise that incorporates historical themes into various product categories provides unique outlets for archival messages. A book of photography, a postcard set, or a calendar may be not only visually attractive but also informational. It signals to the buyer that the creating organization cares about heritage and has systematically preserved documentation in specific subject areas. In a very subtle way, it suggests the depth of resources that stand behind the small representation in a single decorative piece.

Conclusion

The programs outlined above represent a shopping list of marketing techniques; many others can be found. They are applicable to most archival institutions, depending on their staff size, motivation and resources. These assorted approaches arise from the belief that any archival program will improve when more segments of the public learn about them.

Finally, these approaches must be programmatic, not casual; regular, not occasional; integral institutional components, not add-ons. Good managers place a heavy priority on planning and the development of measurable objectives. Taking this approach, archival managers should incorporate marketing elements into their annual business plan, along with such standard components as collections development, processing schedules, and reference service. Just as it is possible to quantify institutional growth in terms of donations, research use, and statistical reporting, archivists need to chart their outreach programs and evaluate them regularly. By monitoring institutional progress in this area over both short- and long-range cycles, archivists can measure accomplishments in terms of program visibility and community support.

Additional Readings

Daniels, Maygene F., and Timothy Walch (eds.). *A Modern Archives Reader: Basic Readings on Archival Theory and Practice* (Washington, DC: National Archives and Records Service, U.S. General Services Administration, 1984).

Howe, Barbara J., and Emory L. Kemp (eds.). *Public History: An Introduction* (Malabar, FL: Robert E. Kreiger Publishing Company, 1986).

Pederson, Ann (ed.). *Keeping Archives* (Sydney: Australian Society of Archives Incorporated, 1987).

Pederson, Ann E., and Gail Farr Casterline. *Archives and Manuscripts: Public Programs.* Basic Manual Series (Chicago: Society of American Archivists, 1982).

Wilstead, Thomas, and William Nolte. *Managing Archival and Manuscript Repositories* (Chicago: Society of American Archivists, 1991).

5

Anniversaries

A Framework for Planning Public Programs

Timothy L. Ericson

Although this chapter ostensibly concerns archivists' participating effectively in anniversaries, its larger, more important purpose is to improve public services and public relations by *anticipating* and *planning* events. Anniversaries provide the context for discussion because they are predictable. Archivists can anticipate anniversaries and plan programs that will best serve the needs of those who call upon them for assistance. But it is important to remember that anniversaries are not unique in their predictability. An accreditation review or homecoming weekend at a university, an annual meeting at a church or business, or the annual observance of Black History month can provide the same opportunities because each is a predictable event that archivists can anticipate, plan for, and use to their advantage.

Being able to anticipate, plan, and participate in anniversaries and other events effectively is important for a variety of reasons. Perhaps the most important is that doing so enables us to provide better public service and create a more positive public image. Archivists are expected to be a resource for events such as anniversaries. If patrons come seeking information that we cannot deliver effectively, their frustration confirms the "dusty shelves" image against which archivists continually battle. By failing to plan and deliver information and events when they are expected, we undercut our own archival programs.

A second reason to anticipate and plan for anniversaries is that they are ideal opportunities to showcase archival services, programs, and the value of archival records. From an archivist's perspective, they are important less for the centennial histories they produce or the nostalgia they evoke, than for the chance they offer us to establish an identity within the community and strengthen the image of the archives as a source of useful information.

A third reason to prepare for such events as anniversaries is that they provide the archivist a chance to educate his/her constituents. They allow us to teach resource allocators, news media representatives, alumni, retirees, members of the local community, and other clientele some specific ways that archives can be valuable sources of information—not simply shelves lined with curious old stuff of interest only to antique dealers, genealogists, and tweedy, pipe-smoking historians. Anniversaries can bring people into the archives who otherwise would never appear. In the aftermath of such a celebration, most may never

Reprinted by permission: Tribune Media Services

come again. Some will, and those who do are likely to become important donors, advocates, or financial supporters.

For archivists, the first important element in any event such as an anniversary is to understand what drives it and then determine how the archives can become *productively* involved in it. "Productive" has two requirements. The first is to be *prepared* to respond to requests that people make. The second is to work at making the celebration a *meaningful* event, rather than a festival of purely antiquarian or nostalgic interest without substance or long-term consequence. There are five important steps in finding out whether the celebration is significant and if so how the archives can become a producing part of it: to anticipate, investigate, cooperate, participate, and evaluate.

Anticipate

The Archivist's First Law of Outreach:

> Human beings are unable to resist celebrating any anniversary divisible by twenty-five.

What is it about anniversaries that captures our imagination and makes them so irresistible? The motivations behind anniversaries are important because they give us a clue to the types of information and activities that archivists will probably be called upon to support. Perhaps the most useful observation about anniversaries is that they appeal to a wide variety of emotions that complement one another. First of all, anniversaries nurture a sense of community and a shared sense of accomplishment. They validate the effort that it took to build and sustain the business, the college, the church, the local rod and gun club, or whatever institution is the focus of celebration. Anniversaries also affirm the goals of the founders and provide the opportunity to appreciate the effort and dedication that it took to effect change and prevail. In other words, we believe that to have prevailed is to have participated in an important historical process and to have accomplished something worthwhile. The American Revolution Bicentennial, which began in 1976, is a striking example of this impulse. More than creating a yearlong obsession with red, white, and blue souvenir beer cans, key chains, and fire hydrants, it engendered sustained national interest in the ideals of the Declaration of Independence.

The Bicentennial celebration was particularly poignant because it mirrored in so many ways the centennial that our ancestors observed with equal fervor a century earlier. In a similar way, the centennial of the American Civil War in the early 1960s reaffirmed the ideal of the *United* States. The list could continue, but it is enough to say that anniversaries—in whatever context—provide an opportunity to reaffirm basic values that we hold as alumni or employees, as a congregation, community, or member of American society.

In the same way that anniversaries cause us to look back, they are as often used to look forward. Having proved through past success that we have done something worthwhile, we resolve to follow the path that our forebears laid out for us. We look ahead and rededicate ourselves to their goals, expressing our determination to forge ahead with the work they began. This emotion is often apparent in the slogans we compose. For example, a church in North Dakota celebrating its centennial in 1992 adopted as its theme, "In Jesus' name we press on." A graduate academic program recently celebrated its first quarter-century with the slogan, "Twenty-five years of excellence in graduate education and research" and dedicated itself to even greater excellence in the coming quarter-century. Even the Internal Revenue Service is not reluctant to use slogans. In its 1987 pamphlet about the Tax Reform Act of 1986, the IRS sported a special front page logo announcing, "125 Years Service to America"—implicitly promising, one must think, even better service in the future because of the reforms!

Occasionally anniversaries are promoted simply because we fondly remember the past or the images associated with it. The power of reminiscence brings to mind times in almost everyone's life that were particularly meaningful, influential, or happier. Many people recalled the cartoons of their youth when Bugs Bunny celebrated a fiftieth birthday in 1990. A "Beetle Bailey" comic strip celebrated forty years of publication in the same year with no other clear goal than to help readers recall how long they had been laughing at the misadventures of Beetle and the Sarge. *Newsweek* highlighted the art of Vincent van Gogh by remembering the one-hundredth anniversary of his death in 1890. There are similar examples at the local level. Many historical feature articles in newspapers or institutional newsletters pay tribute to our love of reminiscence, as do regular "Pages from the Past," columns which contain the news of 25, 50, 75, or 100 years ago, or "Scenes from Yesteryear" that highlight historical photographs. All of these suggest avenues that archivists can take. Remember that every week brings the hundredth anniversary of something.

Finally, some anniversaries are nothing more than events dreamed up by advertising wizards as tools to promote some product. Companies use anniversaries to stress their history of quality or their dedication to service. How can sugar in a packet that announces its producer's one-hundredth anniversary be anything but pure? How can a 75-year-old hardware store sell less than the best wrenches? More often, anniversaries are celebrated because they can be calculated to catch people's attention, and to this end they need not be significant from an historian's perspective. Nor do they need to be cloaked in high ideals. How else do we explain the seventy-fifth anniversary of the Goo Goo Cluster (complete with a special commemorative hat offer!) other than as a ploy to increase sales? Is there another logical reason to celebrate the semicentennial of the invention of Spam, including a "Spam Air Show" held in Austin, Minnesota, where the product is currently manufactured? Why else gear up to celebrate the seventy-fifth anniversary of the Fig Newton? Or the Snickers Candy Bar? To be fair, such commercial impulses are not the exclusive property of the business community. The effectiveness of anniversaries as marketing tools should need no further proof after the tiny community of Villisca, Iowa, and Lizzie Bordon's hometown of Fall River, Massachusetts, both attracted widespread attention by publicizing axe murders that took place within their boundaries 75 and 100 years earlier!

In the broadest sense, an anniversary does not have to be an event that takes place only within a quarter-century time frame. Some anniversaries come annually, just as couples celebrate their wedding! For example, Black History Month in February is an annual anniversary celebrating the contributions of African Americans to our culture. National Women's History Month in March is observed for similar reasons. The annual homecomings at colleges and universities are anniversaries that recognize the importance of education and of alumni to their alma mater. The link that connects all of these events for archivists is that we can anticipate them and prepare for them. They are vehicles that archivists can use to make their programs more visible.

In fact, if archivists are so disposed, they can even create their own anniversaries. The event need not even be profoundly significant, historically, to work as a promotional vehicle. Everyone will notice an anniversary if it is well promoted, but the working point is that everyone will notice an anniversary. An archivist with a collection documenting the career of a prominent prohibitionist might consider the anniversary of the passage of the Eighteenth Amendment on January 16. Archives with rural school records may want to plan some promotional event for February 13, the anniversary of the establishment of America's oldest public school, opened in Boston in 1635. Agricultural collections might be a topic appropriate to National Agriculture Day, which is observed each March 21. The second week in May is set aside for National Photo week—an ideal time to highlight archival audiovisual resources. Every state in the union has an "Admission Day." The list could continue indefinitely, but two lessons should be clear. First, one does not wait for the next centennial in order to participate in an anniversary. Second, if we begin to look around, we will find that there are actually more events than we could ever hope to participate in. The key is choosing from among the many choices those which are most closely associated with your institutional mission and will most benefit the archival program, then making your choices count by proper planning.

Whatever the motivation, there are practical reasons to take advantage of anniversaries. Foremost is the simple fact that given most people's natural inclination toward such events, it is possible to build on an *existing level of interest* rather than having to promote an event from nothing. More importantly, the natural level of interest commonly associated with anniversaries is usually present among several groups that are important to archives. People who have never visited an archives will be interested in a centennial because they will see for the first time the connection between archival records and an aspect of history that touches them personally. Newspaper and television reporters will be interested in an event that has proven widespread community appeal. Resource allocators will probably be more receptive to committing time and money to events that will attract favorable attention and publicity. As a result, it will be easier for the archivist to generate support, publicity, and other coverage. For archivists, the lesson is simple: When you can attach yourselves to an existing event, much of the work that you might otherwise have to undertake will be done by others with similar interests. Public relations and marketing specialists have been using this piggyback technique for years; archivists can use it to their own ends as well.

In certain respects, effective participation in an anniversary is an extension of our appraisal, arrangement, description, and reference programs, and the success of our efforts will depend on the skill with which we have undertaken our basic mission. An important part of anticipating an event is looking ahead not only to the event itself, but also to the *type of support* you may be called upon to give. What kinds of information will people be seeking? What kinds of questions will you likely be called upon to answer? Such information can help establish short term priorities for our everyday work.

For example, a university archivist anticipating an upcoming centennial should consider acquiring alumni reminiscences or oral histories as a collection development priority in the several years prior to the actual centennial. Archivists with collections documenting American participation in the Second World War would have been well advised to arrange and describe these prior to 1991, when the fiftieth anniversary of Pearl Harbor stimulated interest in World War II. A denominational archivist might find it useful to collect information about the founding dates of individual churches in order to more quickly and effectively respond to expected inquiries about a coming centennial. Archivists in a state anticipating a sesquicentennial might want to prepare pathfinders or study guides on popular topics associated with the coming anniversary. Duplicate prints of historical photographs prepared ahead of time are ready for use in displays or quickly available as illustrations in media publicity. This is not to say that archivists must plan their programs and live their lives according to the dictates of coming anniversaries, but it is wise to anticipate the needs of those who may soon be asking for your help. Sometimes preparing for an anniversary is not so much taking on extra work as it is reordering everyday priorities.

PLANNING TIPS

The following list of planning tips will help the archivist prepare for various types of anniversaries.

1. For events such as centennials, the time you leave for planning should be measured in terms of years rather than months.
2. Plan an early meeting with others in your institution to determine the nature and extent of their interest. If they are interested, you may have moved the planning process ahead by months or even years. You will benefit from this by gaining more preparation time. If others are not interested, you may want to consider scaling back your own preparations.
3. Anticipate well ahead of time what information people will probably want to know. For example, in preparation for a church or synagogue centennial, compile a checklist of basic information such as:

- Date of founding
- Names of and information about founders
- Size of original congregation
- Size of present congregation
- Description, location, and photographs of all previous buildings used for worship
- Time line of major events in the history of the institution (such as fires, building projects, or controversies)

4. In preliminary planning, anticipate as many of the different factors and needs associated with events that you can. These may include:

- The focus or the theme you may wish to emphasize
- The audiences that may be involved
- Staff requirements
- Technical needs (meeting rooms, audiovisual equipment)
- Supplies that will be required
- Financial support necessary to undertake an event
- Publicity requirements
- Evaluation procedures

Investigate

The Archivist's Second Law of Outreach:

> The amount of lead time allotted by a committee to any anniversary activity is inversely proportional to the complexity of the event.

The centennial is fast approaching. What do you do? How do you begin? It is important to be able to anticipate anniversaries, but it is equally important to use your lead time carefully. Only with adequate preparation can we better deliver the information and services that we may be called upon to provide, rather than being obliged to react at the last minute. The Second Law of Outreach means, for example, that someone from the centennial committee will come to the archives breathless with enthusiasm, wanting to produce an illustrated centennial history for a banquet that is being held in two weeks! Or a reporter from the local newspaper will want everyone in the photograph of the "Class of 1908" identified in time to meet a deadline that is only two hours away.

The first step in an investigation should be to consider the mission and goals of the institution you serve. What will the institution want to achieve through the anniversary celebration? What constituencies or publics will it probably want to reach? What activities will be appropriate to these ends?

At the same time, the archives should determine its own goals in participating. What specific outcomes do you want? What objectives do you have for the archival programs that will produce these outcomes? These may include:

- The chance to increase holdings
- A higher community and institutional profile
- An increased number or range of researchers
- Increased human, financial, or other resources
- A larger or remodeled facility

Whatever your answer, goals and objectives should influence how you prepare and define your own role in activities that take place. Your success can only be evaluated in terms of your goals and objectives.

In both cases, it is important to investigate who your probable audiences will be. Will they include institutional administrators? Students and faculty? Alumni or retirees? Members of the general public? Scholarly researchers? Media representatives? All of the above? What are each of these groups likely to want from you? Considering such questions ahead of time is important, because each group is likely to have different expectations, priorities, and needs. Each may be interested in different programs, services, and approaches.

Remember too that not every anniversary is worth the same amount of commitment on your part. For each event, archivists need to determine the *cost-benefit ratio of involvement.* For example, participation does not always mean writing a centennial history. In some cases, it may be best to do no more than send a letter of congratulation, a few photocopied historical documents, or a note conveying best wishes and mentioning documentary resources that the group might use during its celebration. Whatever your choice, it is important to first determine the *level* of participation as well as the *nature.*

Your initial investigation should also seek ways to tie specific anniversary activities to external events, thus multiplying the extent and value of publicity. For example, an archives wanting to mount an exhibit highlighting the contribution of women as a part of its institution's centennial should strongly consider Women's History Month for the opening. Doing so will make the exhibit more attractive to local media and people who otherwise might not be interested. More importantly, the added publicity may attract the attention of resource allocators who will see that such timing gives the institution higher visibility.

The reverse side of the page is equally important. Early in your planning, investigate what programs might *compete* with events that you are scheduling. These may include other centennial programs or outside events such as football games, holidays, and special community days that you might not immediately remember.

As you investigate how and when you will participate, don't forget to consider ways of enhancing your resources so that you will be able to do more. State humanities commissions are a good source of funding for public programming if your anniversary fits within the parameters of their current themes. Every area has a number of small local or regional foundations that may be interested in funding a particular activity or publication.

Consider starting a volunteer or Friends program in advance of the celebration. Initiating a volunteer program shortly before a centennial or similar celebration takes advantage of the natural level of interest. If you bring in volunteers as you begin planning, you will benefit from fresh perspectives as you formulate your programs. Volunteers or Friends also may be helpful in lobbying for institutional and outside support, and by the time the celebration begins they will provide you with additional staff that is well-trained and familiar with the archives operation.

PLANNING TIPS

1. Establish priorities! The world is full of great ideas that we have neither the time nor the resources to undertake and complete well. It is better to make hard decisions at the beginning than to become mired in projects you cannot do properly.

2. Make a thorough investigation of the resources at your disposal that may help to support anniversary-related activities. These should include the following.

Financial Resources

- Travel
- Supplies
- Equipment
- Services

Human Resources

- Archival staff
- Volunteer staff —other institutional staff with special expertise
- Institutional Resources
- Photocopying
- Editing
- Public relations
- Photography
- Computer support
- Audiovisual support
- Fleet vehicles
- Catering
- Meeting room space
- Parking

Archival Resources

- Archival holdings useful for displays
- The facility as a site for programs
- Hobbies and talents of staff

Community Resources

- Historical societies and other groups with similar interests with whom you might work
- Groups that might provide support services such as Boy Scouts and Girl Scouts
- Groups that are likely hosts for programs such as newcomers clubs and church or service organizations
- Commercial groups that might help with publicity, such as the Chamber of Commerce
- Local broadcast and print media

3. Investigate the types of programs that you might undertake, then establish priorities. Remember that although you must do something, you can't do everything. The following checklist includes program possibilities you may wish to consider.

- Coordinate a series of community forums that deals with contemporary issues relating to themes prominent in your anniversary celebration.
- Design a brochure that ties the archives' holdings to the anniversary celebration. Be sure to take advantage of good historical photographs and other attractive illustrations.
- Start a column in the local newspaper or in an institutional newsletter. Such features may contain "news from the past," historical photographs, or short articles describing important past events. (Remember that the "news from the past" format is applicable to radio as well. It is no more difficult or time-consuming to put together a feature that will be read as a script than it is to write a release for publication in the local newspaper.)
- For short news features, select items that contrast past circumstances with the present. Even items as simple as the cost of tuition a century ago as compared to today's will attract attention. This is the type of information that people remember and talk about.
- Use oral history and other audio resources as the basis for radio features highlighting some aspect of your institution's history.
- Use visual resources as the basis for commercial and cable television features.
- Through a series of news releases, publicize donations of archival material that are given during the anniversary celebration period. Include photographs and the names of donors.
- Develop a slide or videotape program that can be presented to groups of students, alumni or retirees, and used for special institutional events such as annual meetings, or to community organizations.
- Organize a series of temporary historical exhibits highlighting important themes in your organization's history.
- Organize a series of temporary exhibits honoring such special groups as retirees, distinguished alumni, or championship athletic teams, or tracing the history of annual events such as homecomings and graduations.
- Create a traveling exhibit that can be used with different audiences in a variety of locations.

- Encourage a centennial publication, but don't become stuck on simply doing a traditional centennial history. Depending on your intended audience and budget, you may wish to consider a series of shorter publications or an album of historical photographic views.
- Produce, or encourage someone else to produce, a calendar featuring historical photographs and highlighting important dates that are a part of the anniversary celebration. The calendar may be used as a giveaway or sold to help raise funds to underwrite other activities.
- Organize a walking tour of historical buildings or sites and publish a guide to accompany it.
- Work with local preservation groups to collect information on historical buildings and sites, and mark these as part of the anniversary celebration.
- Present a series of workshops in which archivists share ways to preserve personal historical materials such as photographs, newspaper clippings, and documents that every family has.
- Present a series of miniclasses in areas related to archival research, such as pursuing local history or genealogy, developing oral history, conducting historical research or dating historical photographs.
- Schedule a series of tours of the archives in conjunction with events and activities associated with the anniversary.
- Organize activities such as "Archivist for a Day" (or an afternoon) and have people help out with indexing, identifying old photographs, and performing routine archival tasks. Use this as the basis for beginning a volunteer program.
- Develop a series of curricular materials that can be used in the public schools.
- Work with schools and local arts organizations to sponsor the production of historical dramas, plays, art shows, or an exhibit mounted in the archives.
- Organize a series of contests or quizzes that involve identifying historical scenes or people or that will increase people's awareness of their own history.
- Support writing contests or research projects in which students or others write themes, essays, short stories, or dramatic pieces on topics of interest during the centennial. Find ways to have contest winners published in institutional or local community media.
- Print a series of historical postcards or document facsimiles that can be used either as promotional items or sold to help raise funds for other anniversary activities.

4. If you plan to seek outside funding, coordinate this effort with the development office in your institution. Possibly another office will have already contacted a foundation or granting agency about funding, and a separate request from the archives may confuse matters and cause bad feelings.

5. For each event that you plan, develop a time line that shows specific tasks that must be done and assigns responsibilities and deadlines for these.

Cooperate

The First Corollary to Oeser's Law:

> "The value of someone else's activity or event is inversely proportional to the amount of time they expect you to spend preparing for it."
>
> Arthur Bloch
> *Murphy's Law and Other Reasons Why Things Go Wrong!*

Just because you're the archivist doesn't mean that you must do everything yourself. Don't offer to design the centennial logo for the commemorative coffee mug, even though your archives may have the only extant copy of the logo used for the fiftieth anniversary mug. Don't plan, mount, and distribute the centennial exhibit alone. Even the great ideas that you have may not be possible because of lack of finances, staff, or time. Such activities are candidates for cooperative action.

Work with others both inside the institution and outside of it. An example: In most instances, your goal should be to provide information for the centennial history, not write it. There are distinct advantages to this: It takes less time to provide the information than to write the history, and in the end you will have avoided the mine fields. (Others can take the blame for neglecting to mention Uncle Harry in the chapter on prominent leaders!) Other examples: The centennial cookbook, plate album, or memoir.

Many times your most important activity is to work with a centennial committee and ensure that planning is started well in advance. A centennial committee is an ideal forum for cooperative action within the institution and with the local community. Although it is important for the archives to be represented on such a committee, the archivist need not be the chair. An active supporting role is frequently more effective. If you are convinced that participation is worthwhile for the archives but institutional interest is lukewarm, you may have to organize the committee or play a more active leadership role, although it may be politically wiser to encourage others in the institution to chair it.

Don't overlook the array of community organizations that might become cooperatively involved in your anniversary celebration as participants, hosts for programs, or contributors. Many activities lend themselves to productive cooperation with outside groups. Boy Scouts and Girl Scouts have programs to earn merit badges. Universities have classes studying oral history or learning the fundamentals of exhibit design, and they may be pleased to help out if they can earn academic credit in the process. Local service organizations are on the lookout for activities that benefit the community generally or serve the needs of a specific segment of the population.

PLANNING TIPS

1. Be sure to schedule a tour of the archives for anniversary planning committees so they have a chance to see your facility and the historical resources you can offer them.

2. Schedule a similar archives tour for top administrators.

3. Make use of public display areas such as those in banks, malls, and other business locations that will help publicize the anniversary (and the archives).

4. Don't overlook any of the following groups in your planning.

- Public and private schools
- Colleges and universities
- Public libraries
- Community adult education programs
- Boy Scouts and Girl Scouts
- Museums
- Genealogical societies
- Local historical societies
- Radio stations
- Television stations (including local access cable)
- Newspapers
- Other archives
- Summer recreation programs
- Chamber of Commerce
- Jaycees, Rotary, or similar service organizations
- Elks, Masons, and other similar fraternal organizations
- Newcomers' clubs
- Churches
- Businesses
- Arts organizations
- Veterans organizations
- Senior citizens organizations
- Recreational, sporting, and social organizations

5. Because one of your most important cooperative relationships is with the local press, you may wish to create a press kit. Archivists from larger institutions should work with specialists from their public relations department or news bureau to accomplish this, but those who must produce their own press kit should know that they may include many different items: press releases (both of the history of the institution and upcoming events); photographs (with dates and captions); admission tickets to any public events in which the archives will be involved; brochures describing the archives and its services; schedules of events, including dates, times, places, the names of notable participants or attendees, and planned activities; and parking permits that will make it easier for media representatives to attend scheduled events (see Chapter 3).

Participate

The Second Corollary to Murphy's Law:

> "Everything takes longer than you think."
>
> Arthur Bloch

Select carefully *how* you will participate. The most productive means often are those that involve your archival holdings rather than your good offices as a community volunteer. Also remember that the way you are represented in an anniversary celebration sends a message to others. Exhibits designed to tell people about the history of your institution are also (rightly or wrongly) telling potential donors what you collect. If the highlight of the exhibit is the first president's gold ink pen and yellowed newspaper clippings about the founding of the institution, you may be sending the message that you want donations of artifacts and newspaper clippings when, in fact, you do not. If you want to tell prospective donors that archives are more than newspaper clippings, letters with the signatures of famous people, or quaint and wonderful artifacts, then you must show them more than this. Whatever you undertake must have substance. Exhibits should be educational, not simply pretty; even frivolous or funny exhibits can be instructive if they have substance. Centennial histories should be thought provoking, not simply laudatory and self-serving. Be careful not to squander your efforts on anecdotal publications, or superficial events that fail to reflect what you are really about or what your archives would like to accomplish.

Don't concentrate exclusively on writing the centennial history or delivering the keynote lecture, to the exclusion of supporting roles that may be less time-consuming and ultimately more productive. Remember to distinguish between ends and means. For most archivists, the centennial history, the exhibition, the reunion, or the lecture, is not the ultimate goal. These are simply means—tools—you can use to accomplish what you want. By serving on an advisory committee, for example, you can influence the activities that are being undertaken and promote the use of your holdings directly.

Also remember that effective participation in an anniversary celebration requires more than knowing the difference between evidential and informational value. You will need skills that are not taught in archival education programs. These may include meeting planning, budgeting, operating audiovisual equipment, writing, editing, making photographs, and negotiating contracts and agreements. Spend some time reading literature that exists outside the archival universe. You will find a great deal of useful information from such fields as management, museum studies, and audiovisual education. Through such means and experience, you will learn some new skills. Remember that you will be judged by the quality of what you produce. Don't be reluctant to ask for help from someone with the knowledge you lack.

Many centennial "veterans" have found that a series of smaller events and projects are more effective and better for their programs than one big splash. A series of events, perhaps extending throughout a centennial year, will draw a more diverse audience and probably reveal a more diverse range of your archival resources. It will also keep you in the spotlight for a longer period of time.

Once you have identified your goals and the audiences you want to serve, you must select the proper means to reach them. Many different options are available; the art is in selecting wisely. You may consider hosting or participating in some type of public event or producing a publication or an audiovisual presentation. Whatever you choose must be appropriate to the audience and something you can deliver in a timely and effective way.

Establish procedures *on paper* that will help administer the activities you have chosen—particularly with regard to money! If you are reimbursing people for expenses, make sure everyone understands exactly what types of expenses are reimbursable, what are the reimbursable limits of expenses, and what receipts will necessary. If someone is writing a centennial history, make sure that the amount of any honorarium is recorded, as well as when it will be paid, any conditions of payment, and who will own copyright. Use letters of contract or contracts whenever possible. These are particularly useful for such services as room setup, printing, or catering, for which you are usually quoted prices. Make sure you know what is and is not included in the charges.

PLANNING TIPS

1. For a series of public programs or activities, have in mind an event that will serve not just as the end but the climax of the celebration. Other activities should build toward this event. For example, if you are planning a reunion as your final event, consider making available the centennial history that has been written as one of the celebratory activities.

2. Be pragmatic: A centennial is a perfect time to get rid of the 500 copies of the 75th anniversary history that have been taking up room on the back shelves.

3. Mail invitations to events or registration brochures at least eight weeks prior to the event's scheduled date.

4. Phase your mailings and other publicity. Publicity for a coming event should come at several intervals: four to six weeks, two weeks, and one week prior to the scheduled date.

5. When budgeting for an event, be careful not to overlook any expenses. The following checklist may help by suggesting common areas you need to consider.

Equipment rental

- Audiovisual (account for all components you need. For example, the screen for a slide projector will often be extra, as will the monitor for a videocassette player)
- Sound, including loudspeakers, microphones, taping equipment, and electrical sources to supply them
- Tables, chairs, tents, or similar equipment

Personnel

- Honoraria for speakers or writers
- Overtime wages for staff
- Miscellaneous expenses, such as security

Postage

- Number of mailings
- Size of mailing list
- Envelopes

Publicity

- Brochures
- Posters
- Paid advertisements

Services

- Charges for room
- Charges for setup
- Catering expenses (don't forget breaks as well as meals)
- Printing and editorial costs
- Cleanup

Supplies

- Paper, folders, and similar supplies for handouts, registration materials, signage, and so forth
- Duplication expenses
- Curricular and workshop materials
- Name badges

Travel

- Mileage
- Lodging
- Meals

6. In arranging for services, don't forget to ask about deadlines for ordering and the amount of time needed to provide the service. For example, by what date do you need to order audiovisual equipment? How much in advance of the mailing date do you need to have your brochure in the hands of the printer?

7. When dealing with print or broadcast media or with outside organizations that publish newsletters, be sure to find out when their deadlines are and the form in which they want news articles or press releases.

In the case of a *public event*, ensure that it is planned well in advance of the date, and be especially careful not to schedule it at a time when another local event will be taking place. Check community calendars and sports schedules. You don't want your open house at the same time as the homecoming football game and you wouldn't want your slide presentation on the history of your community to take place on the afternoon of Superbowl Sunday. Also be sure you have the necessary permissions to hold the event or undertake the project, particularly if it is to use public space or facilities outside your institution. (See Appendix 3 for guidelines.)

For public events, you may be called upon to decide how the tables, chairs, and other equipment should be arranged, so it is a good idea to be at least somewhat familiar with common setups. In general, the setup should be determined by the type of event you are planning. The room setup should reflect the functional needs of the event.

The following are common types of room setups.

Theater or Auditorium Style

Commonly used for events of limited duration such as lectures, audiovisual presentations, awards ceremonies, or events where you expect a large audience. (See Figure 5.1).

Create a center aisle at least 4 feet wide and aisles at the end of each row at least 3 feet wide.

Classroom Style

This seating is more comfortable for longer periods of time. It features rows of tables, as shown in Figure 5.2.

Try to seat no more than 2 people to a six-foot table or 3 at an eight-foot table. Leave aisles between the tables not only for the comfort of the participants but so the instructor can move freely about the room.

Conference Style

The conference style is of three types. The *Board Room* setup features seating around a large table or series of tables as shown in Figure 5.3.

This style lends itself to discussions in a seminar or at a planning meeting. It is best suited for small groups of not more than 24 persons, to ensure that everyone hears and can make eye contact. Be careful to give people seated on corners enough room to avoid their bumping knees. The *Hollow Square* is used for the same purpose as *Boardroom,* but it can accommodate up to 40 people. The *Horseshoe* style setup is a *Hollow Square* with one of the four sides removed. It is ideal for workshops, seminars, discussions, and other meetings of up to 30 persons that feature audiovisual presentations, blackboards, or flip charts.

The Roundtable or Banquet Style

The roundtable or banquet style (Figure 5.4) is seating "in the round" and is often used when the program includes a meal or when a seminar is to be broken into smaller discussion groups. Round tables, 60 or 72 inches in diameter, are best used with no more than 8 or 10 persons around each, respectively.

PLANNING TIPS

1. In general, ensure that the room is set up so that the main entrance is at the rear or on the side, to minimize the disruption caused by latecomers.

2. Public meeting areas almost always have limits set by the fire department on the number of participants that can be accommodated at one time. Learn what these limits are and plan to live within them.

3. For all types of room setups, remember to include registration tables and tables for displays or distributing literature.

4. For any event, don't forget signage that will tell people where to go. For workshops or other several-day events, provide handouts showing the location of lavatories, phones, restaurants and the like.

Audiovisual Presentations

Audiovisual presentations are effective in a variety of different situations. Slides, overhead transparencies, slide-tape programs, movies, and videotape productions can make a program more visually interesting and help illustrate points more effectively. Audiovisuals make it easier to introduce humor into presentations, and in an age when people are more visually oriented, presenters find audiences better able to grasp the message when it is delivered visually rather than via a lecture. Like other aspects of a program, the use of audiovisuals must be carefully planned.

The most widely used form of audiovisual presentation is a few slides or overhead transparencies that illustrate specific points in a public presentation, lecture, or workshop. In certain instances, you may wish to show a commercially produced program for the same purpose or produce your own. This is not the forum to provide detailed instructions on producing quality audiovisual programs, except to say that if you choose to use them, take the time to plan them well. While a few slides or over-

Figure 5.1. Theatre or Auditorium Seating

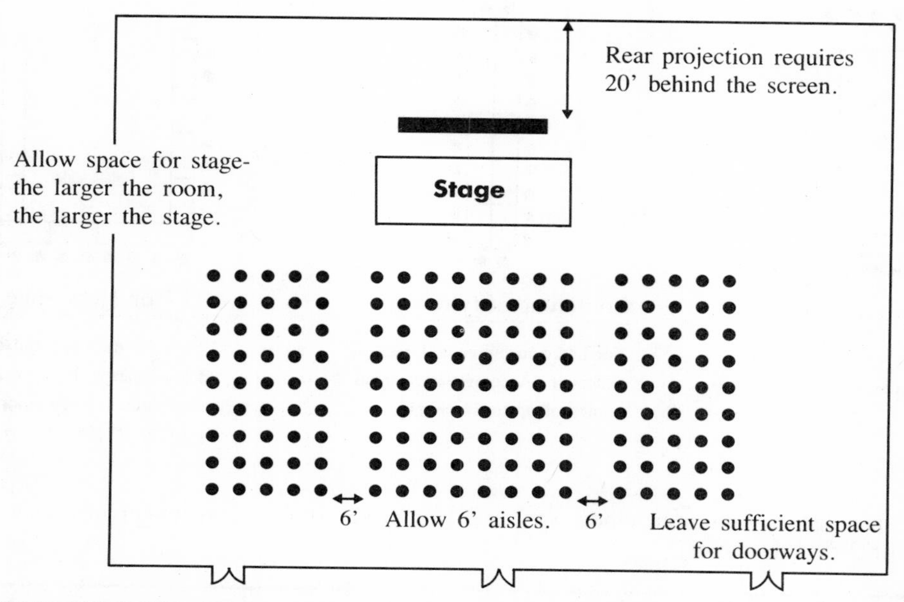

Reprinted courtesy of the 1988 Sheraton Meeting Workbook

Figure 5.2 . Schoolroom or Classroom Seating

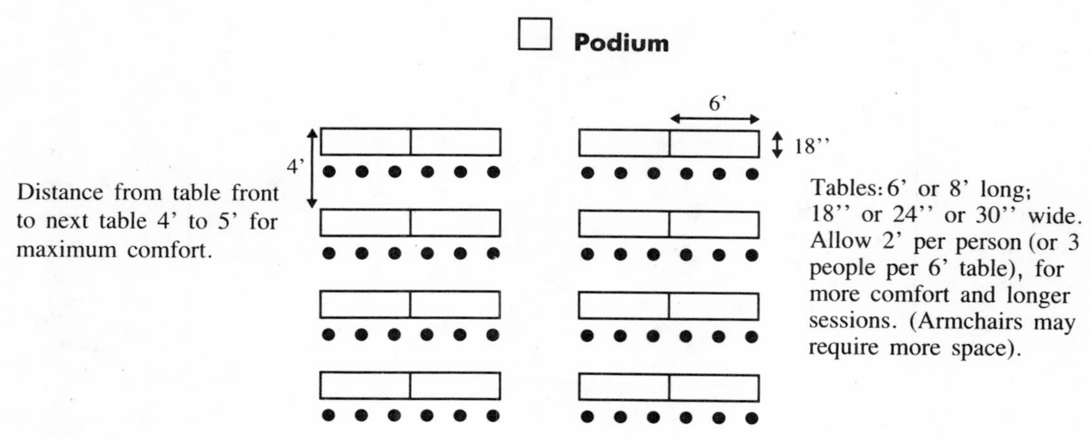

Reprinted courtesy of the 1988 Sheraton Meeting Workbook

Figure 5.3. Conference Seating

Conference Seating

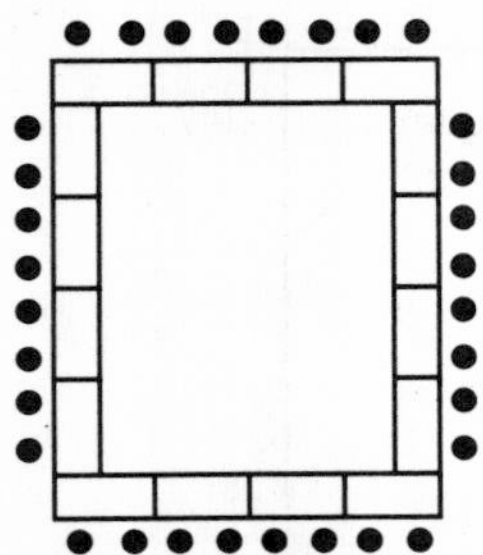

Hollow Square

For idea exchange. Accommodates about 40 people.

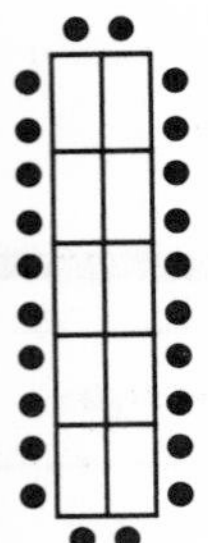

Conference Style

For board meetings and idea exchange. Accommodates small groups of up to 24 people.

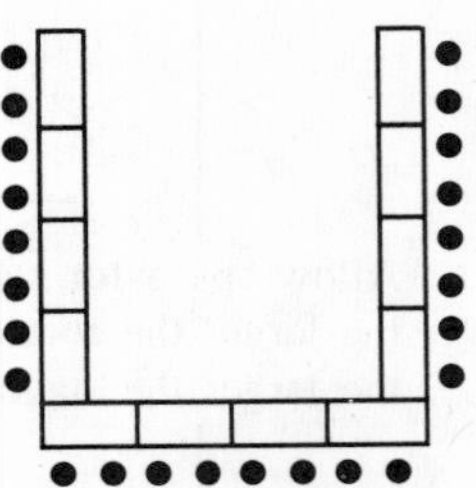

"U" or Horseshoe

For board meetings and idea idea exchange. Best for A/V presentations. Accommodates up to 30 people.

Allow 2' per person minimum elbow space, 3' for more comfort and longer meetings. Use 24″ or 36″ wide tables.

Not drawn to scale

Reprinted courtesy of the 1988 Sheraton Meeting Workbook

Figure 5.4. Banquet or Roundtable Discussion Seating (Rounds)

Banquet or Roundtable Discussion Seating (Rounds)

Used mainly for dining, seminars and small discussion groups

Use 60″ tables to seat 8 people.

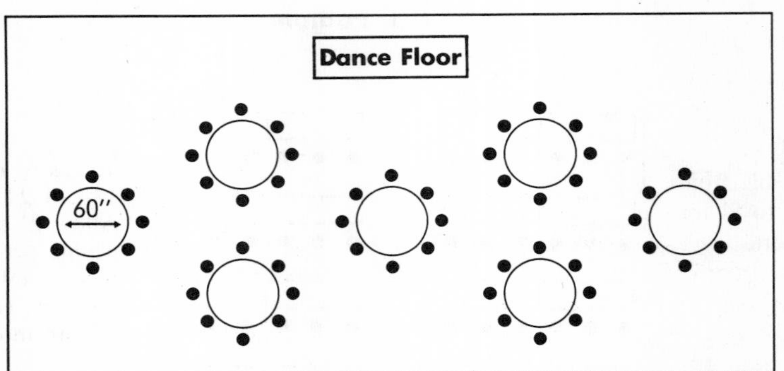

Use 72″ tables to seat 9 or 10 people.

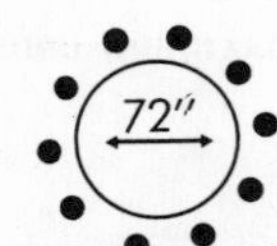

Not drawn to scale

Reprinted courtesy of the 1988 Sheraton Meeting Workbook

head transparencies are easier to produce, a sophisticated program requiring a sound track or videotape editing is time-consuming and expensive. Remember that people see audiovisual programs in various forms daily and a homemade, unsophisticated production may do more harm than good. Use experts whenever you can.

If you plan to produce your own audiovisual programs, use quality equipment. For example, don't use a tape recorder with a built-in microphone or audiotape that is of dubious quality. Consult a good guide to oral history interviewing—many of the guidelines for taping will apply to audiovisual programs as well. But even the best audiovisual programs have been ruined because of poor planning prior to their showing. For example, don't show a videotape on a single 25-inch monitor in an auditorium that you expect to fill with 250 people. Some sources recommend that the greatest viewing distance should be no greater than eight times the height of the projected image. If you are showing slides on a five-foot square screen, the back row of the seating area should be no more than forty feet from the screen.

It is always a good idea to check the room in which you will be showing your audiovisuals well ahead of time, so you will know where outlets are located and whether light from windows will be a problem. Learn ahead of time where light switches are located and whether they have dimmers. Test whether the outlets and light switches work in conjunction with one another. You don't want your projector to shut down as soon as you turn out the lights. Request that the entrance to the room be at the back of the viewing area, so latecomers will not interrupt the presentation.

Make sure you request all the equipment you need. Don't make the mistake of requesting a slide projector and arrive to discover that you forgot to specify a screen. Don't forget that a videocassette player requires a monitor. Remember items like extension cords and extra bulbs. Check the equipment beforehand to ensure that it is in good operating order. Make your checks the previous day, if you can, so there will be time to remedy problems.

The positioning of equipment within the room is extremely important. If you are showing slides, use a zoom lens so the projector can be positioned behind the audience, where the noise from the fan will be minimized. Set the projector on a stand high enough to avoid a "keystone" image. Request a center aisle down which you can project so that when you turn on your projector, you won't see silhouettes of heads along the bottom of the screen. Make sure the screen is placed far enough from the front row so that people sitting there will be able to see easily; the bottom of a slide screen should be at least four feet from the floor. For a videocassette, set the monitor high enough so that everyone can see it easily. If you are using an overhead projector, set it at the front left side, if you can. That way it won't obstruct the view of the audience.

Make sure you know how to use your equipment, and check your setup. Set up your equipment so that when it is turned on, the first image appears—in focus and right-side up! Walk around the room to make sure you can see the images on the screen from every seating position. Check the sound level and make any necessary adjustments.

Finally, make arrangements with someone to turn off or dim the lights as you begin the program and turn them on afterward. If appropriate, have someone assigned to turn off the equipment after the audiovisual is finished. Don't rewind tapes or remove slide carousals until the end of the entire program.

PLANNING TIPS

1. Leave an inch or two around each edge of an overhead transparency. Otherwise you will lose part of the image when you project it, or you may have trouble fitting the entire image on the screen.

2. If you are shooting your own slides, frame them all in the same way, preferring horizontal to vertical. Remember that written text, such as a page from a handwritten letter or a similar historical document, seldom makes for a good visual. Use a blowup of selected passages or make a photocopy handout instead.

3. When you order a slide screen, specify the size you want.

4. Run your slides through once, to make sure that none are upside down and that each image fits on the screen.

Evaluate

Second Corollary to Chisholm's Third Law:

> "If you do something that you are sure will meet with everybody's approval, somebody won't like it."
>
> Arthur Bloch

For many, the process of evaluation is the most difficult aspect of an anniversary celebration or, for that matter, any work that we do. It comes at the time when we have become weary of the anniversary, and it forces us to confront criticism of our efforts. But in many respects evaluation is the most important part of the process, because it documents and sums up, provides closure, and defines improvement. Knowing what went right and what went wrong will help us avoid making the same mistakes the next time and provide insight into better methods of accomplishing our goals.

Evaluations should come not only from archives staff but also from others within the institution—and outsiders. It should be an ongoing process, not one undertaken only at the end of the celebration. Evaluation can take place every time you have a staff meeting to discuss how planning is going. It can take place at the end of each event or program in which you participate. It can take place at the end of the celebration period as you look back and reflect on whether the work was worth the results if achieved. Finally, it can take place a year or two afterward, when the passage of time has given you the facts and the perspective to decide whether you met any, some, or all of the goals that you set at the beginning of the celebration. Ultimately, evaluation can help you answer the all important question: If I had it to do over again, would I? And how would I change it?

The final outcome of evaluation should be a report that tells in specific terms what went well and what did not. At the minimum, it should be written to file for your own reference or the benefit of your successor, who may be planning a similar celebration. Assuming a well-planned celebration has gone well, a copy should certainly be routed to appropriate resource allocators. The report should not attempt to gloss over or ignore problems that were encountered. It should include such documentation as your original planning time line, your original set of goals, and the outcomes you hoped to achieve. It should address such issues as problems that were not anticipated and how these were overcome. It should comment on the planning process and analyze how well or poorly you were able to estimate factors such as time and budget. In short, it should be the first step in planning for the next anniversary or similar event. In all likelihood, the final report will be used as a model for planning similar events in the future. (See Appendix 3d.)

PLANNING TIPS

1. Evaluate all your activities in terms of previously stated goals and objectives. Think of specific measures that enable you to determine whether you achieved the goals you set out for yourself.

2. Get a variety of perspectives:

- Do resource allocators and other institutional staff think the anniversary celebration was worthwhile? What do they see as the archives' most important contributions?
- What were the benefits to the archives? Does the archival staff think the effort of participation was worth the benefits derived?
- Did your publics find the activities and programs you sponsored worthwhile? What activities did they find most beneficial or interesting? Why?

3. Use a variety of tools to complete your evaluation. Follow-up questionnaires are the most convenient tool to use, but they have limitations. Most that are completed immediately following an event will be completed hurriedly and will aim to please. Interviews with participants are a more effective means to evaluate the success or failure of a program, but these are

more difficult and time-consuming to complete. In certain instances, you may wish to do a follow-up survey by mail, which can be costly and time-consuming with a low response rate, or by telephone, which is faster, but more open to interpretation. Despite limitations inherent in each, a combination of these three means will frequently provide a more complete overall picture.

4. Evaluate specific aspects of the planning process, such as budget and the time required to complete certain activities. Also evaluate such things as the audiovisual equipment you used, room in which particular events were held, and any other aspect of the arrangements that were critical to the success of a particular activity.

5. Ask for specific measures of success or failure. If you ask someone to rate on a scale of 1-10 how beneficial a program was, what does a simple numerical rating tell you? A "3" may signal that something was wrong, but you want to know *what* was wrong and how it could have been improved.

Conclusion

Anniversary celebrations are ideal opportunities for archivists to build public support for their programs in a variety of ways. Interest in the anniversary can bring the archives and new constituencies together. The important role that an archives plays in the various activities and events that are planned as part of an anniversary celebration can make a positive impression on resource allocators within the institution. Anniversaries make it easy for the archives to benefit from publicity and become well known in the local community. They are a good time to solicit important new collections of archival records. But perhaps most importantly, the benefits of anniversaries are long-lasting. The effort it has taken to be an integral part of an important landmark in the history of one's institution or community will make an impression that will last for years to come. It will help dispel the "dusty shelves full of yellowing documents" image and promote the archives as a place to which people come to find information that is important to their lives. The key to taking full advantage of these benefits is to anticipate and plan wisely, enabling the archives to use its resources wisely and direct its efforts toward specific goals that will improve both the quality and support for the archival program.

Additional Readings

Chase, William D., and Helen M. Chase. *Chase's Annual Events* (Chicago: Contemporary Books, 1994 ff.). Published annually and widely available, this source is an excellent guide to upcoming events that lend themselves to public program ideas.

Farr, Gail. *Archives and Manuscripts: Exhibits* (Chicago: Society of American Archivists, 1980).

Pederson, Ann E., and Gail Farr. *Archives and Manuscripts: Public Programs* (Chicago, Society of American Archivists, 1982).

Trager, James. *The People's Chronology: A Year-by-Year Record of Human Events from Prehistory to the Present* (New York: Henry Holt and Company, 1992).

Wilsted, Thomas, and William Nolte. *Managing Archival and Manuscript Repositories* (Chicago: Society of American Archivists, 1991).Contains particularly useful chapters on "Planning," "Fund Raising and Development," and "Public Relations."

6

Volunteers and Friends

Recruitment, Management, and Satisfaction

Audray Bateman Randle

Every day thousands of citizens spend a portion of their day as part of the unpaid volunteer American work force. A Gallup poll taken in 1987 showed that more than 80 million citizens do some kind of volunteer work, contributing 19.5 million hours of service in a year. These figures do not include such informal volunteer work as being a good neighbor or visiting with a sick friend, but they represent time spent by people who give service on a regular basis for a special purpose.

Almost any job that is done for financial remuneration in any business, industrial, social, educational, recreational, religious, or cultural enterprise can be done by the right volunteer. The majority of volunteers or unpaid workers (the label is used interchangeably here) serve not-for-profit organizations such as schools, hospitals, religious communities, youth groups, social service agencies, museums, libraries, historical societies, and a variety of other groups, many of which could not exist without unpaid staff.

Volunteers' reasons for doing their work are as varied as the jobs they perform and the organizations that reap the benefits. When asked why they volunteer, citizens give as their number-one reason, "Because I want to do something useful." Many feel that working at a job without financial reward is their contribution to their community or repayment for benefits they have received. Others are motivated by the need to make new friends or simply fill the hours of their lives productively. Some want to gain new skills or brush up on old ones so they can enter the job market. But whatever the reasons people give for volunteering—and archivists take note—many add, "because someone *asked* me to do it!"

Times change, and as economic conditions and life-styles change, so do volunteers. Today's typical volunteer is no longer the upper-class young matron with plenty of free time during the day. More than half of our nation's volunteers are citizens who have full-time paying jobs. Forty-five percent of volunteers are men. Surprisingly, people in the 30- to 45-year age range give the largest amount of volunteer time. Retired citizens and teenagers also make a significant contribution.

Management has changed, too. Supervisors and policy makers who felt that volunteer workers were not appropriate for their institutions or agencies ten years ago are now actively recruiting unpaid workers to supplement the hours of staff time that have been lost by current financial constraints.

Until recently, managers of archival and records repositories have been hesitant to use volunteers. Their chief response to suggestions that volunteers could be a possible solution to budget cuts or depleted program staffing is that the staff is already overworked. That is, they think there is no time for training or supervising volunteers. Archivists may also think that unpaid workers are not dependable. Since volunteers do not receive compensation for their work, the reasoning goes, they tend to show up only when it is convenient. Many in the profession feel that volunteers can do only routine, boring tasks or that a volunteer program won't last very long in their repository. Some archivists think that volunteers are a risk to security; they fear volunteers will misfile or steal valuable documents.

There are, however, many archival repositories, manuscript and local history collections that use volunteers with great success. Volunteers are not miracle workers, but they can be a means of accomplishing work far beyond the scope of the staff.

A good example of this is the use of volunteers at the Center for American History and its Barker Texas History Center at the University of Texas at Austin. Lynn Bell, Assistant Curator of Manuscripts and Volunteer Coordinator, wrote about their volunteers in the April 14, 1989 issue of the *Library Bulletin*, published by the University's General Libraries:

> ...Their contributions have ranged from preparing 19th-century newspapers for microfilming, to applying protective sleeves to historical photographs, to unfolding family correspondence, analyzing and arranging the papers and creating finding aids. Whatever the assignment, the volunteers bring much-appreciated assistance to the archives and manuscripts unit.

Ms. Bell reports that in 1991, volunteers contributed 2,127 hours, equaling 53 work weeks.

As well as completing projects that the staff would not otherwise do, volunteers are great marketers and advocates. They spread the word through the community on the sources of information available at the repository, thus increasing the number of users, and through volunteer contacts help repositories acquire donations of material. Volunteers are also likely financial donors; statistics show that they give more financial support to not-for-profit organizations than those who do not volunteer.

With nearly all archival institutions under severe economic constraints, and with little promise for a brighter future, archivists and manuscript curators are looking for creative ways to make more materials and programs available to more users. Tapping the unpaid work force *is* the answer for many institutions.

Setting Up a Volunteer Program

Determining the Need for a Volunteer Program

A few archival repositories have used volunteers with some success but little prior planning. True value, however, comes with first assessing the needs of the repository and then deciding if volunteers can supplement the work of the staff. The first question for the archivist to ask is whether volunteers can help reach the goals and fulfill the mission of the repository. It is a good idea to involve all levels of the staff in answering this question. In particular, staff who have expressed negative reactions to the use of volunteers should participate.

First, schedule a brainstorming session with the staff. Ask them to list all the tasks that need to be done in processing, reference service, public programming, and administration. Consider the backlog of materials and the many projects that the staff has suggested in the past but never had the time to do. Discourage the attitude that "it would be easier to do it myself." Keep in mind that in the volunteer work force there are people with many abilities and motives for volunteering. Some are suited for and want to do tasks that are simple and repetitive; others may well have knowledge and experience that can augment the expertise of the staff. Insist that the staff have an open mind.

Don't limit the list of possible volunteer assignments to work *in* the repository. Think of work that can be done by people who are homebound or working when the repository is open. Papers written in foreign languages can be photocopied, then translated at home, for example, or duplicates of oral history tapes can be transcribed away from the repository. Businesses, professional people, and artists may be willing to donate their services in creating brochures, newsletters, signs and posters in their own workplace.

This list of job assignments becomes the rationale for a volunteer program. If there are identifiable tasks to be done and staff cannot be hired to do them, then there is justification for using the resources of a volunteer work force. Considerations such as staff time for training and supervision, work space, and security can be dealt with in other planning sessions, which should be conducted regularly.

The creation of job assignments is the first step in using volunteers. Second, you must consider staff reaction to the use of volunteers. The purpose of a volunteer program is to supplement but never replace the staff. It is therefore important to make the staff feel secure about their jobs and unthreatened by volunteers who may take over some of their assigned tasks.

Third, the staff must understand that volunteers are not "free" help. Even though volunteers are not paid for the work they do, the staff must be willing to train, supervise, and in some way reward the volunteers. Staff time pays for a successful volunteer program.

Finally, seek the support of top management, whether it is the director of the parent institution or a board of directors that must be convinced volunteers can make a valuable contribution to the repository. Statistics and examples of successful volunteer programs in other repositories may help get approval. The endorsement and support of top management will encourage staff to be enthusiastic about working with volunteers. Is there work to be accomplished? Does the staff agree that volunteers can help? Are they comfortable with the idea of volunteers? Do they understand that time spent early on training and supervision will be time well spent in the end? If the answer to these questions is yes, then planning for using unpaid workers has begun.

Planning for a Volunteer Program

Following your decision to use volunteers, there are four major elements in planning your volunteer program. These are choosing a volunteer coordinator, creating work space, insuring security, and identifying liability.

Choosing a Volunteer Coordinator

The first item on the planning agenda is to designate a volunteer coordinator or manager who will start and oversee the volunteer program. An affluent repository may hire someone to fill the position, but most repositories will, at first, recruit only a few volunteer workers, and responsibility for the program can be assigned to a willing member of the staff.

Recruiting, interviewing, and selecting volunteers are part of the coordinator's assignment. The volunteer coordinator should be convinced of the efficacy of a volunteer program and skilled at interacting with other people. He/she should also be able to work closely with staff in determining job assignments and matching volunteers to the jobs. The coordinator is also the link between the unpaid and paid staff. He/she will work with each to help resolve problems.

The coordinator's responsibilities also include scheduling, record keeping, program evaluation, and seeing that the volunteers are rewarded for their services. The coordinator will also plan and direct general volunteer training, including orientation to the archives and approaches to the public. The staff member in charge of each project to which the volunteer is finally assigned will train and supervise the volunteer for that particular work.

A good coordinator is the key to a successful volunteer program, but setting up and managing a volunteer program takes time. The staff person appointed to the job may need to put other projects on hold. Changing priorities to include the volunteer coordinator's responsibilities will in the end greatly enlarge the work force and increase the amount of work done.

Creating Work Space

One of the best ways to ruin a well-intended volunteer program is to assume that a workplace can be arranged when the volunteer arrives. A volunteer must have a reserved work space, just as does any paid staff member. Nothing is more discouraging to the volunteer than to arrive for work and find the place that he/she worked the last time covered with documents from another project or discover that he/she is constantly moving from one temporary space to another.

Consider available work space and equipment early in the planning with your staff. Even in a crowded repository, problems can be solved by engaging the ingenuity and cooperation of staff.

In addition to assigned work space, volunteers also need the equipment it takes to do their job, such as a typewriter or computer, and a place to store such personal belongings as a purse, coffee mug, or brown-bag lunch. Everything they need must be available to them when they arrive for work, so that their time is maximized. Several volunteers whose working hours do not overlap can use the same desk, with a drawer assigned to each. Work space can also be a table or a reserved carrel, with document boxes on a shelf for storage.

Most volunteers do not want to work alone or in remote storage areas. Work space should be provided near other people. New volunteers should work near their supervisors, but volunteers who are trained and require less direction should not be sent to work alone. If shelving books or materials in isolated stacks is a task that must be done by volunteers, then a staff member should work with them or the coordinator should schedule two or more volunteers to work at the same time in the same area.

Insuring Security

Consider security when you use unpaid workers. Certainly a repository would not allow volunteers access to staff work areas and storage areas, any more than such areas would be open to the public. Carefully selected volunteers do not present a security problem, and most repositories can find good projects for volunteers that do not run the risk of the loss, theft, or misplacement of materials. But if the volunteer project includes handling valuable documents, then the work should be closely observed by a member of the staff. In short, security measures for volunteers who work on restricted, confidential, or especially valuable materials should be the same as those for the staff.

Liability

As part of the planning for a volunteer program, investigate both accident and liability insurance. If the parent institution carries insurance that adequately covers users, employees, and volunteers, no further attention to this matter may be necessary. But if volunteers are a new addition, or if a volunteer program is in place in your institution but no thought has been given to insurance, consult top management or the institution's attorney about the need for insurance coverage. Get answers to such questions as: Who is responsible for medical expenses or hospitalization if a volunteer falls down a flight of stairs or sustains a back injury from lifting a heavy carton? Who is responsible if a volunteer's purse is stolen? Who is responsible if a volunteer gives a user misinformation that affects the user adversely? Some insurance companies issue group policies especially written for volunteer services. If insurance premiums are not a budget item, some institutions ask each volunteer to contribute his/her own share for group coverage. The cost to the volunteer is usually just a few dollars a year.

Recruitment

Selecting the best volunteers and matching them with the right assignment and the right staff member are two of the most important jobs of the volunteer coordinator.

The coordinator will create volunteer projects from the list of job assignments compiled by you and your staff early in the planning. The project supervisor will eventually write complete job descriptions. For recruiting alone, the supervisor need only give the coordinator a brief description of each project and the skills, knowledge, and approximate hours needed to complete it. With these requirements in mind, the coordinator will anticipate the number of volunteers needed and look for volunteers who match the needs of each project.

The recruitment of volunteers is a *selection* process. The repository need *not* accept every potential volunteer who comes forward with an offer to help. Taking time to choose volunteers who have an interest in the mission of the repository, the time to commit, and the skills to do the work will guarantee their success and avoid most problems in supervision and turnover of volunteers.

Where to Find Volunteers

Volunteers can be attracted from many sources, but the coordinator must be very selective about where he/she looks, to avoid unsuitable candidates. Do not invite volunteers to work on first contact. Have them fill out an application form. With this information, the volunteer coordinator, with help from the staff, can select the volunteer for further consideration.

Repositories use a variety of methods to recruit volunteer help. Most volunteer coordinators say that the very best method is word of mouth. One volunteer suggests a friend, or staff may know someone who has time and interest. Word spreads quickly, and with little effort, the coordinator soon has a list of potential candidates without having done any actual recruiting.

Repository users must not be overlooked in the search for volunteers. At one library, for example, a user wanted access to unprocessed papers not yet available to the public, so he offered to help with the processing. The papers were written in German script, which no one on the staff could read. The archivist and the user, with his ability to translate and his knowledge of the subject, processed and created finding aids for materials that had been in storage for years.

Cultural groups (symphonies, museums, and libraries) and social service agencies (hospitals, big-brother, big-sister programs, battered women's shelters, and literacy projects) have long depended on volunteers to do much of their work. Although repositories must compete with these agencies in recruiting unpaid workers, archives and manuscript collections can attract many people who have a special interest in the subject area of the repository or in working with historical materials.

If the community has a volunteer bureau that matches volunteers to agencies of all kinds, the volunteer coordinator can talk to that office. The coordinator must make clear to the volunteer bureau the specific needs of the repository and must be allowed to make the final selection of volunteers.

Other sources to explore for recruiting volunteers are civic and professional organizations, senior citizen groups, and historical and genealogical societies. Many cities and towns have organizations such as the Junior League and the Assistance League, whose purpose is to give financial support and volunteer hours to not-for-profit community projects. A partnership with such a group can be an enormous benefit to a repository in search of volunteer help.

The use of student intern programs has also been successful in many archives, fulfilling both the repository's volunteer needs and certain current educational objectives, including community participation and applied work experience. In cooperation with a nearby junior college, technical school, or university, the archivist or coordinator can develop a project that provides students with an opportunity to have on-the-job experience in exchange for course credit. Students majoring in library science, archival programs, or history are clear choices for internships, but the coordinator should also consider students in other fields who would benefit the repository. Art students can produce posters or set up exhibits. Computer science majors can develop computer programs for appraising, scheduling, or describing records; and students of journalism, photography, public relations, and architecture are also candidates for projects.

Handicapped citizens and restitution volunteers are also good sources for potential volunteers. Agencies can be found in almost every community seeking volunteer opportunities for people who have the skills to do a job but have various disabilities that keep them from entering the job market.

Offices of the local courts in many communities are looking for agencies where citizens convicted of certain crimes can make restitution through volunteer service to the community. Driving-while-intoxicated is one of the most common crimes in which volunteer service is part of the sentence. Since restitution volunteers include people from every occupational and social level, they are able to fill many volunteer jobs in the repository. Professional people with skills needed for a processing project or office workers who can assist in clerical work will be found among them. Others can help with building maintenance, transfer heavy materials, or assemble shelving. Restitution volunteers must complete the number of hours assigned in a set period of time, and fulfilling their obligation is carefully monitored by the courts.

Articles in local newspapers and group newsletters, or notices on appropriate bulletin boards, can bring responses to a call for help from a repository. One university archives put a public-service announcement on the classical music radio station with good results. The National Archives lists itself in a *Washington Post* column on volunteers.

Some institutions request a commitment of three or four hours a week for one year from their volunteers. This requirement excludes many citizens who are willing to give volunteer hours but are looking for opportunities that do not require a long-term commitment. They prefer to contribute for a shorter, more concentrated time. Teachers, for example, might be interested in working four hours two or three times a week for a month or two in the summer. Retired persons may leave the area three to four months of the year for cooler or warmer climates. If the repository is open some evening and weekend hours, people who work full-time can be added to the list of potential volunteers. Whatever the circumstance, the volunteer coordinator may be able to work out concentrated, short-term assignments for volunteers with limited or confined work times.

Application for Volunteer Service

In order to decide if working in an archives or manuscript collection will fill their individual needs and goals, potential volunteers need information about the repository as much as the repository needs information about them. At the Austin (Texas) History Center, a call went out for volunteers. Those who indicated an interest were invited as a group for coffee at the center. They were given information on the volunteer program, the available work times, and a guided tour of the facility. At the end of the meeting, they were invited to complete and return an application form.

An application form can serve several purposes. It gives the volunteer coordinator information about the knowledge, skills, interests, and available work hours of each potential volunteer and can supply other useful information, such as where to reach the volunteer between scheduled work times and who to notify in an emergency (see Appendix 4b).

Application forms also serve as a permanent file of the names of people who are interested in volunteering. Although there may not be an immediate project to match the skills of the volunteer, there may be one in the future. Notes should also be made on the form about applicants who are not suited for any project in the repository, now or later. Information of this kind is often needed when the volunteer coordinator's responsibilities have been assumed by another person.

Interviewing the Potential Volunteer

A personal interview for unpaid workers is just as necessary as an interview for paid staff members and is another step in matching potential volunteers to projects or rejecting those who are unsuitable.

By the time the volunteer coordinator is ready to interview, the staff should have prepared job descriptions for each assignment. The potential volunteer should not be made to feel that the interview is an interrogation, rather that it is a time for both parties to get acquainted.

Having read the application form, the coordinator will know the skills, knowledge, and interests of the volunteer. During the interview, the coordinator should ask open-ended questions that will help determine if the candidate is suited for the type of work to be done. Examples of open-ended questions are

- "What did you like most about your last volunteer placement (or paid work)?"
- "What type of work do you like most? What least?"
- "Do you prefer to work alone on your own project or be part of a group?"

Open-ended questions will help to determine how well the potential volunteer will work with the staff. Clues to this include whether the person is a constant talker or not, whether he or she appears to be a decision maker or a follower, and what his or her work habits are likely to be.

From the interview, the coordinator can learn what volunteers expect from the repository in return for their service. They may want training that leads to employment or an assignment that helps them make a decision on their choice of career. Volunteers may have a special interest in a subject area collected by the repository, or simply want to make new friends.

The coordinator should explain possible volunteer assignments, the training that will be required, the length of service and schedule required of the volunteer, and the policies governing the paid staff that an unpaid worker must adhere to. The potential volunteer should also be told about the benefits of volunteering for your repository. In an archives or manuscript repository, volunteers can work with unique materials, acquire information about unusual subjects, and meet interesting people. They should also be told about the rewards they may receive for their work, which might include an annual appreciation luncheon or dinner, discounts on publications, or free parking.

End the interview by telling the interviewee that you will be in touch with him/her soon.

After the interview has ended and the potential volunteer has gone is the time for a final decision about his/her suitability. The candidate has a chance to think about the placement, and the volunteer coordinator has time to match volunteers to job descriptions. The coordinator should select only the number of volunteers that can be effectively used.

Be able to say no to those who are not suitable. It's hard to reject anyone who wants to donate time and effort, but careful selection of volunteers prevents many problems in volunteer management. There are some ways to say no politely, but firmly.

- "I don't have anything suitable for you."
- "I don't think work in this repository is what you are looking for."
- "As an alternative let me give you the name of the person at the Volunteer Center (or another agency) who knows of many volunteer placements."

The coordinator should call or write each person who has been interviewed within a few days of the interview. Notify by letter potential volunteers who are rejected permanently. For those who are accepted for immediate placement and those who will be needed at a later date, a telephone call will serve to explain the next steps. The coordinator begins by welcoming the volunteer and talking about specific work assignments. If the volunteer is suited for several assignments, he or she may be given a choice. The volunteer should be told when the project begins, what the work schedule is, the time for orientation and training, and who will supervise the work. This conversation should assure the new volunteer that he/she will be making a significant contribution to the mission of the repository, and make him/her enthusiastic about starting work. Send a follow up letter to confirm the information.

Many repositories ask volunteers to sign an agreement that outlines the commitment of both the repository and the volunteer. Often the parent institution requires that the volunteer be notified in writing that unpaid workers are not entitled to Worker's Compensation Insurance, employee benefits, or unemployment compensation. Such a statement can be incorporated in the agreement.

Training

Job Description

Complete written job descriptions are as important for volunteer workers as for paid staff. Staff members who will supervise a project should write the job description.

In writing the job description, the supervisor must think not only of the skills and knowledge the volunteer must bring to the job, but also about the amount of time required to train and supervise the volunteer.

A large part of planning for effective use of volunteer workers is done when the supervisor writes the job description, because thinking through the project and deciding what a volunteer will do helps define training and supervisory procedures. It also confirms whether or not the work assignment benefits the repository and will interest the volunteer. Answers to the following questions may be helpful in creating job descriptions.

- What special qualifications and skills are needed?
- Can the volunteer work on this project three or four hours a week without repeated training to compensate for the length of time between work periods, or would the project be better suited to a volunteer who wants to work in a concentrated time period?
- What are the scheduling requirements?
- Is the project such that the volunteer can set his/her own work pace and work methods?
- Is errorless performance necessary?
- What decisions must the volunteer make to do the task?
- Is the work described worth the staff time it takes to train and supervise? Do not create busywork jobs to occupy a volunteer's time. Volunteer assignments must be significant and satisfying to the volunteer and productive for the repository.

Orientation

Whether there is one volunteer or many, begin training with a general orientation. Every volunteer should know some facts about the repository.

- The history of the repository
- The kinds of materials collected by the repository, their subject matter and sources
- The repository's place in the parent organization
- Its allocation and sources of funding
- The nature of the repository's clientele
- The organization and work of each section
- The numbers and responsibilities of the staff, and the line of supervision
- The contribution that unpaid workers make to the repository.

Volunteers should also understand work rules.

- What kind of training they will get
- How assignments can be changed if the volunteer and the job do not match
- How volunteer-staff problems are resolved
- What the volunteer must do if he/she cannot come to work, i.e., how to make up the hours, or if the volunteer is assigned a job that deals with the public, how replacements are found
- What rules and regulations for security and parking govern paid and unpaid staff
- What record keeping volunteers are asked to do (signing in, signing out, and recording hours worked)
- What the repository telephone number is at which the volunteer can be reached when he/she is working, and the policy about using the telephone
- With whom will volunteers work. Introduce new volunteers to the staff either at the orientation session or the first work session.

A genuine welcome and expressions of appreciation will go far to make the volunteer feel that your repository is the right place to contribute his/her time and service.

Volunteer Manual

A volunteer manual is a practical complement to the volunteer program, if there is staff time to create it. Given to each new volunteer, the manual repeats in written form the information that is given to the volunteer at the interview and the orientation session.

The manual may also contain a letter of welcome from the director of the parent institution or the repository director, a floor plan of the facility, and copies of the repository's brochures and newsletters. A list of books and articles about the materials collected by the repository is also helpful. If there is a Friends of the Archives, the volunteer manual provides information about how Friends help the repository, how one benefits by being a member, and how one joins.

The format for volunteer manuals varies. They can be professionally designed and printed or typed and photocopied. They can be held together in a colorful binder with pockets for brochures and other enclosures, stapled, or sewn. Whatever the form, remember that the volunteer manual conveys an image of the repository; be sure that it is the image you want to convey.

On-the-Job Training

The effort you expend to select the best volunteers and match them with the right projects pays off for the project supervisor at on-the-job training time. Volunteers who have the necessary skills and are enthusiastic about their projects will learn quickly and, most importantly, will retain what they have learned between their scheduled work times.

If several volunteers are working on the same assignment at different times, it will save staff time to do an initial group training session, even though this may mean meeting when the repository is closed. Whether you offer a group or individual session, begin by giving a detailed description of the project, the work that the staff will do, and how the volunteers will help accomplish the project. The assignments should be explained thoroughly.

Provide written instructions that contain step-by-step procedures for completing the assignment. The more complicated the task, the more explicit must be the instructions. Very often the staff procedure manual can be used by volunteers who are performing jobs once done by a staff member. Since the volunteer may not come to work for a week or more, written instructions will serve as a review of the assignment, often answering the volunteer's questions and saving the trainer's time.

The volunteer's work should be checked frequently at first, and errors corrected. As with a new paid employee, the unpaid worker wants to know what is expected of him/her and how to do a good job.

If the volunteer finds the training difficult, then it may be necessary to review the matching process. Ask yourself whether the volunteer actually has the skills and interests that he/she indicated on the application or at the interview. If not, then an immediate change of assignment will save the staff and the volunteer both time and frustration.

Management

Supervision

The reason most often given by volunteers for losing interest in or leaving a job is that they received little or no supervision. Once trained, the volunteers report they are left without support. No one checks their work or corrects mistakes, nor does anyone tell them they are doing a good job.

Ideally, trainer and supervisor are one, but when training ends, it may happen that the supervisor does not work near the volunteer or their schedules do not overlap. The project supervisor must be creative in establishing a means of communication with the volunteer when face-to-face contact is not possible. At one repository, for example, the supervisor, who worked during the day, created a bulletin board for general announcements and changes in instructions for a group of volunteers who worked during the repository's evening service hours. The supervisor also posted appropriate cartoons and words of appreciation. Notes correcting errors or messages concerning individual assignments were left where the volunteers' work was stored.

In such situations, it is important that the supervisor also periodically schedule time to talk with the volunteer, evaluating completed work and getting feedback from the volunteer. Volunteers may suggest changes that will improve procedures. A good supervisor listens and considers new ideas.

Volunteers should be given as much responsibility as the supervisor thinks they can carry. They should not feel that their work is a dead-end. With new knowledge and experience, volunteers should advance in their assignments. They can also train and supervise other volunteers under the supervision of a staff member.

In short, volunteers can provide many essential services in every size and every type of repository, but successful volunteer programs require constant interaction between paid and unpaid workers and careful supervision and monitoring. What constitutes good supervision for paid workers is also good supervision for volunteers.

Volunteer Organizations

In institutions with large volunteer forces, the volunteers frequently establish their own organization, often called an association or guild, electing officers and establishing governance. These groups recruit volunteers, recognize service, and provide social events for members. The volunteer coordinator plays an important part in maintaining a good relationship between the volunteers' organization and the repository. Volunteer organizations should *not* be concerned with the policy, operation, or management of the repository. But volunteers, whether part of an organized group or not, must feel that they are contributing members of the staff and must understand from the beginning that they work under the same management guidelines and through the same channels as the paid staff.

Dismissing a Volunteer

Not all volunteers turn out to be as they were perceived during the selection process. If the unpaid worker does not meet the performance standards set by the supervisor or causes problems with other volunteers and staff, then the volunteer coordinator must change the situation. The coordinator acts as the mediator between the supervisor and the volunteers and should discuss the problem with the parties concerned. If the problem lies with the supervisor, assigning supervisory responsibilities to another staff member or changing the volunteer's job assignment may be necessary. But if the volunteer causes a problem that cannot be solved, then it is time to end the relationship. The fact that a volunteer is doing work without pay does not mean that he/she cannot be dismissed.

It is wise to use the same procedures before dismissing a volunteer that are used for paid employees. Giving the volunteer additional training, changing assignments, counseling, and documenting the reason for the dismissal are important so that the institution has justification for the action taken if the rejected volunteer retaliates. For example, a volunteer may file suit against an institution asking for reinstatement or damages, but well documented performance or attendance reports can be used to address these demands.

The dismissal should be done with the utmost tact. You will also find it helpful to recommend another agency that might use the volunteer's services, if this is appropriate.

Record Keeping

Personnel files should be kept for unpaid workers as well as for paid employees. It is the responsibility of the volunteer coordinator to see that these files are created and maintained.

Information on how to contact the volunteer between scheduled work hours and when and whom to call in case of emergency should be readily available. Other data on assignments, projects completed, and the number of hours worked will be used periodically to evaluate the program. This information is also useful if the volunteer requests a recommendation for employment.

Retain the application form, notes from the interview, and documentation of any problems. Keep a record of the skills and interests of the volunteer to solve problems that may arise between the volunteer and the staff or to make changes in work assignments.

Statistics on the work volunteers perform can serve to justify the time paid staff uses to train and supervise them, as well as having other uses.

Keep a time sheet on which the volunteer records the date, the time of his/her arrival and departure, and the hours worked. This record is not only valuable in assessing the program, but may be helpful for purposes of security. The time sheet also serves as a record of service for volunteers who are fulfilling the requirements of an organization such as the Junior League or are part of a court restitution program. Records of frequent absences, tardiness, or early leaving will indicate that a volunteer may be losing interest in the assignment or that a long-time worker is about to burn out. Many repositories keep individual monthly time sheets in a notebook that is easily accessible to the volunteers.

Keeping volunteer records should not burden the coordinator, and they are part of a successful volunteer program.

Evaluation

At least twice a year, the volunteer coordinator should take time to evaluate the volunteer program, analyze the statistics, and discuss each project with the staff supervisor. Among the questions that the coordinator and staff will consider are

- Is the amount of work accomplished by volunteers worth the time the staff must give to train and supervise them?
- Are the duties of the volunteer coordinator an effective use of his/her time?
- Are the volunteers motivated, satisfied with their assignments, and rewarded for their work?

Affirmative answers mean a successful volunteer program. No's suggest reevaluation.

Recognition

Recognizing the contribution of the unpaid worker is as important to a successful volunteer program as matching the right person to the right project thorough training and good supervision. What motivates paid staff also motivates volunteers.

Recognition begins with making the volunteer feel that he/she is part of the staff, not an outsider who assists in the work of one staff member and is tolerated or ignored by the others. Such simple things as calling the volunteer by name, greeting him or her at the beginning of the work period, frequently taking time to say thank-you, and listening to and accepting good ideas gives the volunteer a feeling of importance and belonging.

Volunteers also want to know what is going on in the repository. If volunteers and staff have little interaction other than training and supervision, consider inviting them to selected staff meetings, creating a simple volunteer newsletter, or posting notices on a bulletin board to provide information about new acquisitions, new procedures or policies, changes in staff, and fluctuations in budget. If the repository's volunteers come from the volunteer program of a parent institution, then the institution should also have its own kinds of recognition.

Whether the volunteer coordinator is responsible for two volunteers or two hundred, he/she must be creative in finding ways to say thank you. The coordinator can express appreciation by placing articles about the volunteers' contributions in the local newspaper or the institution's newsletter, by sending greeting cards on special occasions to the volunteers, or by celebrating birthdays at coffee break.

A volunteer coordinator who calls or writes a volunteer who is absent because of illness or family problems, or one who is not coming to work at the scheduled time helps reinforce the value of that person's work.

Recognition should fit the repository's resources. It can range from yearly recognition ceremonies at a fancy luncheon or elaborate banquet, with certificates or pins for years of service and small gifts given to the honored volunteers, to setting aside time for the staff to say thank-you at a simple coffee.

Some repositories recognize their volunteers by prominently exhibiting a plaque with brass plates bearing the names of the volunteers and their years of service or by giving an appropriate gift, such as a publication from the repository, a copy of a photograph or other document from the collections, or a special name tag.

A word of caution. When you plan recognition, consider first the motivation for service and the desires of the volunteer. Some volunteers do not want special recognition ceremonies or handsomely framed certificates. Others look forward to such celebrations and mementoes. Although public recognition ceremonies may be good public relations for the repository, they are not necessary to a successful volunteer program. What is necessary is recognition that fits the wishes of the volunteers and the resources and style of your institution. (See Appendix 4a for additional guidelines.)

Friends

Volunteer organizations are a vital part of American life. People want to be part of a group that supports their special interests. Think of a cause, and you will find an organization that supports that cause. Friends of libraries, museums, and other cultural institutions are common in every city.

There is a difference between volunteer workers and Friends organizations, however. It is often the primary function of a Friends group to supply extra funding for an institution. Friends can provide a repository with money to prepare exhibits, purchase collections, hire a consultant, support a publication program, or send a staff member to a workshop. A Friends organization can support public relations projects, host receptions, or be a lobbying force.

Volunteers, on the other hand, are usually recruited independently by the repository's volunteer coordinator to work under the direction of the repository staff on projects that might otherwise be done by staff. Members of Friends are a primary source for potential volunteers for a repository.

If the parent institution of an archives does not already have an organized Friends or an active support group, consider establishing one. No matter who takes on the job of organizing a Friends group, the repository director will need approval from top management and must plan to expend time on the project, but if there is a need for the kinds of support and services that Friends can give, then the time is well spent.

Organizing the Friends

Timing is important to organizing a Friends group. A special focus also helps attract people to such an organization. The time is right to form a Friends group when a repository is moving into a new facility, undertaking a major renovation of an old building, acquiring a major acquisition, or getting publicity because of a special project. Such activity will draw public attention to the repository and interest potential new Friends. On the other hand, if another cultural institution in the community is in the midst of a big membership drive, money-raising event, or another attention-getting project, you may want to wait a few months before publicly announcing the organization of a Friends of the repository.

A Friends group often begins as a committee of a larger or different organization. The research committee of one local genealogy society helped found a Friends group for a county's historical museum and archives, for example. In Austin, Texas, a group of citizens banded together temporarily to raise funds to finance the renovation of the old public library building to house the local history collection. After this goal was reached, the group stayed together as the nucleus of a permanent support organization for the collection.

When there is no start-up group, find one person who will take up your cause and, with the help of the head archivist or director of the repository, organize an initial committee. Choose that person carefully. Find someone who has serious interest in the work of the repository, who sees the need for a support group, and who can convince others of that need. The organizer should also be philanthropic by nature and reputation. If he/she is a leader in the community, other prominent citizens will be attracted to the group. The initial committee, often called founders, should represent the diversity that exists in the community and be able to lend expertise and breadth to the institution. It is ideal to have a mixture of men and women, varying age groups, professions, and ethnic representation. Lawyers, accountants, people in other professions, labor union heads, and citizens with connections to civic organizations, corporations, and businesses are assets to any organizing committee.

This founding committee should fully understand the mission of the repository and agree on the purpose of the proposed Friends organization. The committee should write, and the archivist or director of the repository approve, a statement of purpose. Such a statement is helpful as the planning progresses, and will help avoid misdirected efforts.

The organizational committee should consider the following items.

1. What will be the official name of the group?

2. What are the immediate and long-range goals of the repository and how can the Friends help accomplish them?

3. What structure will best serve the Friends? Most not-for-profit organizations are governed by a board of directors or by an executive committee, steering committee, or council. The organizational committee must also consider what officers and committees are needed; what will be the makeup of the board of directors and who will fill those posts; and how the organization will conduct business and fulfill its purpose.

4. How will the Friends incorporate? Establishing a tax-exempt not-for-profit organization is necessary if one of the purposes of the group is to raise money. Requirements and fees vary in each state, and the advice of a lawyer will speed the process and assure that it is being done correctly.

5. What bylaws are needed? Study the bylaws of similar organizations and use appropriate sections to create the rules that will govern the Friends. Again, the advice of a lawyer simplifies this task.

6. What are the financial considerations? Sources of funding for the organization, fund raising, and how money will be spent must be decided. An accountant will help greatly to set up a system to record and account for income and expenditures. The organizing committee must also choose a banking institution. It will need seed money. It must send mailings about meetings, pay for light refreshments, and provide other incidental expenditures. If the repository does not have the resources to pay those costs, then it may be necessary to ask each founder for a small contribution.

7. What insurance will be needed? As with volunteer workers, the initial committee must decide whether liability insurance is needed. Some community leaders will not serve as officers or board members of an organization that does not have liability coverage.

8. Who will be members, and how will they be reached? How does one become a member of the Friends, and what are the benefits of membership? In the early stages of planning, the committee will appoint a membership chairman for the initial recruitment who will create a file of names suggested by members of the committee and drawn from membership roles of other historically oriented organizations. A membership directory to be distributed to all members can be published and updated regularly after the support group is well established. Besides the names, addresses, and telephone numbers of the current members, the directory can also contain such information as a statement of purpose, accomplishments of the Friends to date, the bylaws and articles of incorporation, names of the officers and committee chairs, and a calendar of events and meetings.

9. What is the timetable for final decisions? If the group was organized to accomplish a special project, establish a schedule for completing stages and finishing the projects.

Then set a date for the organizational meeting of the membership and decide how potential members will be notified of the formation of the new organization. At the first meeting, the new members will pay their dues, consider the bylaws, decide on incorporation, and vote on a slate of officers and board of directors. An initial board is named on the proposed corporate charter. The membership will also approve any other items concerning organization. The planning ends, and the operation of the Friends begins.

The part the director of the repository plays in the organization and operation of a Friends group is extremely important, and not always an easy task. Sometimes the initial committee or the Friends board of directors will make final plans for projects, membership, or fund raising that clash with the goals and objectives of the repository. To avoid this, the director should participate from the outset in the organizational planning and the deliberations of the board and committees after the support group is organized. The director must be open to new ideas but ready to question any decision that is not in the best interests of the repository.

The relationship of the Friends to the repository must be made clear to everyone from the outset. Those who govern the Friends must understand that the policy, operation, and management of the repository is *not* their responsibility, but that of the director.

The director, in turn, must do all that is necessary to assure the Friends that the group is making a valuable contribution to the repository. The Friends board, with guidance from the director, will make decisions about meetings of the organization, fund raising, spending money that will be raised, special events and projects, and membership dues and benefits.

Fund Raising

Few archives, manuscript or local history repositories have adequate funds to completely achieve their mission. Every repository needs additional funds, not only to perform the basic tasks of preserving and making the materials entrusted to it available to users, but also to do the special projects that are increasingly part of core archival programs. Friends groups are a good fund raising vehicle.

In every community, support groups for social services and cultural agencies find various ways to make money. Some hold bake sales or sell candy bars, T-shirts, calendars, or greeting cards. Others sell high-priced tickets to fancy galas, sponsor lectures, trips, performances of big-name stars, or hold used book and garage sales. Such fund raising methods usually take the time and effort of many members of the support group and keep members interested. Success in fund raising is measured by the amount of profit the group realizes. Most agencies aim for 50 percent profit over the cost of the product or up front expenses of an event. Fund raising projects are initiated and carried out by members of the support group; the repository's staff time on such projects should be kept to a minimum.

Friends groups for archives and manuscript collections have created fund raising projects that are good money makers and also provide visibility for the holdings of the repository. Successful projects include making reproductions of old photographs on postcards, notepaper, posters, and calendars and reprints of old maps or rare books. Friends of archives have sponsored activities as varied as lectures on subjects relating to the repository's collections delivered by authorities or celebrities, lecture series celebrating national events, such as the Bicentennial of the Declaration of Independence, and workshops on how to care for family photographs or do family oral history.

Many organizations simply ask for contributions, either by mail or by telephone. People are more likely to give to a cause when they are asked by someone they know well. Members of the Friends, who have influence in the community, can contact local corporations and businesses for contributions or pledges.

Dues for membership are another source of funds. These usually cover the operational expenses of the organization, but different categories of dues can be developed to raise money for the repository with little effort. For example, to be a life member of your Friends may cost $1,000; a benefactor, $500; a sponsor, $100; and a contributing member, $10. Another institution may start at $100, working down as the local economy dictates. Corporate membership can be one such category. Memberships higher than the contributing category can be noted in the membership directory. Be sure that your Friends dues are consonant with those of similar groups in your community; don't set a reduced fee because you are "just an archives."

Fund raising should not be limited to solicitation of money, selling a product, or holding a benefit, however. Members of Friends groups experienced in writing proposals for grants from federal and state agencies or applying for funding from local foundations can perform this task for your repository. In today's economy, government agencies and foundations are asking for matching funds, and Friends are often the source of these.

A project well chosen and well planned by dedicated, hard working members does not always insure successful fund raising. Some factors are beyond the control of the organization. Economic conditions in the community and the competition for contributions affect giving. Museums, performing arts organizations, libraries, and other cultural institutions must compete for available funding with public service agencies, environmental interests, and religious groups. To get their share, Friends of archives and manuscript repositories must market the purpose and services of their repository clearly and often in order to motivate givers to enlist in their cause.

A Friends group can work miracles, because Friends can accomplish objectives that the repository's paid staff cannot. Friends can be volunteers, public relations agents, and lobbyists, and they can supply funding for projects that were once only dreams.

7

Troubleshooting

James Bressor and Julie Bressor

A former three-term governor has arranged to turn over all his papers to your archives. With your office, he plans a 2:00 P.M. news conference at the archives to announce his gift, timed to gain maximum exposure on the evening news. Forty-five minutes before reporters are scheduled to arrive, a pipe in your archives bursts, seriously damaging the collections of two other former governors and a U.S. Senator.

Word of the damage spreads quickly. Reporters begin to arrive, wearing their best smirks; a pair of acid-pen columnists you hadn't expected also appear. Your donor, known for his temper and capriciousness, begins to treat you and members of your staff brusquely. As a local newscaster makes her entrance, the governor begins to question, rather loudly, how you spent the capital improvement money he helped appropriate for the archives just a few years ago, because it's abundantly clear, at least to him, that it wasn't spent on plumbing...

What do you do?

It doesn't always happen to someone else. Sooner or later, it may happen to you: the stolen manuscript, the collection of letters lost to fire, a file thrown out in a series of misadventures. Reporters begin calling to ask how something like this could occur. Your job is to respond to a difficult, unexpected situation quickly, honestly, and thoroughly.

Avoiding Problems

There's no getting around bad news. You can, however, reduce the potential for negative publicity by recognizing the causes of bad news. The impact of bad news can be further mitigated by carefully managing information and responses in a crisis situation through careful preparation and an understanding of the dimensions of the crisis. But the best way to handle a public relations problem is to prevent it from happening. In the hypothetical situation described above, someone was probably not doing his/her job. Just because a pipe hasn't burst in the past 50 years doesn't mean you will go another 50 years without a disaster of this kind.

In planning for the unexpected, you must recognize that danger can come from a variety of natural environmental or human causes. A natural disaster can strike in the form of a flash flood, hurricane, or earthquake. Crises linked directly to the public include arson, theft, injury, legal suits and death. Environmental disasters such as a burst pipe, positive testing for toxic substances in the air or in building materials, and chemical spills now happen often. By understanding the potential causes of problems, you can begin to take steps to protect your organization, your collections, your staff, and your users from the problem itself and the adverse publicity that will follow.

Assessing the Physical Plant

The best place to begin an assessment is close to home, beginning with a thorough inspection and understanding of your facility. Set aside at least several hours to do a condition survey of your physical plant. You can do this yourself or, better yet, bring along an engineer or building maintenance expert. A survey should include information on the overall condition of the physical plant and specific notes on the condition of particular parts of your structure such as the roof, flashing, ceilings, pipes, and wiring. When you plan a survey, it's a good idea to first familiarize yourself with preservation and industry standards for your type of facility and its maintenance. A number of publications relating to physical plants and preservation are available. (See Additional Readings at the end of this chapter.) A good starting place is the appropriate chapters in GRASP, a self-assessment model for preservation planning released by the National Association for Government and Records Administrators (NAGARA) in 1990. Most regional and national preservation and conservation organizations offer helpful reprints and bibliographies.

Study carefully the building environment that surrounds your archives. Many older—and some newer—buildings have heating and condensation problems, old wiring, and aging copper and iron pipes. Identify problem areas and remain vigilant about potential problems. Carry out a top-to-bottom inspection of the building at least once a year. This inspection should not be a cursory walk through the facility. Look carefully. If, for instance, you have heat or water pipes in a room housing collections, don't study the pipes alone; look also at the floor or shelves below for signs of water stains. Again, have an expert accompany you. Call in a professional to look at problems as they appear; most will visit without charge or for a nominal fee. Some regional preservation organizations offer facility surveys, and grants for facility and conservation surveys such as the Conservation Assessment Program (CAP) offered through the Institute of Museum Services (IMS) are available. A survey should also include information on whether the facility is in compliance with the accessibility requirements outlined in the Americans With Disabilities Act (ADA), which became effective January 26, 1992, and recommendations on how to comply with the Act.

The inspection should result in a list of what, if anything, needs to be fixed, altered, or replaced, how soon this should be done, and what should be monitored and how often. If you know your electrical wiring or pipes are old, replace them as soon as possible. Clean and recalibrate climate control systems regularly. If you notice loose flashing on the roof, have it fixed without delay. The survey should help you persuade a miserly board of directors or an unsympathetic government agency to underwrite additional maintenance and renovation costs. Point out that if the collections are to be kept, they must be protected and preventative maintenance and repair are far more cost effective than the alternative of doing nothing, which inevitably leads to collections loss, personal injury and litigation, increased maintenance costs in the future and, most likely, bad publicity.

In addition, know the physical limitations of the space you use, and work around possible problems. Take precautions and implement practical solutions if you can. If humidity or dampness is a problem, take action. Determine what the year-round humidity level is and do something to control it. Consider your priorities. Uppermost should be the proper stewardship of your collections, not the sentimentality associated with keeping material in a drafty, moist, 200-year-old historically correct fire hazard. Not fulfilling your obligation to properly care for the materials you are responsible for reflects badly on you, your organization, and the profession as a whole. That reflection usually appears first in the media.

A note of caution. Most renovations result in exposure to hazardous substances from lead paint to asbestos insulation. Many present-day paints, fumigants and sealants contain a variety of toxins. These hazards are very real and of concern to the public. Before undertaking any work, be sure the appropriate contractors and staff are fully aware of the variety of potential hazards that could be encountered during a renovation project. Renovations also require that you keep on your toes. Statistics show this is the most likely time for a disaster to occur, whether it results from fire, water damage, theft, or exposure of hazardous materials.

Assessing the Human Factor

Not all problems stem from your physical plant. Probably half of all bad publicity can be traced to a human source. In the case of an archives, the source can be a negligent staffer, a thief, a disgruntled patron, or an arsonist. Often the source can be traced to an internal problem.

The first place to look for potential problems is your organizational structure and day-to-day operating procedures. Do you have a procedure by which more than one person makes certain the lights are off, doors and windows locked, and alarm system armed at the end of the day ? Are areas for specific activities separate and clearly marked—such as those in which papers are being processed, recycled or discarded? It is certainly possible that a janitor can throw away valuable documents. Legend has it that Thomas Carlyle had to rewrite the first volume of his *History of the French Revolution* when he loaned it to John Stuart Mill, whose maid mistook it for trash and burned it. Do you train every new employee, intern, or volunteer in your facility to understand thoroughly the nature of your collections? Each new staffer should have a complete introduction to your entire archives, from your basic mission to collections highlights and procedures for use, including guidelines on what to do and whom to contact in an emergency. Periodically update and review these procedures.

Consider also how well you work with your staff. A good manager lessens the likelihood of public relations problems by fostering a positive atmosphere and cooperative team spirit among employees. In a well-managed archives, the staff shares responsibility for helping the organization fulfill its basic mission every day. It is essential to regularly evaluate your managerial and communications skills and improve and refresh them as needed.

Theft of documents is often internal. Whether or not you can trust staff members not to steal begins when you hire them. Ask for and follow up on references. If you or your board members are considering special procedures as part of an interview and hiring process, be aware that some tests, especially those relating to drug use and activities outside the workplace, can generate negative publicity and demoralize staff. As for trusting your users, minimize opportunities for theft or damage to the collections by using accepted archival security procedures.

A frequently overlooked area of potential trouble is how the archives deals with its users. How many patrons walk through your door seeking information to be confronted with a sign describing what can't be done at the archives? Does someone ask a patron to register, closet briefcases, or surrender a driver's license or student card before he/she can ask a question or sit down? Has it been a few years since you've updated your signs (if you have any)? Or do you assume patrons know what to look for? If you answered yes to any of these questions, it's time for public relations rebuilding in this area.

Put yourself in the user's shoes. An archives reading room is often a complicated place, with numerous indices, shelf locations, procedures for requesting material and various printed resources. Does your signage and staff explain what services are available and where to go for more information? Do you accentuate the positive—what can be done at the archives—or do you specify the negative—what can't be done at the archives? Are your chairs, tables, and lighting adequate for researchers? Think of your role as a service provider and helpful professional, and take another look at what the public sees and experiences when it visits your archives. Do what you can to make a patron's experience at the archives a positive one.

Assessing Your Relations with the Media

Public relations gaffes can be of your own innocent making. Always hear what you say when speaking in public or with reporters. A damaging quote won't go away, and you can never erase it from a newspaper or the evening news. It will live on forever, for future reporters to use over and over again. One of the first public relations troubleshooters in this country was hired by William Henry Vanderbilt in 1882. His job was to diffuse the damage done by a simple, four-word quote. In an interview on railroad rates and fares, Vanderbilt responded to a question with two sentences. The second sentence, "What does the public care for railroads, except to get as much out of them for as small a consideration as possible?" is now forgotten. It is the first sentence, short and to the point, that is remembered: "The public be damned!" Mr. Vanderbilt's troubleshooter was probably paid handsomely for his efforts, but to little advantage. The quote eventually found its way to Bartlett's *Familiar Quotations* and nearly every reference and period textbook in print.

During an interview, speak clearly, slowly, and if necessary, repetitively. As hard as it is for us to admit, it is not the typical reporter's first choice to write stories about archives. Pork-barrel politics, double murders, and sexual or fiscal impropriety by members of Congress are the sought-after assignments. Furthermore, you are likely to be interviewed not by a seasoned reporter but by a cub, a recent college graduate who knows nothing about your institution. Follow-up is important. Don't hesitate to ask a reporter at the end of an interview, "Do you want me to go over anything again?" Invite the reporter to call back with questions.

Especially when speaking with a veteran reporter, beware of manipulative questions such as "Wouldn't you agree..." or "Isn't it true that...." Answer on your own terms. State facts as you see fit. Answer the question you have been asked, not one you have not been asked. If the reporter says, "Many people say that your institution...," ask who those people are and find out what they have for specific comments. If the reporter can't answer, you don't owe him or her a response. But never say, "No comment."

Be precise about facts; never walk away from an interview thinking you can clean up mistakes in a correction. A next-day correction or clarification never has the same impact as a first-day error. Asking for a correction or clarification can also jeopardize your relations with reporters, editors, and sometimes the whole news organization, because you are asking them to publish a public notice admitting that a staff member made a mistake. Although very few reporters will agree to such a request, you can ask to see the reporter's finished story before it goes to the editors. Be aware that an experienced reporter may infer you don't trust his or her ability to do a good job.

Assessing the Impact of Special Events

Not all potential problems come from within the archives. Outreach and special events in the archives often require additional specific public relations planning. The activity must meet the needs of the archives and the needs of your institution at the same time, or trouble can result. It's essential to think through the purpose, goals, and responsibility for any special activities that will result in publicity for the archives and, by extension, for your parent organization.

Let's say that a widely respected lawyer, a national leader in the prosecution of on-the-job sexual harassment cases, has arranged to donate her papers to your repository, the archives of her alma mater. The collection is within your collecting scope, and your institution is happy to have a high-profile alumna make such a donation. It provides an excellent public relations opportunity. But take precautions; assume nothing. Before you draw up a press release, for example, review your institution's sexual-harassment history and its current policies. Do these live up to your donor's standards? If you learn of any problems, be prepared to explain to the press (and to your donor) what your institution has done to correct them.

For donations of any current, issue-oriented material, explore the possible political repercussions. Be sure the archives, the donor, and the parent organization understand potential press and public reaction. Explore the ramifications from different perspectives. Talk quietly with staff, colleagues, researchers, and administrators about the possible publicity this donation might generate. Imagine different ways reporters might approach the story. Decide if the publicity can be positive or whether it will reflect badly on your program or your parent organization. You may want to document your decision and the process by which you reached it. If your decision affects future collecting activities in this area, note this change in appropriate policy documents.

Many of these points are simple, but they are frequently overlooked. It is important to remember that many public relations crises can be traced to just such administrative oversights.

Anticipating Crisis

Despite your best efforts to avoid problems, they will occasionally arise. By expanding your concept of disaster planning to include the following steps, you will be better able to deal with the public, the press, and your organization when trouble occurs and better able to manage the flow of information and activity in a crisis situation. Again, many of these steps may seem to be elementary office and administrative procedures. But in an emergency situation, daily functions become public relations functions as all activities come under scrutiny.

1. Have up-to-date fact sheets about your repository available for public relations use. Make this information readable, using such easy-to-understand details as number of feet of material, collection scope, staff size, significant holdings, and collecting areas. The fact sheet should also contain highlights, including biographies of luminaries whose papers reside in your archives and notable products of research in your holdings. The fact sheet has a wide variety of public relations and development uses, but it will save valuable time when a crisis occurs and can help you organize your thoughts so you can speak with reporters succinctly and clearly.

Why prepare a fact sheet about a local institution for local media and local public? Because not even they know what you want them to know about your institution. For example, many residents of Shelburne, Vermont, confuse Shelburne Farms, a conservation education organization and former agricultural estate, with the Shelburne Museum, which houses an outstanding collection of Americana. While both are well-known attractions, the two have completely different missions and are several miles apart. Yet many area residents consider them one and the same. Given the high turnover rate at many small and midsize newspapers, no one working for your local news organization is likely to know more about your repository than do local residents. One look at a fact sheet gives a reporter a clear picture of what you do and what makes it newsworthy.

Fact sheets and related material serve several useful functions beyond providing information in an emergency situation. They can be public relations tools to draw upon in interviews, to be used in staff and volunteer training, and to help with development and donor-related activities.

2. Your office should also have a regularly updated procedures manual, where all the fact sheets, day-to-day operations, special events checklists, and crisis management guidelines are compiled. Procedures for regular archives activities, staff responsibilities, and administrative guidelines should be spelled out. Clearly delineated procedures for regular activities in the archives certainly lessen the likelihood of theft, loss, or damage.

An entire section of the manual should be devoted to managing a crisis situation and should include procedures on responding to each of the following.

- Natural disasters, such as earthquakes and floods
- Human disasters, such as arson, theft, injury, and death
- Environmental disasters, such as water damage or the presence of toxic materials

Clearly describe what actions need to be taken, who is in charge, and how to communicate with volunteers and the press. All procedures should be based on standards established in recent professional journals and publications. Develop plans cooperatively where possible, and always work closely with local emergency management personnel in writing and updating plans.

3. Guests at any kind of public facility have the right to emergency care in case of injury or illness. At least one person, and preferably several people, on your staff should have training in first aid and CPR (cardiopulmonary resuscitation). Your health unit should be available to visitors in an emergency. The view that you should avoid assisting a visitor in an emergency because you might be the subject of a lawsuit is counterproductive when you consider the alternative—and the public outcome—of doing nothing. Most states have laws protecting Good Samaritans. If you are properly trained in the basics, you can be sure of taking the right action in an emergency instead of second-guessing someone's needs. If you are still hesitant, check your rights and responsibilities with your organization's attorney.

4. Keep emergency numbers by every telephone in your repository and on file with your buildings and grounds manager or other appropriate person. These numbers should include emergency medical services, police, the local fire department, plumbers, heating and ventilating crews, and anyone else you would consider crucial in an emergency. Update the numbers regularly and keep a copy in your wallet.

5. Stay constantly alert to the danger of damage to collections during renovations. During any facility work, collections are vulnerable, and this is a likely time for disaster to strike. Prepare a safety checklist for contractors and staff. Ask for briefs of appropriate local, state, and federal regulations (building codes, lead-based paint and asbestos removal, permitting, access for people with disabilities), weekly reports, and other pertinent information so you remain informed at all times. Renovations should provide positive publicity for your organization; don't lose these opportunities by inadequate planning and poor documentation. Keep pertinent information as part of your permanent files.

6. Be fully conversant with state and federal laws and regulations relating to public access to information and facilities. The federal Freedom of Information Act guarantees public access to specific information; state constitutions, statutes, and regulations govern access and exemptions to access to both public and private records. Your own organization may have policies regarding access. In addition, know your rights and responsibilities relating to copyright law and its applicability to materials in your care. The Americans With Disabilities Act (ADA) is a landmark piece of civil-rights legislation relating to access to facilities and programs. Know how you comply with ADA and what steps you should take to comply fully. Your statewide historic preservation office, state agency of human services, and the U.S. Department of Justice can offer assistance in learning more about ADA.

7. Always be aware of ways your institution can offend its neighbors. If you purchase acid-free paper produced a thousand miles away when a local paper mill also produces acid-free paper, be prepared to explain why. Don't just say there's a significant cost difference. Provide a written policy saying that your facility will pay up to a certain percentage more for locally made material. If you choose not to buy recycled paper and folders because of acidity concerns, or you choose not to recycle paper used in daily office work, state your reasons.

Your organization will be most often talked about in your local community, and you can have an impact on what is said. When planning a special event, don't overlook the needs and interests of the local community; that is where your volunteers, reporters, and local donors live. A well-planned special event has everyone talking, but never as much as when the event overlooks someone or something important next door. Imagine an archives presenting a special series on its state's labor movement but ignoring the vibrant labor history at nearby stone quarries, particularly if those quarries provided the stone for the building in which the archives is housed. That's the type of gaffe area residents remember for a long time.

8. All special events require adequate planning. Modify a universal checklist for each special event. Be sure your facility is adequate and appropriate for the event. Double check to see that all of your contracts are signed and legal, the publicity material is correct, and the right people have been invited to the right place at the right time. If you are reaching out to a new audience, include directions and informational material in your publicity material. Incorporate a welcome and introduction to your collections into all of your special programs.

9. Prepare for criticism from various interest groups, then practice handling it. There is an increasing possibility that archivists in academia, for instance, might be vulnerable to charges of political incorrectness (are your collections gender balanced and ethnically balanced, for example?). Role play issues with your co-workers. You'll be surprised at how hard it can be to respond carefully and thoughtfully to their passionate rhetoric. Learn to respond reasonably, briefly, and calmly.

10. Be consistent in your convictions. If you subscribe to a published code of ethics, stick to it. If your collecting activities are part of an overall plan, keep to the plan. Don't make exceptions to the rules, since it is the exception to the rule that inevitably gets publicity.

Responding to a Crisis

Taking precautions and being prepared are only half of a crisis management plan. The most difficult activity is responding to an actual disaster. When you are faced with a crisis, it is essential to act promptly and to follow the plans you have developed for such an emergency. It is equally important to keep calm and proceed with care. Your role will probably be that of crisis manager and spokesperson; therefore your lead will be followed. People will listen to your every word. First and most important, be honest. Be frank about the status of the crisis, and how it is being handled. Be clear about who is in charge, and be prepared to handle at least part of the publicity relating to the crisis. Don't stonewall and don't blame.

Talking to the Press

The designated spokesperson should be knowledgeable about your organization or the issue at hand. Reporters will quote anyone if they believe that person will give them correct information, and they can't always call around to confirm the information they've been given. Any person who speaks with a reporter must provide correct information, thereby avoiding responsibility for an incorrect story. Never lie to a reporter. Not only do you compromise your capacity to remain honest in the future, but if you are found out, reporters and others will not only lose faith in you and your organization but also target you. If you don't have the answer to a reporter's question, don't hesitate to say "I don't know" and promise to get back to the reporter with the information, if possible. Know the reporter's deadline and get back to him/her.

All of this doesn't mean you can't seek to control what is written or broadcast. If something happens that might bring negative publicity, try to lessen the damage by discussing the situation positively. You can remain both plausible and truthful, as the following draft releases in Figure 7.1 suggest. Compare Release A with Release B.

Each release contains the required who, what, where, when, and how. Each describes the scope of the collections, what was damaged and how, and contains a quote from an appropriate administrator. But the first release emphasizes the extent of the loss, then places the blame for this loss on its parent organization, the university. The tone is one of complaint. The second release emphasizes the extent to which the loss was contained, what was saved, and places no blame. The spokesperson appears to be accessible and prepared, suggesting that plans go forward for assessing damage and monitoring the situation and the staff is to be commended. The tone is upbeat. Both releases give correct factual information, but the second release is both informative and positive.

Figure 7.1. Two Sample Releases for the Same Story

(Release A)

FOR IMMEDIATE RELEASE June 1, 1992

Burlington, VT—A burst water pipe at the State University's Ethan Allen Archives Monday destroyed several boxes containing the papers of former U.S. Senator Jack Smith and 19th-century Governor Joshua Williams.

The four-inch line burst open and destroyed the valuable records in the early afternoon while the entire archives staff was present. After custodial staff turned off the water, archivists removed the damaged material as best they could before closing time.

"We're just lucky it happened before we went home," said chief archivist Anna Jones. "It's tragic we lost as much as we did. If the university hadn't asked for budget cuts for the past two years, this wouldn't have happened."

(Release B)

FOR IMMEDIATE RELEASE June 1, 1992

Burlington, VT—Staff at State University's Ethan Allen archives saved thousands of personal papers donated by former U.S. Governor Jack Smith and the family of 19th-century Governor Joshua Williams Monday when a pipe burst in the archives.

The affected collections were immediately taken to a nearby facility for further analysis.

Chief archivist Anna Jones credited her staff with responding quickly to move the papers to safety when the four-inch line broke open at 1:35 P.M.

"We lost some papers, and any loss is painful," Jones said. "But we've practiced how to handle such an accident, so we could get all the papers and photographs out of the affected area quickly. The Administration and Buildings staff have been most helpful in dealing with the situation."

A press release alone will not satisfy reporters in a serious crisis, especially one that involves the public or extensive damage to property. You will quickly receive requests for interviews. Unless you have had many successful years dealing with the press, practice how you will respond to a reporter. Work with another person in your organization, just as politicians sit down with staff for mock press conferences and debates. Learn to respond to hard or unexpected questions, and be open to criticism during these practice sessions. Chances are, in a crisis, you will have to answer some difficult questions.

Anticipate questions; don't evade them. If you don't know the answer or don't have the information at hand, say so and promise to do your best to get the information. If there are specific questions you can't answer, be prepared to explain why, because a reporter will try different tacks to get the answer to a question an interviewee won't answer. Return telephone calls. When you duck an issue, a reporter smells a story.

Reporters always want to know who is responsible for what happened. Don't place blame on your organization, your superiors, or your staff. In the two releases shown in Figure 7.1, the first specifically links the university's decision to cut the archives budget with the burst pipe. In effect, the responsibility for the disaster is placed on upper-level administration. Not only will this comment upset the administration and public relations office, but you must also ask yourself what was gained. The second release places no blame, and it implies that the crisis was handled responsibly by everyone involved. If the administration has been neglectful of your facility and a disaster occurred because of this neglect, use that information when it can best be used, during the next budgeting cycle. A one-time jab is ineffective and will harm your cause.

As the spokesperson, you should also be prepared to be faulted or to take responsibility in a crisis situation. If that is appropriate, accept it. If not, respond carefully, loyally, and thoughtfully. Draw up a list of words you should avoid using when dealing with the press, such as blame, fault, tragedy, unprepared, unnoticed, sloppy, ill-conceived, irresponsible, and any others that suggest culpability, incompetence, or bad intentions.

If your repository is just a small department in a large organization, work closely with the official spokespersons in your public relations office during a crisis. It is the job of the spokesperson to protect the organization as a whole and his/her superiors in particular. Plan ahead to avoid any miscommunication. Keep the public relations office on your mailing list for special events announcements, alert them to renovations and the reasons for them, share fact sheets, and respond quickly and professionally to their requests for information. The surest way to cause bad blood between you and the public relations office is to let the public relations officer be caught unaware when a reporter calls to ask about a crisis, or a repository spokesperson speak unwisely.

When a number of people in a large organization are responding to questions about a crisis, speak with one voice. If a variety of people attempt to speak on behalf of the institution without coordinating their replies, your office will look disorganized. Establish clear lines of communication with others who might get a call from the media.

Follow-up

Reporters covering a crisis are single-minded. A reporter pressing you for details on why you stored valuable papers under leaky pipes will have no immediate interest in an upcoming exhibit of trade catalogs from the 1920s. The reporter asking you questions on this day has come for one story. But you can, near the end of the interview, ask, "For months now I've been trying to get someone at your paper to get out here occasionally. Whom should I call when I put up a good exhibit?" You'll probably get a name.

When the crisis has passed, don't assume the troubleshooting is over. For all of your thoughtful and vigorous efforts, your organization may have some public relations rebuilding to do. The disaster has provided you with media contacts, some worth cultivating. Make follow-up calls when you have good news, and update your list of media contacts regularly.

If nothing else, the reporter who covered the crisis that shut down your repository will probably want to do a story when you reopen. The same reporter may also express an interest in the interim events, such as major goals met in a capital campaign to rebuild your facility. Treat that person as an ongoing ally, keep him/her informed, and he/she will eventually become an ally.

If you fail with the reporter, call the editor or, for radio and television, the producer. If you are dealing with a large newspaper or station, remember that it probably has several sections—sports, business, food, and health—each with different editors or producers. Consider various collections within your archives that might interest these editors and producers and direct your press release or call to the appropriate person. Don't overdo it; most reporters like to think they came up with the story idea themselves. And remember that big papers and radio and television stations aren't the only fish in the sea. You can work with community papers, public-access cable television, weekly or monthly publications, and community-oriented weekly television and radio shows.

After you receive publicity—either good or bad—evaluate it. Ask your staff and others how the story comes across to them. Remember past successes and failures when you plan for future publicity. Keep a clipping and videotape file as a record of your media exposure. Bad publicity can be painful but instructive.

Remember too that the crisis involved not only the media, but your organization as well. Follow up and rebuild internally, with appropriate staff, board members, and administrators. Your performance in the weeks and months following the crisis says as much about your management abilities as your actions during the crisis.

Summary

The essence of troubleshooting is planning. Good planning consists of two broad categories: avoiding problems by anticipating them and handling them well when they occur. You must plan to avoid problems, but you must also be ready for crises when they arrive—and they will, despite your best efforts.

Remember to constantly evaluate your archives, checking for potential trouble spots. Remain vigilant for potential crises in all areas, including policies, personnel, and facilities. Never assume that an aging electrical system or steep stairway might not lead to a headline-grabbing liability suit. Never assume that your kindly not-for-profit organization can't offend someone. And never assume that everyone in your community, reporters included, knows what you're talking about. Learn how to be an effective communicator. Keep appropriate records and checklists relating to your facility and collections for easy reference.

Once the bad news happens, remember to remain calm, be honest, and prepare for the tough questions that will come. Avoid negative statements, and don't lay blame. Work closely with others to resolve the situation, and look for opportunities to give the story a positive spin.

Follow up, both internally and with the media, on information as it arises. Expect the process to take weeks, months, and perhaps longer to be fully resolved. Monitor and communicate what's being done to ensure that this particular problem won't reoccur.

Evaluate all of your media exposure and ask others for their reactions. Incorporate lessons learned into daily policies and procedures.

As unlikely as it may seem at the time, a well-managed response to a crisis will often result in something positive—improved facilities, better procedures, and a renewed appreciation of the value of your collection and staff.

Additional Readings

"ACRL Guidelines for the Security of Rare Books and Special Collections." In *C & RL News*, vol. 51, no. 3 (March 1990).

Adams, G. Donald. *Museum Public Relations* (Nashville, TN: American Association for State and Local History, 1982).

Allen, Susan M. "Thefts in Libraries and Archives." *C & RL News*, vol. 51, no. 10 (November 1990).

Associated Press. *Stylebook and Libel Manual* (Associated Press, 1984).

Bussey, Holly, and Susan Swartzburg. *Libraries and Archives: Design and Renovation with a Preservation Perspective* (Metuchen, NJ: Scarecrow Press, 1991)

Ferré, John P., and Shirley C. Willihnganz. *Public Relations Ethics: A Bibliography* (Boston: G. K. Hall, 1991). Don't miss the Appendix, which includes the Public Relations Society of America's Code of Professional Standards.

Guidelines and Resources for Archival Strategic Planning (GRASP). (National Association of Government Archivists and Records Administrators, 1990).

Peterson, Gary M., and Trudy Huskamp Peterson. *Archives and Manuscripts: Law* (Chicago: Society of American Archivists, 1985).

Studies in Public Relations

Politicians and the Press in the Archives: Milwaukee

Matt Blessing

Henry W. Maier served as mayor of Milwaukee for seven consecutive terms between 1960 and 1988, a national record for a big-city mayor. Soon after Maier retired from public office, the records of his administration—nearly 700 cubic feet of textual documents, audiotapes, photographs, and memorabilia—were transferred to the Milwaukee Urban Archives (MUA) on the campus of the University of Wisconsin-Milwaukee. (The MUA is a regional branch of the State Historical Society of Wisconsin and the University of Wisconsin-Milwaukee Archives.) About one year after Maier's mayoral records were accessioned at the MUA, a processing archivist and a graduate student began to arrange and describe the materials, completing the project in slightly less than two years.

Henry Maier's longtime battle with the local press corps, particularly the *Milwaukee Journal,* was legendary in the city. Throughout his long tenure as mayor, Maier and the press had debated both the most important and most trivial issues of the era. At the height of their conflict, Maier had stubbornly refused to acknowledge reporters from the *Milwaukee Journal* at his weekly press conferences. Maier's bitter conflicts with the press did not end after he retired. The mayor-turned-professor emeritus kept it no secret that his forthcoming political memoir would set the record straight about the local press corps, while the *Journal* continued to publish wry news bits and satire about the former mayor and his staff.

Because the mayoral records were to be made available soon after Maier's retirement from a long career, many issues remained acutely sensitive. Staff at the Milwaukee Urban Archives were not surprised when journalists from several metropolitan newspapers requested access to Maier's mayoral records. The archives staff was fully aware of their responsibility to provide equal access to all public records as prescribed by both the Wisconsin Open Records Law and standard archival ethics, but they also saw the potential for a serious conflict.

At the root of the problem was Maier's belief that the mayoral records were his personal papers. Soon after the records had arrived at the archives, Maier asked that they be closed to researchers until he had completed his biography. The senior archivist explained that the records were public records available to any researcher and could not legally be restricted. On subsequent visits, however, the archives staff chose not to correct the former chief executive when he spoke of "my papers." The records were, in fact, closed for a period of time during the early stages of processing, temporarily delaying the conflict.

The archives staff permitted access to Maier's mayoral records as soon as intellectual control of the materials had been established. The senior archivist sent Maier a memorandum telling him that the records were being made available, but did not receive an acknowledgment from him. A copy of the memorandum was also sent to the library administration. Researchers, most of whom were journalists, were required to use a rough draft of the inventory while the processing staff completed the descriptive portions. Not surprisingly, patrons immediately selected materials on many of the most important and controversial decisions and policies of the Maier administration, materials related to urban renewal programs of the 1960s, political campaigns, civil rights leaders, and other prominent individuals with whom the mayor dealt. A popular neighborhood weekly, the *Southside Spirit,* was the first Milwaukee newspaper to publish articles based on Maier's mayoral records. For four consecutive weeks a feature-length investigative article on the Maier administration appeared on the front page of the *Spirit.* Based almost entirely on records available at the MUA, the first article captured the tension and fears inside the mayor's office during the city's 1967 civil disturbances. Lengthy and often unflattering quotations by Maier and his staff about several civil rights activists drawn from the mayoral records were used in the article. Subsequent articles in the *Spirit* highlighted mayor Maier's campaign tactics and strategies, internal conflicts among his staff, the mayor's disputes with the press, and other topics likely to embarrass him.

Preparing for criticism from Maier and his former staff, the senior archivist decided to issue a memorandum to the student and paraprofessional staff who provided much of the reference service. The intent was twofold: 1) to prevent any violation of Wisconsin's Open Records Law by the staff and 2) to provide the paraprofessional staff with the information it needed to handle basic phone inquiries about the mayoral records. The memorandum reminded staff that the mayoral records were unrestricted public records belonging to the people of Wisconsin and available to any patron who agreed to follow the rules of the reading room. It also noted that the archives staff was not responsible for interpretations and conclusions drawn by researchers. Finally, students were warned not to violate state privacy statutes by releasing the names of researchers to other parties. The memorandum was routed to all staff, then posted on the reference room desk for all part-time assistants to read. Copies of the memorandum were sent to library administrators.

What happened next remains unclear. Staff think that a journalist using the archives overheard and misinterpreted a conversation between archives staff members, then conveyed the misinformation to reporters at both the *Milwaukee Journal* and the *Downtown Edition,* who contrived juicy news bits about Maier's causing difficulties at the MUA and complaining to the library administration about open access to his papers. The *Milwaukee Journal* chose to include the information in its humor and gossip column, a popular section read by many of the paper's 300,000 subscribers. The other newspaper, the *Downtown Edition,* chided Maier and several former aides that "tampering with archives is a no-no!" Journalism based on uncorroborated secondhand information had placed the archives staff in the midst of the decades-old conflict between the press and Henry Maier.

Less than a week later, the *Milwaukee Journal* published reproduced portions of a magazine article about Maier in which the former chief executive had annotated the margins with dozens of colorful expletives. Next, *Milwaukee Magazine,* a monthly periodical, published a lengthy story about Maier's covert strategies in dealing with the press, with lengthy quotations drawn from documents in the mayoral records.

Maier was infuriated by the articles, and angry phone calls to the library administration became more frequent. Maier again requested that the archives staff find a way to restrict the records. A career politician, Maier also contacted many of his old political allies in state and local government to pressure the library administration to conform to his wishes. To explain the archive's mandated responsibilities and public records laws now appeared futile. For years Maier had been allowed to believe that the mayoral records were his personal property. Soon after the *Spirit* articles appeared, the senior archivist made the decision to relay every development in the Maier situation to his supervisor, the library director. Issuing two or three memoranda weekly for several weeks, the staff was able to describe precisely what had been said during each conversation with Maier. Because the library administration was kept abreast of developments from the very beginning, they came to view the situation as much their problem as that of the archives staff. The archivist's reports also served to educate library administrators in archival principles and public records laws, with which they were not familiar. Most importantly, the memoranda reduced the chances that management would be surprised or embarrassed because of a lack of information. This was made clear when the library director was able to respond to requests from the chancellor's office about problems in the archives. It is important to note that communications with the library administration were not significantly different from those during routine times. Many public relations specialists argue that crisis situations are best handled by more intensive application of standard communications practices. The standard form of communication in this case, the FYI memorandum, had effectively built confidence and trust within the library administration. A simple, straightforward, and consistently practiced communications system allowed the staff to manage this problem, knowing that they already had the support of the library administration.

A similar communications strategy was subsequently pursued with the local press, especially with the staff of the *Milwaukee Journal*. This was a relatively easy task, since no news-gathering organization wanted to damage a working relationship with a source of free, easily accessible, one-of-a-kind information. The newspapers always respected "off the record" explanations when they were requested by the archives staff. The senior archivist typically asked to review press quotations before they were printed. Journalists were cooperative and agreed to print retractions when they had erred.

It is important to remember that most news agencies depend heavily upon public relations personnel for information. The preeminent scholar of public relations, Scott M. Cutlip, has shown that nearly 45 percent of all stories published in newspapers originated from public relations practitioners. (Ironically, Professor Cutlip's studies were conducted in Milwaukee.) With a bit of skill, a good public relations practitioner will rarely experience any difficulty getting a story printed.

Nevertheless, relations with the press in this case might have been better as might the reporting itself. That no reporter from the *Milwaukee Journal* contacted the archives staff before issuing a story based on secondhand information is evidence of this. Better communications with the local press might have prevented publication of damaging information and produced more substantive, high-quality articles in some of the publications. Dealing with the tabloid press or individual "scoop artists" is, of course, infinitely more difficult. Overall, the Milwaukee press corps was consistently cooperative in printing retractions but careless in releasing unsubstantiated news. Archivists would be wise to consider the individual nature of their own community newspapers and television stations, establishing and building a working relationship with a contact person at each media outlet. Never assume, however, that today's journalists will regularly check all information or seek second and third party confirmation.

The conflict between Henry Maier and Milwaukee's press corps was more than a quarter-century old when attention focused on the Milwaukee Urban Archives. The dispute over access to the mayoral records consisted of one short chapter in a very long story. There is no doubt that the episode permanently damaged the MUA's relationship with Henry Maier. Preliminary planning for an oral history project involving Maier and his staff was canceled. Celebrating the official opening of the records was, of course, out of the question.

In sum, the controversy resulted in an overall improvement in communications, understanding, and mutual confidence between the archives and the library administration. To a somewhat lesser extent, the relationship between the archives and several reporters improved. Journalists increasingly came to recognize a common interest with the archives, insuring that all individuals have equal access to information as required by the state's open records law. Each party seemed to become more sensitive to the other's needs. The publicity also attracted more journalists to the archives to examine other archival and manuscript collections.

Lessons

1. Recognize a public relations problem when you see it. Anticipate adversarial use and public controversy, and practice responding to it.

2. Instruct staff carefully in how to respond to contentious donors, aggressive journalists, and other users. Keep a uniform public position, if you can.

3. Find ways to check on the accuracy of a story *before* it is published. "Could you repeat my quotes?" or "How do you understand these events?" are legitimate interviewee-to-journalist questions.

4. Keep upper-level administration aware of what is happening by written memos. Report daily, if necessary. Also tell public relations staff in a large institution. Avoid surprises at upper levels. Help administration to own your problem.

5. Have written fact sheets available about collection policy: what public records are, who can access them, when, etc.

6. Understand the habits and constraints of journalists today—time, the tendency not to check sources, pressure to do the attention-grabbing story. Adapt to these habits and constraints.

The Pope and the Archives

A Study in Archival Public Image

James M. O'Toole

What is the impact on an archives when the pope comes to town? Very few archives have had the chance to discover the answer to that question, and only a few ever will. Even so, all archives can capitalize on the visits of dignitaries and other special occasions. The experience of the Archives of the Roman Catholic Archdiocese of Boston during the visit of Pope John Paul II in the fall of 1979 offers lessons to other archives about how to improve their public image.

When rumors first circulated in late summer 1979 that the leader of the world's 850 million Catholics would come to Boston for two days in November, the reaction was eager anticipation of a historic event. After all, we had been accustomed to think, popes simply didn't do this kind of thing. John Paul's subsequent travels have, to a large extent, set a different standard—that of the peripatetic pontiff—but at that time the pope was still a self-styled "prisoner of the Vatican." Elected barely a year before, John Paul II adopted a highly visible approach to his office. This scholar, poet, resistance fighter, sometime actor, and avid mountain climber intended to see as much of the world as he could and, in turn, to let the world see him. That plan included a visit to six cities in the United States, with Boston the first stop.

From our perspective in the basement (yes, the basement) of the archdiocesan chancery building, the staff of the Archives shared the general excitement. More particularly, we recognized that the visit would place special demands on us because the archives was still a new department of local church administration. Organized Catholicism in Boston could trace its origins to 1789, and a diocese had been established in 1808. Since that time, institutional and personal records of enduring value had been accumulating at a steady pace, but there was no formal archival program to care for them. The authors of an archdiocesan history had performed some rudimentary archival work in the 1930s, and a secretary in the archbishop's office had traditionally held the title of archivist. (That is, she answered the few genealogical inquiries that came by mail, usually responding that she had been unable to locate the desired information in the unorganized collections.) There were no systematic means for identifying and acquiring permanently valuable records, however, no procedures for maintaining intellectual and physical control over the holdings, no efforts to make them broadly available for use.

In the middle 1970s, however, the archdiocese began a concerted effort to institute a professional archives and records program. Spurred on by the interest of the archbishop, Cardinal Humberto S. Medeiros, a talented linguist with an earned doctorate, and his chancellor, Bishop Thomas V. Daily, a genealogist and avid reader of history, the archdiocese received grants from the National Historical Publications and Records Commission and other foundations to begin the program. When I was hired as archivist in January 1978, fresh from three years on the staff of the Massachusetts State Archives, I found a 200-year processing backlog, but I also found an atmosphere congenial to the development of a full, many-faceted archives.

Like any new effort, the archives had to find ways to assert its legitimacy among the established departments of institutional administration. The problem was the more acute in our case because, since we started with "soft" money and only vague assurances that the archdiocese would continue the program in some form after the grants ended in 1980, there was no guarantee that the archives would continue to exist. Accordingly, we had two related and immediate goals. To address the historical interest that had led to the establishment of the program, we moved at once to expand access by scholars, students, genealogists, parish historians, and others. We did this through traditional archival processing of key records series and a network of contacts with local colleges, historical societies, and other organizations. I also began to write a regular column highlighting interesting documents from the archives, which appeared twice a month on the op-ed page of the archdiocesan weekly newspaper, the *Pilot*. This column put the archives and its activities in the public eye and, as we later realized, helped fix it as part of the mental universe of archdiocesan administrators. Our second goal was to make the archives a central feature of church administration by emphasizing the practical usefulness of archival records to current concerns. This we accomplished by acquiring some critical records series—blueprints and architectural records of parish buildings, for example, and accounting records of recent vintage—and by working closely with offices and administrators "upstairs."

The papal visit was a crucial event in achieving both of these goals. From the very first announcement, business as usual stopped in all archdiocesan offices, including the archives, and everyone's attention was turned to planning for the historic occasion. With a scant six weeks to get ready, church administrators faced a multitude of details. The pope would be in Boston less than twenty-four hours, but the questions surrounding every minute were legion. John Paul would be greeted by civic officials at the airport on Monday afternoon and would then proceed to Holy Cross Cathedral for a prayer service with the priests of New England. Next would come a motorcade through the neighborhoods of the city, followed by an open-air mass on historic Boston Common. After a second motorcade, he would retire to Cardinal Medeiros's residence for the evening and, after breakfast with archdiocesan seminarians on Tuesday morning, he would leave for New York to address the United Nations.

As planning got underway, the archives deliberately converted itself into a general research bureau. Drawing on its own collections as well as other sources, we let the planners know that we could find answers to all sorts of questions. What was the history of the various places, civil and ecclesiastical, that the pope would visit? What important local sites was he bypassing, and could they be worked in at the last minute? What had been the nature of relations between the United States and the papacy, and how might that affect protocol? What did the papal coat of arms look like? What made this unusual man tick? While he was still Cardinal Karol Wojtyla, the Archbishop of Krakow, John Paul had visited Boston twice, and the evidence from those trips, now preserved in the archives, was scrutinized for what it revealed about the man, his American contacts, and the likely themes of his visit. The archives, for instance, answered many demands for the text of his 1976 lecture at Harvard Divinity School. Entitled, with deceptive approachability, "Participation or Alienation?" the address was a complex theological discourse on the intricacies of Hegelian philosophy, the topic of the pontiff's doctoral dissertation, and those who asked for a copy of it surely got more than they bargained for.

Practical problems, some of them having little to do with the archives, demanded attention as well. I was pressed into service to help oversee the printing of program booklets and the distribution of tickets for the various events. (Needless to say, we were dealing here with the hottest ticket in town.) Admission to the cathedral prayer service was by pass only, and a reserved section had been set aside at the outdoor mass for local dignitaries, members of religious communities, representatives of parishes, youth groups, and other denominations. I helped design the booklets containing the prayers and hymns to be used at these ceremonies, writing introductory texts and historical prefaces, selecting photographs and shuttling back and forth to the printer.

Of more serious import were questions of security during the visit. Here the archives was able to contribute to the planning with records from its collection, particularly the extensive holdings of architectural drawings. The Secret Service, which was charged with protecting John Paul throughout his American visit, demanded to see blueprints of every building the pope would be in or near at each stop along his route. This proved especially problematical in the case of the 104-year-old Holy Cross Cathedral, of which few original records had survived, but enough information was finally assembled to satisfy the Secret Service agents. Representatives of the local police and fire departments came next, looking for all likely access points and the location of fire hydrants in case of emergency. This was the first—and only—time that a "researcher" came into the archives clad in heavy rubber boots and fire helmet. Finally, there were workmen from the telephone company, seeking help in installing new lines in archdiocesan buildings to handle the increased demand from administration and the news media.

About ten days before the pope's arrival, reporters from local newspapers and television and radio stations discovered the archives, frantically searching for anything they could use as background to their coverage. We had already had contact with the news media through my column in the *Pilot* and a close working relationship with the Archdiocesan News Bureau, which was coordinating coverage of the event. Now journalists of all kinds, especially from the nonprint media, called on the archives for materials that would help them fill gaps in the long hours of continuous live coverage. We made our large collection of historical photographs of churches and special parish events—detailed cataloging of which had, fortunately, just been completed that summer—available to film crews. Watching them work, we made it a point to learn how the visually trained eye could find several different uses for a single photographic image by focusing now on this, now on that. Over the telephone I recorded several radio interviews, to be broadcast as background pieces, adjusting myself to the initially disconcerting technology involved. When the interviewer asked a question, I could hear everything perfectly well; when I was talking, however, I heard nothing but a blank line, almost as if we had been disconnected. Speaking smoothly, with confidence and without pauses, took some practice, but by the third or fourth interview I felt comfortable with the medium.

Working with the news media this way, gaining recognition not only for the archdiocese in general but also for the archives in particular, required other adjustments. First, reporters have chronically unpredictable schedules. If we wanted coverage, we had to be ready when they were, even if that meant dropping something else in midstream. These interviews also demanded that I adjust my expectations of the kinds of questions that would be asked of the archives and, accordingly, the kinds of answers that were needed. We were quite at home with traditional inquiries from scholars and students embarked on "serious" research. Reporters, however, ask very different questions. One said to me, with a perfectly straight face, "When I say 'history of the archdiocese,' what immediately pops into your mind?" All these questions need appropriate answers. They wanted the pithy story, the example that sums up a larger historical trend, the one recognizably human individual whose life embodies a larger movement. There is room for nuance and complexity, but these must be presented simply, without the measured "on the one hand, on the other hand" of academic discourse, and without jargon. As an archivist, I had to think about my collections and the stories they told in a new, though not unfamiliar, way. It was the difference between talking to the local business lunch club and reading a paper at the American Historical Association. Once that adjustment had been made, I realized what an advantage I had. The reporters came to the archives with very few preconceptions, leaving me entirely free to determine what larger story I wanted to tell and how I wanted to tell it. Preparation paid off, and in every case the reporter let me tell that story.

Finally, I learned that the information in the archives was what might be called malleable. I never invented information, but I sometimes modified my sense of what was important. The most archivally valuable records we held were not necessarily the most useful in reaching a larger audience. The core records of archdiocesan administration were less likely to attract interest and answer broad public questions than one old-looking document with flowery penmanship or a famous autograph. A run-of-the-mill photograph, picked out from several that looked more or less the same, could be manipulated to seem like several different images, each telling a unique story. A picture of one person or event could become, in effect, a picture of something else. The statistical and demographic records (those of parish baptisms and marriages, for example) that would support a perfectly valid and interesting scholarly paper were less likely to get attention than the amusing story selected from the pages of a thirty-year run of weekly parish bulletins. In any archives, not all information is created equal, and with different audiences we emphasize the unexpected and otherwise insignificant.

Despite the torrential rain that drenched everyone gathered on Boston Common (the archives staff included), the pope's visit was a tremendous success. Even as life returned to normal, the archives took advantage of the euphoria by working to collect a complete record of the event. These efforts, a form of *ad hoc* records management, also served internal public relations by keeping the archives at the visible center of church administration. Making what was our first contact with many archdiocesan offices, we gathered up the records of the various planning committees. We acquired the architectural drawings and scale model of the striking platform and canopy that had been built for the outdoor mass. The event's official photographer provided a full visual record of the day. Some artifacts came our way as well: candles and mass books we accepted, though we managed to head off a plan to wheel the specially constructed fifteen-foot altar into one of our storage vaults. Papal visits do not happen very often, but if another one comes, the archives will have a reasonably complete record of precedent.

The involvement of the archives in the visit of Pope John Paul II to Boston proved to be an important step in the ongoing development of our public relations image, a step that paid handsome benefits. Six months later, the archives' budget was completely absorbed into the archdiocesan budget, exclusive of grants and without any reductions in staff size, at a time when other departments were suffering serious cutbacks. I do not suggest that our work during the papal visit was the only reason for this critical transition, but the highly visible role we had played certainly did no harm.

The experience of those few weeks in 1979 was also to prove very useful a few years later, when the archives got the chance for more extended work with the local media. Having established a public relations presence, the archives found other occasions to reach a wide audience. During the observance of the 175th anniversary of the archdiocese in the spring of 1983 and again at the time of the unexpected death of Cardinal Medeiros that fall, the archives worked closely with administrators and reporters. By then, their turning to the archives for helpful information and lively interviews was second nature. During the installation of a new archbishop, Bernard F. Law, in the spring of 1984, the archives received even more coverage. One television station broadcast an interview in which I showed documents and photographs as I reviewed local Catholic history. This interview appeared on the evening news in a segment that lasted 6 to 7 minutes, a near eternity in television time. The final triumph for archival public relations came in the spring of 1985, when Archbishop Law was elevated to the rank of Cardinal at a ceremony in Saint Peter's Square, Rome. I attended that ceremony as part of the official entourage from Boston and, though I was there in part as the archdiocesan archivist, I was also carrying press credentials. That was a small but symbolic accomplishment, demonstrating that the public role of the archives had been accepted as an essential part of our responsibilities.

What might other archivists learn from these admittedly unusual experiences?

Lessons

1. Always keep an eye out for public relations possibilities in the definition and administration of your archives program. If you hide in the basement, others will think of you as belonging there. If you are more active "upstairs," others will accept and come to rely on you. Act at all times as if you belong.

2. Seize opportunities for creating good archival press whenever they come, adjusting your archival priorities when necessary to emphasize public outreach. The papers you will always have with you—pardon the Scriptural paraphrase—and you can always go back to process them and produce finding aids that are works of archival art.

3. Evaluate the materials in your collection for their public relations value as well as their traditional archival value. Be constantly on watch for the eye-catching document and the good story, even if these are not the most historically significant items you have. You will always find a use for them.

4. Most importantly, think of the archives as an all-purpose information source for all kinds of people, not just the scholar or administrator. You are excited about caring for your resources. Why shouldn't you share that excitement with others?

Once in a Hundred Years

The Centennial Opportunity

Michael F. Kohl

Clemson University celebrated its centennial in 1988-1989, an event that served as the catalyst for transforming the university's Archives. Basic to the successful strengthening of this program was the support of key university administrators, start-up funding from the National Historical Publications and Records Commission, and the identification of viable, high visibility projects for its various constituencies.

Background

As the land-grant university for South Carolina with a current enrollment of over 17,000, Clemson has played a major role in the state's higher education since its founding in 1888. Planning for the Clemson centennial began in the spring of 1984 after the university's president appointed a planning committee made up of university faculty and the Special Collections staff of the Library, students, and administrators, as well as representatives from the Clemson community, alumni, and South Carolina media. This committee, made up of a number of subcommittees, created a framework for the centennial celebration, including deciding when the centennial would be celebrated; what would be its major themes; what level of participation would be sought from the entire "Clemson Family," that is, alumni, area residents, and the citizens of South Carolina; what would be the level of financing.

Planning a wide variety of centennial events sponsored by different parts of the university drew a broad range of people into the celebration process. The subsequent creation of centennial committees in every college and the university libraries also allowed academic departments to participate in this event. Committees for exhibits, publications, town and gown, and events such as the laying of a centennial cornerstone enlisted a variety of talents. The creation of centennial memorabilia and the linking of some centennial events with other university activities became the means for financing this celebration.

Beginning this planning several years ahead was important to the centennial's success. Although there were significant changes in the university's senior administration, (three university presidents and three vice-presidents for development served during the period between 1983-1988), the key administrator entrusted with the overall management of the centennial, the vice-provost, stayed the course and provided the critical continuity necessary for the centennial's success.

This study focuses on archival program development and the demands placed upon Special Collections, which includes the university archives. Special Collections identified opportunities within the broad context of this event to create public programs that built upon an incremental approach to archival outreach and interpreted the archives function to the public.

Creating a University Archives and Records Management Program

During the fall of 1983, the head of Special Collections at the university libraries alerted his administrators to the potential adverse impact of a centennial celebration on the unit's ability to help researchers. Special Collections lacked staff to handle the increase in research use and process the records researchers would use, and it lacked a functioning university archives and records management program.

To deal with these problems, the libraries first requested from the university administration permanent positions for a university archivist and records manager, as well as increases in the student assistant budget and supplies. The answer was no. Because the university's Development Office had other priorities to steer donors toward, including the libraries' book budget, the libraries did not seriously consider obtaining private funds to establish the university archives. At this point, the National Historical Publications and Records Commission (NHPRC) provided the catalyst for developing the university archives and records management programs. Preliminary discussions between the head of Special Collections and the NHPRC indicated that a proposal would receive more serious consideration if the university would agree that the positions of university archivist and records manager become permanent.

The provost, who approves the addition of all new permanent positions for academic departments, decided that the value of outside funding outweighed the low priority of these archival positions. With some reluctance, he agreed to this condition as part of the proposal submitted to the NHPRC in May 1984. Agreeing to fund these positions permanently was a gamble for the provost. On the positive side, he encouraged the libraries to seek outside funding, thus "solving" the problem since the libraries would stop requesting immediate funding from the university. There was the chance that the grant would not be funded, but if it were, it would be during a fiscal year when he had more money to fund positions. His thinking demonstrates the willingness of administrators to agree to lower priority projects whose sources of funding include outside resources.

With the assurance of continuing program support, the NHPRC awarded a $50,000 grant in November 1984 that provided a year's salary for each of the two positions as well as funds for archival supplies and student assistants. The grant eventually covered a period from January 1985 to December 1988. Tying the long-term needs of the university's archives and records management program to the specific needs generated by the university's centennial proved to be a winning combination that transformed Special Collections activities. For the first time, the university had a professional records manager who could devote full time to inventorying records, updating general schedules, preparing special schedules, transferring records to the archives, and creating a records center. With the hiring of the university archivist, there was for the first time someone responsible for the acquisition, arrangement, and description of Clemson's own records.

The creation of a records center was not a centennial project. However, its creation was a direct outgrowth of the revitalized records management program. Beginning in 1983, the head of Special Collections had begun scouting out potential locations for a records center. He identified the unfinished basement of a university office building as a suitable site. In 1986, the director of libraries convinced appropriate administrators to remove bales of cotton stored there and begin the conversion. After funding was obtained, a 3,000-square-foot records center with a 6,000-cubic-foot capacity emerged. Once again, the libraries looked outside their own budget. The vice president for business affairs, who faced a crisis in storing routine financial records then crammed into the administration building offices and closets, recognized the value of a functioning records management program. Business Affairs provided the funding for the renovation and equipment as well as one paraprofessional po-

Use of Archives During Clemson Centennial Planning

Fiscal Year	University Archives as % of Special Collections Holdings Use	University Archives Use Increase (Decrease) From Previous Year
1983-84	16%	5%
1984-85	17%	1%
1985-86	28%	11%
1986-87	37%	9%
1987-88	24%	(13%)
1988-89	28%	4%

sition to help the records manager. In 1989, Business Affairs supported the addition of a micrographics supervisor.

The NHPRC grant had a multiplier effect upon program development such that, by the end of 1989, there were five full-time permanent staff members working on university archives and records management activities, as compared with none in 1985. Because of the centennial, archival problems caught the attention of Clemson's administrators. The grant provided a means to solve both short-term problems and long-term deficiencies.

Reference in Overdrive

The Clemson centennial provided the impetus for archival program development, but Special Collections also experienced a great deal of pressure from centennial-related projects. The examination of its centennial projects, however, illustrates the successes and problems an archives can encounter during such an event.

Reference use related to the university archives unexpectedly peaked before the centennial officially began at Clemson, as shown in the table above. The early start to university centennial planning and the emphasis upon research projects produced a large increase in the use of the collections. Scholarly researchers, undergraduate students, and the general public all dramatically increased their use of Special Collections. Besides biographies of Clemson's presidents, a number of the university's colleges produced their own histories. The author of a popular history of the university also used the archives.

Although Clemson undergraduates had always been the largest single user group, even larger numbers of them came to the archives, often for the first time, to work on centennial-related assignments. Usually, the Special Collections staff knew ahead of time about these projects and could gather the material the students needed, but this did not always occur. One noon hour for example, some thirty freshmen descended upon the one reference archivist on duty and demanded to use the same material. The addition of a full-time university archivist and a records manager helped stabilize this kind of stressful situation.

Publications

In the spring of 1985, the university centennial committee sponsored a scholarly publication of the biographies of Clemson's presidents to be ready at the centennial's start in April 1988 and to serve as a ready reference source. But the volume that most engaged Special Collections was a pictorial history of Clemson, which had been the most popular centennial proposal. This project required both research in the photograph collections of Special Collections and an active public acquisition program, from which was assembled a large research collection. The project had several advantages. It satisfied a need as seen by the Centennial

Committee—the creation of an historically sound, popular publication. It engaged an enthusiastic member of the faculty, Professor Alan Schaffer. It would cost little money, other than project staff time and the resources of the university's communication center and libraries; and it would create a product with high visibility.

It also presented a number of challenges for the University Archives. Special Collections provided space during the summer of 1987 for Dr. Schaffer to systematically review its holdings and have hundreds of copies of prints created by the university's photo lab. This took longer than expected, and some confusion arose over refiling photos, resulting in more changes in reference procedures. The production of the photo album also took longer than expected, but during the spring of 1990, *Visions: Clemson's Yesteryears*, was published. More than a standard illustrated photo history, it was evocative of the spirit and values that created and shaped the university. Moreover, the project brought the archives several hundred photos related to Clemson from donors throughout the nation which were, with their index, an important addition to the university archives.

Exhibits

Exhibits with centennial themes became highly visible projects for which Special Collections participated with other university departments. This attention translated into the creation of a permanent position. During the course of the eighteen-month centennial celebration, Special Collections mounted exhibits in the main lobby of the university library, outside the Special Collections reading room, and elsewhere in the university as part of specific centennial events. Several exhibits included archival material. Two, exhibits of historical photographs and the cornerstone, emphasized archival preservation. These exhibits were successful in raising the public's archival awareness at Clemson.

Special Collections staff nevertheless found these exhibits to be a great burden during a time when a variety of other centennial activities, as well as the relocation of Special Collections to a new facility, also demanded attention. The library technical assistants in the unit assumed much of the responsibility for the coordination, creation, and mounting of these exhibits. By early 1989, the libraries' administrators recognized that the success of the exhibit program had rested upon its good fortune in having extremely capable paraprofessional staff ready to assume additional duties beyond those in their job descriptions. In fairness to the staff who did this work, a full-time professional position, the Director of Exhibits, was created in Special Collections to insure that the exhibits program would maintain the momentum gained during the centennial celebration.

Oral History Projects

Clemson's centennial celebration produced some oral history activities, but oral history never developed the momentum that characterized other centennial activities. The centennial planning committee concluded that, unlike the photograph project, there was no ready market for tapes and no means to recover costs or create a profit. Equally important, the products of such a project would lack appeal to the general public. There were several small, subject-specific projects undertaken. In the end, there was no major oral history project undertaken during the centennial celebration. The lack of a serious oral history project during Clemson's centennial celebration reflects the limits under which any commemorative celebration labors: It must link available financial resources with the scholarly interests of its researchers, the priorities of the organization's administrators, and the interests of its public.

Time Capsule Activities

Opening the cornerstone located in Clemson's first college building and its replacement with a new time capsule generated more public attention for Special Collections than any other centennial event. When the members of the Board of Trustees dedicated the cornerstone for the Main Building in 1891, they put in it a variety of items, some of historical interest. According to a contemporary newspaper account from the university archives, the items in the cornerstone included: Mr. Clemson's diploma as a graduate of the Royal School of Mines at Paris; his sketch of the life of John C. Calhoun; a phrenological chart of Mr. Clemson; a sketch of the life of Mr. Clemson by Col. R. W. Simpson; a record of the proceedings in the case of *Isabella Lee vs. R. W. Simpson*, and a variety of other material about the college or its founders. The centennial committee administrators recognized that retrieving material documenting the lives of John C. Calhoun and Thomas Green Clemson had potential historical significance and value as a newsworthy event. During the autumn of 1987, a committee planned to remove and open the cornerstone.

During the spring break of 1988, university maintenance staff loosened the cornerstone from its place in the wall. With the university's president and senior members of its administration standing by, TV cameras rolled as the outer shell was chipped open to uncover a copper box with only a piece of lead solder and a pencil in it. Fortunately, a perceptive maintenance supervisor advised prying the box out of the cornerstone. It was then discovered that the copper box had a false bottom.

The box was transferred to the university library and opened while cameras clicked and video cameras rolled their tape. It was a moment of high local drama. First a series of newspapers were removed, then a printed copy of the court case that settled the question of the Clemson will. But hope of an archival coup was dashed when we saw that the remaining contents of the box were badly damaged by water. The solder in the box had apparently melted in an earlier fire, and water had solidified the remainder of the box's contents into a glob of material the consistency of papier mâché. We decided to send the box and its contents to conservators at the South Carolina State Archives, who were able to deacidify the newspapers and recover a number of items, primarily coins. But many of the most interesting items were lost. Newspapers throughout South Carolina printed articles about the event, nevertheless.

During the fall of 1988, the university made plans to install a new time capsule in the cornerstone. Designed to survive anything short of a direct hit from a wrecking ball, it consisted of a stainless steel container with a screwtop lid, sealed with epoxy glue and placed in a copper box lined with sheetrock. Everyone at Clemson had ideas about what should go into the new time capsule. The committee selected a variety of items that documented the full extent of the university's activities and programs, then loaded the time capsule at a press conference in late March of 1989.

The following weekend, two thousand spectators saw the time capsule placed inside the Tillman Hall cornerstone and mounted again on the side of this historic building. Special Collections staff prepared special exhibits and helped with some of the event's logistics. As the crowd watched, the university's president, members of the board of trustees, and other administrators participated in the ceremonies, which drew statewide media attention.

These events raised people's awareness of Special Collections' activities well beyond that of the research community already familiar with its holdings. Staff interviewed on TV and for newspaper articles explained the importance of archival records and how to preserve and restore them. The time capsule activities captured the excitement of discovery, an experience that usually occurs in the archival processing area and search room. The emphasis on preserving the contents of the new time capsule made people aware of preservation problems related to modern paper. The public's interest in the fate of the contents of the Tillman Hall cornerstone demonstrates archivist Joel Wurl's suggestion that preservation may be a tool for reaching the general public, "perhaps the most important constituency," those who may never enter our reading rooms but whose taxes often pay for our repositories.

Conclusion

A centennial is a superb opportunity for an archives to reach its various constituencies: researchers, resource allocators, and the general public. One should recognize the potential benefits. In this case, developing programs that appealed to a variety of constituencies during the event laid the foundation for permanent improvements. The centennial provided the opportunity to expand programs to meet increased public service demands. Today the six-full-time permanent staff members whose positions were created during the centennial period continue to provide service to the university through a functioning records management program, a revitalized university archives, and an expanding exhibits program. Their contributions to the university will continue long after the last centennial event is a distant memory.

Lessons

1. Start early and expect researchers before the event begins.

2. Make sure you are well represented on committees during the planning of special events. Visibility counts.

3. Expect the unexpected. Then find a way to turn the unexpected to your advantage.

4. Meet the needs of the immediate event with permanent programs that solve long-term needs. Have a long-term plan ready.

APPENDIX 1
WORKING WITH THE MEDIA

This appendix contains sample press releases, event announcements, flyers, and a newsletter page and portions of a media plan created by the staff of the National Archives created for a major exhibition and accompanying public programs.

SIMMONS COLLEGE
300 THE FENWAY
BOSTON MASSACHUSETTS 02115

THE COLLEGE ARCHIVES

FOR IMMEDIATE RELEASE
CONTACT:

Megan Sniffin-Marinoff
College Archivist
617-738-3141

The Simmons College Archives announces the opening for research of the records of the Simmons College School of Public Health Nursing (later reorganized into the School of Nursing), covering the years 1902-1970. Important correspondents in this collection include M. Adelaide Nutting, Mary Beard, Isabel Stewart, and Anne Hervey Strong.

In the first years of the twentieth century, Boston nursing leaders were working toward the establishment of a central school for nurses that would teach preclinical subjects, both separate from established hospital training schools and academically affiliated. The movement toward this goal was led by Mary E.P. Davis, Superintendent of Nurses at the Boston Hospital for the Insane and a founder of the American Journal of Nursing.

At the invitation of Davis and Sophia Palmer, editor-in-chief of the Journal, a group of eight leading nursing superintendents from the Boston area formed a committee and met in 1902 to discuss plans for a preparatory course for nurses, eventually recommended to the administration of the newly formed "Simmons Female College." Included on the committee was Linda Richards,

-more-

Simmons
Page 2 of 2

the first woman to receive a diploma from an American nursing school.

By 1904, a special four-month program for nurses was begun at the College. By 1918, as a result of the increasing need for public health nurses recognized during World War I, Simmons College opened a School of Public Health Nursing. The courses, originally taught by Mary Beard of the Boston Instructive District Nursing Association, were ably directed by Anne Hervey Strong, a Bryn Mawr graduate, 1898, and a student of M. Adelaide Nutting, Teacher's College.

Beginning with Strong and her contemporaries, the leaders of the Simmons school exhibited a great awareness of the historical importance of their work, documenting in correspondence and reports their experience both as a part of an emerging profession and an academic discipline. Of particular interest are Strong's records as Committee Chair of the Education Committee of the National Organization for Public Health Nursing, 1918-22, which was responsible for granting approval to public health nursing programs as diverse as those in Berea, Kentucky and Halifax, Nova Scotia.

The records at Simmons College document the general development of American nursing education from the early 1900's to the 1960's. Evolving from an original curriculum of preparatory science courses undertaken in 1904 to a broad-based and varied professional school awarding degrees in nursing and graduate certificates in public health nursing, the changes in curriculum, degree requirements, field-work affiliations, and instructional methods experienced in the Simmons College nursing program, reflect national philosophical trends in nursing education.

#####

For Immediate Release
29 April 1989

One of Vermont's most interesting historic homes will open its doors for free guided tours on the weekend of May 13 and 14. Shelburne House, the century-old mansion on the shores of Lake Champlain in Shelburne will be offering "Upstairs, Downstairs and Behind the Scenes" tours from 10 am to 4 pm both days.

Built in the Gilded Age of the 1880s, Shelburne House was the country home of W. S. Webb and his wife Lila Vanderbilt Webb, a 100 room "cottage" where they entertained visitors from all over the world, the rich and powerful figures of the day. Today it is a luxurious seasonal inn, with its rooms restored to their Victorian magnificence, authentically decorated and furnished.

Before Shelburne House opens for its third season, the tours will provide an opportunity to see the guest bedrooms with their period or monochromatic color themes, the charming third-floor childrens' playroom, the grand Marble Room Dining Room, the imposing Games Room where the gentlemen guests gathered for brandy and cigars after dinner. The tours will also take a look behind the scenes including visits to the modern and well-equipped kitchen.

The tours are free, but reservations are required to ensure that the size of each tour group is kept small enough to allow for easy two-way communication. Come to Shelburne Farms Visitor Center at the gate of Shelburne Farms in Shelburne to make a reservation and pick up your tickets, or call 985-8686. Make your reservation early, as tickets are expected to go quickly.

The Visitor Center, at the corner of Harbor Road and Bay Road is open from 10 am to 5 pm daily.

Media Contact: Rosalyn Graham
802-985-3423

Shelburne Farms • Shelburne, Vermont 05482 • 802-985-8686

The Simmons College Archives announces the opening for research of the records of the Simmons College School of Public Health Nursing (later reorganized into the School of Nursing), covering the years 1902-1970. Important correspondents in this collection include M. Adelaide Nutting, Mary Beard, Isabel Stewart, and Anne Hervey Strong.

In the first years of the twentieth century, Boston nursing leaders were working toward the establishment of a central school for nurses that would teach preclinical subjects, both separate from established hospital training schools and academically affiliated ones. The movement toward this goal was led by Mary E. P. Davis, Superintendent of Nurses at the Boston Hospital for the Insane and a founder of the *American Journal of Nursing*.

At the invitation of Davis and Sophia Talmer, editor-in-chief of the *Journal*, a group of eight leading nursing superintendents from the Boston area formed a committee and met in 1902 to discuss plans for a preparatory course for nurses, which was eventually recommended to the administration of the newly formed "Simmons Female College." Included on the committee was Linda Richards, the first woman to receive a diploma from an American nursing school.

By 1904, a special four-month program for nurses was begun at the College. By 1918, as a result of the increasing need for public health nurses recognized during World War I, Simmons College opened a School of Public Health Nursing. The courses, originally taught by Mary Beard of the Boston Instructive District Nursing Association, were ably directed by Anne Hervey Strong, a Bryn Mawr graduate, 1898, and a student of M. Adelaide Nutting, Teacher's College.

Beginning with Strong and her contemporaries, the leaders of the Simmons school exhibited a great awareness of the historical importance of their work, documenting in correspondence and reports their experience both as a part of an emerging profession and an academic discipline. Of particular interest are Strong's records as Committee Chair of the Education Committee of the National Organization for Public Health Nursing, 1918-22, which was responsible for granting approval to public health nursing programs as diverse as those in Berea, Kentucky, and Halifax, Nova Scotia.

The records at Simmons College document the general development of American nursing education from the early 1900s to the 1960s. Evolving from an original curriculum of preparatory science courses undertaken in 1904 to a broad-based and varied professional school awarding degrees in nursing and graduate certificates in public health nursing, the changes in curriculum, degree requirements, field-work affiliations, and instructional methods experienced in the Simmons College nursing program, reflect national philosophical trends in nursing education.

Megan Sniffin-Marinoff
College Archivist

Bulletin of the History of Medicine, Volume 57, No. 3, Fall 1983

The Simmons College Archives has opened the records of the Simmons College School of Public Health Nursing (later reorganized as the School of Nursing). These records, which cover the years 1902-70, document changes in nursing curriculum, degree requirements, fieldwork affiliations, and instructional methods and reflect the general development of and national philosophical trends in American nursing education. For more information, contact Megan Sniffin-Marinoff, College Archivist, Simmons College, 300 The Fenway, Boston, Massachusetts 02115.

From: *Signs: A Journal of Women in Culture and Society*, Winter 1983; vol. 9, no. 2.

For Immediate Release
11 September 1989

10th annual Harvest Festival:
A tradition of Vermont traditions

The season of the harvest has always had its unique traditions in Vermont: the fall fair, the corn roast, cider pressing, walks in the woods. For the past ten years the Harvest Festival at Shelburne Farms has offered a day of entertainment, education, food and fun that has become an autumn tradition itself.

This year's Harvest Festival will be held on Saturday, Sept. 23 from 10 am to 5 pm in and around the Shelburne Farms Coach Barn on the shores of Lake Champlain. There will be entertainment in the courtyard, educational exhibits and craft demonstrations in the East and West Halls, activities for children, hayrides, and lots of food.

On stage during the day will be old favorites and newcomers with programs of music, dance and spoken word. The will include Banjo Dan and the Midnight Plowboys, Jon Gailmor, TomFoolery, Mac Parker, Green Mountain Cloggers, Baroque Court of Montpelier, Margaret MacArthur and Family, Juliet McVicar and Friends, Ed Larkin Old-Time Contra-Dancers, and the Highland Weavers.

There is also entertainment for the children under a tent in the children's area including Singers Bob and Andrea Teer, Gary Dulabaum, Masquerades Storytelling Theatre, Mary Ann Samuels and Karen Downey.

-2-

There will be a special grand finale performance at 4 pm under the tent by the talented and creative Gould & Stearns "Two Men Talking Mime". This special feature is sponsored by Ben & Jerry's Homemade of Shelburne.

A highlight of the day, which has become a "must-do" September event for many families, is a hayride behind the handsome teams of the Green Mountain Draft Horse Association.

Corn roasted in its husks over a huge bed of charcoal is another tradition. The sweet corn is planted with the Harvest Festival dates in mind, and the special roasting technique guarantees a most flavorful treat.

There are many other food specialties at the Harvest Festival including lamb kabobs and barbecued sausage, maple glazed donuts and maple coffee and Shelburne Farms own Farmhouse cheddar cheese.

Children are guaranteed an exciting and creative day with many hands-on craft and take-home projects to explore, as well as the wild animals of the Discovery Museum and VINS to meet.

The Shelburne Farms Harvest Festival, organized and executed by an army of community volunteers, provides an opportunity for the public to enjoy the historic estate and learn about the many ways Shelburne Farms is accomplishing its mission of teaching stewardship and the conservation of natural and agricultural resources.

Admission to the Harvest Festival is $2 for adults and $1 for children with free admission for members of Shelburne Farms. The Harvest Festival is supported jointly by the Vermont Council on the Arts and the National Endowment for the Arts with special thanks to Vermont Tent and Catering. For information about the Festival, call 985-8686.

New England Historic Genealogical Society

101 Newbury Street • Boston, Massachusetts • 02116-3087

A National Research Center for Family & Local History

Ralph J. Crandall, Director • (617) 536-5740 • Fax 536-7307

NEWS
For Immediate Release
Boston, Massachusetts

Contact:
Emer O'Keeffe
(518) 584-5414
June 30th, 1993

Historical and Genealogical Significance in
Classifieds of Yesteryear

One of the highlights of a Boston newspaper for nearly a century was a "Missing Friends" column, and the information contained in its advertisements is of particular interest to the 40 million Americans who claim Irish heritage. It also provides historians and genealogists with the broadest range of data yet available on Irish immigrants of this period. This vital deposit is put together in a readable series from the New England Historic Genealogical Society entitled: *THE SEARCH FOR MISSING FRIENDS: Irish Immigrant Advertisements Placed in the Boston Pilot.*

The first three books - in a projected nine-volume series - are currently available from NEHGS, and are especially important in that they deal with immigration in the decade following the Great Famine of 1845. During this period, 1845-1855, over two million fled the chaos of Ireland, and most found their way to America in what is truly one of the epic sagas of nineteenth century history.

For Irish immigrants, separated from their families at dockside or by jobs taking them hundreds of miles away on railroads or canals, the Boston *Pilot*'s "Missing Friends" column was an essential information network. For us today - historians, genealogists and laypersons alike - the ads are windows on the world of the immigrants.

The *Search for Missing Friends* is an indispensable addition to available sources for tracing Irish roots and understanding the vagaries of the Irish immigration experience. The text, a meticulous transcription of the ads in chronological order, provides an outstanding social commentary on the times with an abundance of colorful, vivid detail. The introduction to each volume, replete with tables and graphs, provides in-depth analysis of the material in the ads, and makes extensive use

-- MORE --

of available scholarly literature, discussing conditions in Ireland and Irish America, and providing background and context. The ads include such key identifying information as place of origin, year and port of arrival, destination in North America, occupation, etc., and do not simply reflect the Irish in Boston. The *Pilot*, called "the bible of Irish America," had a national distribution of over a million in the mid-1800s, and queries came from all over the United States.

The most valuable finding is, undoubtedly, the substantial number of townland and parish origins. "It supplies this vital link missing from official immigration records," says Dr. Ralph Crandall, Director of NEHGS. Each book contains full name and place name indexes, and Volumes I and II include guidelines on how to continue the research, offering a bibliography and a list of other sources available to the historian/genealogist.

To the social historian, *The Search for Missing Friends* offers a bounty of social and demographic data on Irish immigration to North America. To the genealogist, it provides thousands of possible ancestors and their exact place origins in Ireland. To the layperson, it presents another invitation to see, feel, and be touched by the experience of mid-nineteenth century immigration.

The series has already received acclaim: the *Journal of Irish Social and Economic History* considers it an "important resource," while the *Boston Globe* recognizes in each paragraph "a paradigm of immigration lore and the cry of an aching heart." *Familia* declares it "brilliant in conception," and the *Detroit Society for Genealogical Research Magazine* asserts: "the value of this massive compilation cannot be overstated." With this publication, the New England Historic Genealogical Society has seized the opportunity to be identified as *the* East Coast resource for Irish ethnic studies. Founded in 1845, the Society is the oldest of its kind in the United States, and its family heritage collection today reflects its commitment to a larger, culturally diverse American community.

The Search for Missing Friends (Volume I: 1831-1850; Volume II: 1851-53; and Volume III: 1854-56) is available from the New England Historic Genealogical Society, at $45 + $4.50 P&H for each volume. Address orders to: Sales Department, NEHGS, 101 Newbury Street, Boston, MA 02116.

National Archives
Commemorative Committee

NEWS RELEASE

7th & Pennsylvania Avenue, NW
Washington, DC 20408
(202) 501-5525

FOR IMMEDIATE RELEASE July 22, 1993

WORLD WAR II MUSICAL REVUE "IN THE MOOD" RETURNS TO THE NATIONAL ARCHIVES

Washington, DC... Back by popular demand, the National Archives presents "IN THE MOOD," a World War II musical revue, on Friday, September 10, 1993, at 8 p.m. The performance will take place on the front portico of the National Archives Building on Constitution Avenue, between 7th and 9th Streets, NW. The performance is free and open to the public and seating is on a first come/first seated basis. "IN THE MOOD" will be followed by dancing to the big band swing music that was popular during the 1940's. (Raindate: September 11, 1993.)

The vocal quartet "String of Pearls," accompanied by Bud Forrest's 17-piece "String of Pearls" Orchestra, will perform old favorites such as "Boogie Woogie Bugle Boy" and "Chattanooga Choo Choo." Tom and Tina, the 1992 Virginia State Swing Dance Champions, will be on hand to dance the jitterbug and the lindy hop during the presentation.

According to James Morris, who wrote the script and directs this musical production, "swing music holds a unique place in American cultural history. World War II was probably the first time - and maybe the last time - when we all listened to the same music," said Mr. Morris.

The quartet, "String of Pearls," is composed of Washington-area performers Cindy Hutchins, Ann Johnson, Brenda Brody and vocalist and dancer Brian Donnelly.

(MORE)

DID YOU KNOW:

Color photographs fade rapidly when exposed to sunlight?

Videotape has an average shelf life of a few years?

Color slides last for 50 years or more?

Some chemically treated album pages can destroy photographs and memorabilia?

LEARN HOW TO PRESERVE YOUR FAMILY HISTORY

AT A WORKSHOP BY SHELBURNE FARMS ARCHIVIST JULIE BRESSOR

WEDNESDAY, JUNE 6

7 to 8:30 pm

AT SHELBURNE FARMS VISITOR CENTER

FREE

BRING ONE OR TWO ITEMS ALONG FOR ADVICE

SAMPLE SUPPLIES, HANDOUTS AND CATALOGUES WILL BE AVAILABLE

SHELBURNE FARMS

THE NATIONAL ARCHIVES

Invites  *to*

A World War II Commemoration
The 1940's Musical Revue

Written & Directed by James Morris

featuring

BUD FORREST and his "STRING OF PEARLS"

followed by dancing to the Big Band Sounds of the
"STRING OF PEARLS" ORCHESTRA and VOCAL QUARTET

FRIDAY, SEPTEMBER 10, 1993
8:00 p.m. - 11:00 p.m.
(RAIN DATE: September 11. Call (202) 501-5000 for updated information.)

On the steps of the National Archives
Constitution Avenue between 7th and 9th Streets, NW

Bring your own seating. Dance the night away!

ADMISSION FREE

This program is part of the National Archives commemoration of the 50th anniversary of World War II.
Produced by Bud Forrest Entertainment

For more information call (202) 219-2316

NATIONAL ARCHIVES
National One-Act Playwriting Competition

For
Original, Unpublished, Unproduced
One-Act Play Scripts

CASH AWARDS

1st place — $750
2nd place — $500

Entries must be *unpublished* (not available to amateur or professional theaters for royalty payments) and *unproduced* (not previously staged for a paying audience).

Production will be at the discretion of the National Archives

ALL SCRIPTS MUST BE SUBMITTED BY JANUARY 15, 1992

- **A script must be based on events, episodes, or personal experiences related to U.S. involvement in World War II from 1941 to 1946, i.e., the home-front, sabotage, the Office of Strategic Services (OSS), Pearl Harbor, propaganda, rationing, WACs, etc.**
- **A script must be based on records held by the National Archives in Washington, DC, its regional archives, or any of the Presidential libraries.** Evidence of this must be presented in the form of citations of record groups and series used, the name of the institutions used, and the names of assisting archivists in those institutions. Scripts without this information will be rejected automatically.
- Scripts will be returned only if accompanied by a self-addressed stamped envelope.
- Send a duplicate copy, not the original. Only one entry per playwright.
- The National Archives shall have the right to produce the performances of selected scripts without payment of royalties.
- All production and publication rights remain the property of the playwright.
- The National Archives reserves the right to withhold any or all awards.
- Only stage plays and musicals will be judged. Film and TV scripts will not be accepted.
- Musicals must be limited to the use of no more than three instruments.
- Scripts will be judged on historical reliability, concept, characterization, and dialogue.
- Judges will look most favorably on plays that:
  - —have a running time of no more than 90 minutes and no less than 45 minutes.
  - —**have few scenes, minimal set, costume and lighting requirements, and a minimal number of characters.**
  - —have a description of each character preceding the script.
  - —**(PLEASE NOTE: stage dimensions are 12′6″ deep by 26′ wide; it is a basic lecture stage, no front curtain, no wings.)**
- Employees of the National Archives and Records Administration, its regional archives, and the Presidential libraries are not eligible to enter this competition.

SEND SCRIPTS TO: Chairman, National Archives Playwriting Competition, Education Branch (NEEE), National Archives, Washington, DC 20408.

CALIFORNIA ORIGINALS

Volume 6 Nos. 2 & 3 1991

Interim Site Search Continues

by Genevieve Troka

Efforts to locate an interim site for the Archives got underway in August. The search was initially confined to an area close to downtown Sacramento where the State Capitol and many state agencies are headquartered.

Just when an ideal facility was located, serious concerns were raised about flood dangers in the site area. A historical geographer serving on the Archives' advisory board, determined after extensive research that the site was "prone to periodic flooding". Work to upgrade the condition of levees in the immediate vicinity will not be completed until 1995--the year the Archives leaves to move into the new building. Needless to say, the site search is redirected towards higher ground.

Dept. of General Services Project Director Richard S. Teramoto, State Archivist John F. Burns, and Assistant Secretary of State Jerry W. Hill study flood zone map. (Photo by Genevieve Troka)

In addition to being conveniently located for users, the facility would have to possess or be modified to include, the appropriate environmental controls, security systems (including a vault), and fire detection/suppression systems. The space would have to be laid out so that during the three-year interim period, all Archives' programs could continue to function effectively.

From its inception, the construction of the new Secretary of State/State Archives complex has been planned as a two-phase process. The site around the old Archives building would be built out during phase one and the Archives would then move into its new quarters. During the second phase, the old building would be demolished and the balance of the complex be constructed.

As efforts to complete working drawings progressed, the project managers and architects became increasingly concerned. The Archives would have a limited time period between phases to move. Building the phase one and two structures within three feet of one another, not only produces considerable engineering challenges, but lengthens the construction schedule by two years.

Monetary issues were not the only ones weighing against the original plan. The Archives' collection and day-to-day operations would be subjected to continuous disruptions, high noise levels and vibration, as well as dust and air pollution associated with construction activities. All these issues were studied in depth. The advantages of single-phase construction outweighed those of a two-phase project even when potential damage resulting from moving the collection twice was taken into account.

Our staff hopes that an even better interim facility will soon be identified.

(Sample Page)

I. PRE-EXHIBITION CONTACTS

February 16, 1993: A **press release** was distributed to approximately 525 magazines on the NXI magazine list (Attachment A). Follow-up calls were made to a number of these publications, including The Washingtonian, Southern Living, Amtrak Express, several airline magazines, Life Magazine, American Heritage and Parade.

May 1, 1993: An updated **exhibition press release, backgrounder** and **press releases on the symposium and film series** were issued (Attachments B-E). They were distributed to approximately 965 contacts:

- NXI's general press release list received all releases;
- The releases and a **flyer** (see Attachment F) promoting the symposium were sent to East Coast college and university classics departments, local Greek Orthodox Churches, local Greek cultural organizations, the American School of Classical Studies' list of Washington-area alumnae and patrons and the American Institute of Architects' mailing list.

Letters (see Attachment G) and exhibition information (including the backgrounder) were sent to approximately 15 journalists who covered the National Gallery "Greek Miracle" exhibition.

Public service announcements were mailed approximately 55 radio stations, including NXI's list of local radio stations and Greek-American radio programs in Baltimore and Washington (see Attachment H).

A number of exhibition **posters** were distributed to local Greek Orthodox churches and Greek cultural organizations.

An exclusive photo opportunity was offered to CBS Sunday Morning (with Charles Kuralt) to shoot the arrival and unpacking of the documents. Although they committed to the exclusive, they were unable to coordinate the timing. Jim Houtrides (the producer) visited the exhibition after installation had been completed and unfortunately decided not to cover it.

<u>May 26, 1993</u>: A **media alert** for the press preview was sent on US Newswire to all local media outlets (Attachment H). During the weeks prior to the press preview, the media alert was faxed to more than 75 local media outlets, including the three wire services, 7 local television stations, CNN, CBS, ABC, NBC, National Public Radio, 10 news bureaus, the Washington bureaus of three Greek newspapers, Time, Newsweek and U.S. News & World Report.

Follow-up calls were made to all of these organizations to pitch the story and remind them of the press preview.

An interview was arranged on a **public service program** on WRQX-FM (Mix 107.3), a local radio station. Diana Buitron-Oliver (curator of the exhibition) and Linda Brown (NE) were interviewed by the host, Barbara Britt. The show aired on Sunday, June 13.

A number of press kits were mailed to members of the press who were unable to attend the press preview.

II. PRESS PREVIEW

The press preview was held on June 8, at 9 a.m. Several objects were displayed on art carts in Room 105 so that the press could have a better photo opportunity. The curator, conservator, coordinator for the National Archives, a representative of the Greek government and a representative of the American School of Classical Studies were available to answer questions and describe the exhibition and the objects. (For a list of objects on display, see Attachment I.)

Fifteen people attended the press preview. They represented the following organizations:

The Washington Post
The Washington Times
Newsweek
The Associated Press
The Embassy of Greece
The Voice of America – Greek Service
USIA – Worldnet
USIA – Wire Service
USIA – Greek desk
The American Enterprise Institute
Society for the Preservation of the Greek Heritage

III. FOLLOW-UP

- NXI sent out approximately 40 press kits to various media outlets. The journalists who covered the exhibition received copies of the exhibition catalog.
- Several political commentators, including George Will, Art Buchwald and Richard Cohen, received press kits and catalogs.
- Press releases will be issued for subsequent film series, lecture series and the fall symposium.

National Archives

Washington, DC 20408
(202) 501-5525

NEWS RELEASE

For Immediate Release February 16, 1993

National Archives to Open Exhibition Celebrating 2500th Anniversary of Democracy

Washington, D.C....To celebrate the 2500th anniversary of the origins of democratic government, the National Archives, in cooperation with the American School of Classical Studies at Athens, will open a major exhibition exploring the world's first democracy, which was born in ancient Athens. This exhibition, "The Birth of Democracy," will feature a number of ancient artifacts, some of which have never before been displayed outside of Greece. It is free and open to the public in the National Archives Rotunda from June 15, 1993 through January 2, 1994.

The exhibition focuses on the roots and workings of a radically new political system that the Athenians called demokratia, "the rule of the people." "The Birth of Democracy" will be located in the 26 cases flanking the Charters of Freedom -- the Declaration of Independence, the Constitution and the Bill of Rights -- which are on permanent display in the National Archives Rotunda. Archivist of the United States Don W. Wilson said, "The National Archives is proud to offer our visitors the opportunity to examine some of the rare antiquities of this ancient Greek democracy. Here, within sight of the great charters of American democracy, one may consider this first democracy and ask if 'the Past is Prologue.'"

The unique objects in the exhibition, dating back as early as the 9th century B.C., and spanning many centuries of Athenian history, tell the story of the beginnings of democracy, how it functioned and how it developed. Inscriptions, decorated pottery, jewelry and other artifacts were used by scholars to piece together the exciting chronicle of the city of Athens and the rise of a democratic form of government at the dawn of the Classical Age. The majority of objects were excavated by the American School in the Ancient Agora (marketplace) in Athens. Among the items that will be displayed are:

* Fragment of a water-clock, or klepsydra, used to time speeches before a jury. In the Athenian court system, individual litigants spoke on their own behalf, but their time was strictly limited, regulated by water-clocks;
* Bronze ballots from the 4th century B.C. given to jurors to vote on the innocence or guilt of the defendant;
* Terra-cotta statuettes showing stock characters in Greek drama. Public festivals in honor of the god Dionysos were the beginnings of Western drama, one of the many art forms that flourished in ancient Athens.

The exhibition was organized by the prestigious American School of Classical Studies, drawing for the most part on artifacts excavated in the Agora, the political and commercial heart of Athens. Many of these objects will be seen for the first time outside of Greece thanks to the generosity of the Ministry of Culture of Greece as part of the Greek participation in the celebrations for 2,500 years since the establishment of Democracy. The exhibition was designed by Michael Graves Architect, and is circulated by Art Services International. Partial funding was received from the National Endowment for the Humanities.

* * * *

For additional PRESS information and color and black and white images, contact the National Archives Public Affairs staff at (202) 501-5525.

93-25

National Archives

Washington, DC 20408
(202)501-5525

NEWS RELEASE

BACKGROUND INFORMATION ON "THE BIRTH OF DEMOCRACY"

In a recent Presidential proclamation commemorating Greek Independence Day, President Clinton said, "In creating a new Nation, the American Founding Fathers drew upon the Greek writings for inspiration as to the purpose of government and in order to define the common good of society... This summer the National Archives will... display artifacts from the 5th century B.C. which demonstrate the great degree of participation of Athenians in their government. It is appropriate that our own Constitution will be juxtaposed against these artifacts."

As we near the end of the 20th century, democracy is the political watchword. Today democracy is virtually synonymous with fair, free government; new democratic systems are emerging in all parts of the world, and citizens of established democracies are rediscovering their political power. It is particularly appropriate that the National Archives will host this extraordinary exhibition, "The Birth of Democracy." Conceived by the American School of Classical Studies at Athens, the exhibition focuses on the roots and workings of a radically new political system that the Athenians called demokratia, "the rule of the people."

The goal of "The Birth of Democracy" is not simply to celebrate the classical past or to lay claim to classical Greece as a cultural ancestor, but also to expose viewers to the weaknesses of early democracy, through artifacts and documents about slavery and the exclusion of women from citizenship, shortcomings initially reflected in our own Constitution. The exhibition draws on original materials, thousands of years old, that re-create a vivid image of the ancient democracy that has greatly, if indirectly, influenced our own.

(MORE)

-2-

"The Birth of Democracy" begins with an examination of pre-democratic Athens, where rich aristocratic families vied for power, and tension between the classes brought Athens to the brink of civil war. Jewelry, figurines and vase paintings in this section reflect the great differences in the lifestyles of wealthy and poor Athenians.

The exhibition then explores early Athenian democracy, explaining how citizens were encouraged to participate in every aspect of government, from making laws and sitting on juries, to controlling the weights and measures used in the marketplace. Scale models of the Pnyx, the meeting place of the full citizen body, and of the Bouleuterion, the meeting place for the Senate (boule); and artifacts illustrating daily government activities, such as a bronze juror's ticket and crockery from the dining room where the Senate executive committee dined at public expense, will be on display. A fragment of a water clock shows how the Athenians limited the time that speakers could address the law courts.

Sections on the unique Athenian practice of ostracism and the strong Athenian military explore how this first democracy defended itself from internal and external threats. Ostracism was used by the Athenians to protect the democracy and prevent any recurrence of tyranny. Each year a vote was taken using terra-cotta "ostraka" (ballots), on which citizens inscribed the names of men they thought were becoming too powerful and a threat to the democracy. If enough people voted, the man with the most votes was exiled for 10 years. There are a number of these ostraka displayed in the exhibition.

"The Birth of Democracy" includes a discussion of criticisms, both ancient and modern, of this early democracy. The same system that encouraged widespread participation by its citizens excluded much of the population - women and foreigners - from citizenship, and allowed slavery to flourish. One section illustrates the life of Socrates, one of the most famous critics of Athenian democracy. Another includes artifacts from theatrical productions, which were an important forum for both praising and satirizing Athenian politics and politicians.

The Athenians were careful and thorough recordkeepers and valued the written word as an open record of the workings of the

(MORE)

-3-

government. "The Birth of Democracy" includes a small section on the sources and documents we use to understand the workings and history of Athenian democracy. The central archives building, the Metroon, housed many records of the Athenian democracy, now lost; and overlooked the central Agora square, just as the National Archives overlooks the Mall in Washington. Although the archival records on perishable materials are now lost, thousands of inscriptions on stone survive.

Finally, the exhibition reminds us that if we say that democracy began in Athens, we imply that modern democracies are somehow continuations of this great political experiment. The Founding Fathers of America certainly looked to the ancient governments of Greece and the Roman Republic in drawing up our Constitution. In the final cases of the exhibition some of their writings on the subject of Athens and its political history are featured.

The majority of the artifacts displayed in the exhibition were excavated from the Agora, the commercial and political heart of the ancient city. The American School has fielded the Agora excavations almost continuously since 1930, interrupted only by World War II and its aftermath. Through the generosity of the Ministry of Culture of Greece, many of these unique ancient objects will be seen for the first time outside of Greece. Other items included in the exhibit come from museums in Europe and the United States. Funding has been received from the National Endowment for the Humanities and from The Morris and Gwendolyn Cafritz Foundation.

"The Birth of Democracy" uses various artifacts, documents and other material to illustrate the roots, evolution and institutions of the first democracy. Displayed next to the Declaration of Independence, the Constitution and the Bill of Rights, "The Birth of Democracy" allows us to consider the history and future of our own democracy and ask if "The Past is Prologue."

* * * *

93-44

National Archives

Washington, DC 20408
(202) 501-5525

NEWS RELEASE

For Immediate Release April 21, 1993

NATIONAL ARCHIVES ANNOUNCES NEW FILM SERIES:
"THE BIRTH OF DEMOCRACY"

Washington, DC... In June, the National Archives begins a new film series that is part of the celebration of the 2500th anniversary of the beginnings of democracy in ancient Athens. The series, entitled "The Birth of Democracy," complements a major exhibition of the same name on display in the National Archives Rotunda. All screenings are free and open to the public in the Theater of the National Archives Building, Pennsylvania Avenue between 7th and 9th Streets, N.W.

* **Thursday, June 17:** "The Greeks: The Classical Age," 1988, takes a broad look at the fifth century B.C. The film explores the nature of Athenian democracy, the achievements of Pericles, the consequences of the rivalry between Syracuse and Athens and presents an overview of the architecture, sculpture, pottery and writing of the period. The program will begin at noon in the Theater. (53 minutes.)

* **Monday, June 21:** "The Greeks: The Minds of Men," 1988. This documentary presents a detailed look at the life and teachings of Socrates and his pupil Plato, and at the work of the two founding fathers of history - Herodotus, the first Greek historian,

(MORE)

and Thucydides, the first to write a thorough and fair account of his own times. Their work exemplifies the vital curiosity of the Greeks about the nature of man and his place in the world. The film will begin at noon in the Theater. (52 minutes.)

* **Thursday, June 24:** "Barefoot in Athens," 1984, is the film adaptation of the Maxwell Anderson play that focuses on Socrates' trial for "introducing new divinities" and "corrupting the thinking of our young men." This film is an outstanding introduction to classical Athens, and stars Peter Ustinov, Geraldine Page and Anthony Quayle. It begins at noon in the Theater. (76 minutes.)

"The Birth of Democracy" exhibition explores the world's first democratic government through ancient documents and artifacts, and offers a unique opportunity to compare this ancient democracy with our own system, the first modern democracy. The exhibition will feature a number of artifacts, some of which have never before been displayed outside of Greece. Conceived by the prestigious American School of Classical Studies at Athens, "The Birth of Democracy" focuses on the roots and workings of a radically new political system that the Athenians called <u>demokratia</u>, "the rule of the people." Funding has been received from the National Endowment for the Humanities and from The Morris and Gwendolyn Cafritz Foundation. The exhibition is free and open to the public in the National Archives Rotunda from June 15, 1993 through January 2, 1994.

* * * *

For further PRESS information on either "The Birth of Democracy" film series or exhibition, please contact the National Archives Public Affairs Staff at (202) 501-5525. Contact this number for information on another film and lecture series on Greek democracy scheduled for the fall of 1993.

93-37

Washington, DC 20408

PUBLIC SERVICE ANNOUNCEMENT

FOR USE THROUGH JUNE 15, 1993

:30

ON JUNE 15, 1993, THE NATIONAL ARCHIVES, IN COOPERATION WITH THE AMERICAN SCHOOL OF CLASSICAL STUDIES AT ATHENS, WILL OPEN A MAJOR EXHIBITION EXPLORING THE WORLD'S FIRST DEMOCRACY, WHICH WAS BORN IN ANCIENT ATHENS. THIS EXHIBITION, "THE BIRTH OF DEMOCRACY," CELEBRATES THE 2500TH ANNIVERSARY OF THE ORIGINS OF DEMOCRATIC GOVERNMENT. ANCIENT ARTIFACTS, SOME OF WHICH HAVE NEVER BEFORE BEEN DISPLAYED OUTSIDE OF GREECE, ARE FEATURED IN THE EXHIBITION. IT IS FREE AND OPEN TO THE PUBLIC IN THE NATIONAL ARCHIVES ROTUNDA FROM JUNE 15, 1993 THROUGH JANUARY 2, 1994, CONSTITUTION AVENUE BETWEEN 7TH AND 9TH STREETS, NW.

National Archives

Washington, DC 20408
(202) 501-5525

NEWS RELEASE

MEDIA ALERT

FOR IMMEDIATE RELEASE

May 26, 1993

CONTACT: Susan Cooper
Stephanie Allin
(202) 501-5525

PRESS PREVIEW OF "THE BIRTH OF DEMOCRACY"
A MAJOR NATIONAL ARCHIVES EXHIBITION

WHAT: This is the only opportunity to view and photograph ancient Greek artifacts that are part of the exhibition, "The Birth of Democracy," before they are installed in their display cases. These unique objects, some of which are being displayed outside of Greece for the first time through the generosity of the Ministry of Culture of Greece, are thousands of years old. They chronicle the story of the first democracy, born in ancient Athens 2500 years ago.

WHEN: Tuesday, June 8, 1993, 9 a.m. - 10:30 a.m. (Artificial light in the Rotunda may be used until 9:45 a.m.)

WHERE: Archivist's Reception Room (Room 105)
National Archives Building
Pennsylvania Avenue Entrance
Between 7th and 9th Streets, NW
Washington, DC

The National Archives will conduct special preview tours of the exhibition for the media. The American School of Classical Studies at Athens, which conceived of the exhibition, and the National Archives will present some of the most remarkable objects in the exhibition, including:

* Fragment of a water-clock (klepsydra) used to time speakers in an assembly. The vessel was filled with water that ran out of a spout at the bottom, allowing the speaker to continue until time literally ran out.

(MORE)

-2-

* Tholos crockery from the dining area of the executive committee of the senate marked with delta-epsilon ("demosion," or public), presumably so that senators, dining at public expense, would not walk off with the official table settings.

* Ostraka (potsherds) were used as ballots, on which citizens inscribed the names of men they thought were becoming too powerful and a danger to democracy. The man with the most votes was ostracized for 10 years. A group of 190 ostraka, which were found together and bear the name of a powerful Athenian politician, is an early example of ballot-stuffing; an analysis of the handwriting revealed that the 190 ballots were written by just 14 people.

* Ballots (bronze disks, pierced in the center for innocence or solid for guilt) were ingeniously designed to insure a secret vote.

PHOTO OPPORTUNITIES: These and other ancient objects may be photographed before they are installed in the display cases. The exhibition in the Rotunda may also be photographed.

INTERVIEW OPPORTUNITIES WITH SUBJECT MATTER EXPERTS:

- **Dr. Diana Buitron-Oliver**, curator of the exhibition;
- **Dr. Catherine Vanderpool** of the American School of Classical Studies;
- **Niki Prokopiou**, archaeologist and representative of the Greek Ministry of Culture;
- **Alice Paterakis**, conservator for the American School of Classical Studies' Agora excavations;
- **Chris Rudy Smith**, National Archives coordinator of the exhibition.

The Public Affairs Staff can arrange individual interviews with any of these experts on request.

* * * *

93-47

Washington, DC 20408

INTERVIEW OPPORTUNITIES AT THE "BIRTH OF DEMOCRACY" PRESS PREVIEW

- **Dr. Diana Buitron-Oliver**, curator of the exhibition;
- **Dr. Catherine Vanderpool** of the American School of Classical Studies;
- **Niki Prokopiou**, archaeologist and representative of the Greek Ministry of Culture;
- **Alice Paterakis**, conservator for the American School of Classical Studies' Agora excavations;
- **Chris Rudy Smith**, National Archives coordinator of the exhibition.

OBJECTS ON DISPLAY AT THE "BIRTH OF DEMOCRACY" PRESS PREVIEW

* Tholos dining crockery, black glaze kylix (drinking cup), incised inscription; small olpe (jug). Both from the Agora Museum, Athens.

These pieces are marked with delta-epsilon (demosion - public), presumably so that the senators would not walk off with the official table settings. The senators served on the executive committee for one-tenth of a year and were fed at public expense. The menu in the Tholos might have included cheese, barley cakes, olives, leeks, wine and possibly meat and fish.

* THE PRACTICE OF OSTRACISM: After the battle of Marathon in 490 B.C., the Athenians began to use a special procedure, ostracism, to protect the democracy and prevent any recurrence of tyranny. Each year a vote was taken using potsherds (ostraka) as ballots, on which the citizens inscribed the names of men they thought were becoming too powerful and a danger to democracy. If enough people voted, the man with the most votes was exiled for 10 years.

- Ostrakon of Perikles, terra-cotta, Agora Museum, Athens. Perikles rose to power as leader of the democratic party in the 460's B.C. Year after year, Perikles was elected general of his tribe. He built a power base that made it possible for him to divert the funds of the Delian League, which had been established for the defense of Greece, to the building of the magnificent temples of the Acropolis. He may often have been a candidate for ostracism, but was never ostracized. He lived from 495 B.C. to 429 B.C.

(MORE)

• Ostrakon of Aristeides, terra-cotta, Agora Museum, Athens. When Aristeides was a candidate for ostracism, an illiterate citizen approached him and asked him to write the name of Aristeides on an ostrakon. Aristeides was surprised at this request, and asked the man what harm Aristeides had ever done him. "None whatever," was the reply. "I do not even know the fellow, but I am sick of hearing him called 'The Just' everywhere." When he heard this, Aristeides said nothing but wrote his own name on the ostrakon and handed it back. Aristeides was ostracized in 482 B.C.

• Ostrakon of Themistokles, terra-cotta, Agora Museum, Athens. Themistokles was among the most prominent politicians of fifth century Athens and responsible for the growth of Athenian naval power. His numerous political enemies finally had him ostracized in 472 B.C. A group of 190 ostraka bearing his name were found together and show the nature of early factional politics; an analysis of the handwriting revealed that the 190 ballots were written by just 14 people.

• Athenian (Attic) red-figure kylix (drinking cup), terra cotta, courtesy of the Visitors of the Ashmolean Museum, Oxford, England. This unusual scene has been interpreted as the counting of votes at an ostracism. The man with the stylus and writing tablets seems to be tallying the votes.

* Fragment of a water-clock (klepsydra): This was used to time litigants in a court. The vessel was filled with water that ran out of a bronze-lined spout at the bottom, allowing the speaker to continue until time literally ran out. Individual litigants spoke on their own behalf, though occasionally using speeches prepared by professionals; skillful rhetoric was necessary in order to sway a jury.

* THE ROLE OF WOMEN IN ANCIENT ATHENS: Women in Athens were denied the rights of citizenship. Although they participated in religious festivals and marched in civic precessions, they could not attend the Assembly or sit as jurors. They had few legal rights. Some ancient social critics pointed out that this situation was unfair, but participation in government remained an exclusively male prerogative.

• Athenian (Attic) red-figure fragment of a kylix (drinking cup) with the image of a hetaira, terra-cotta, Agora Museum, Athens. This fragment preserves the partial image of a nude woman, who holds a castanet in her left hand. She is probably a hetaira, a woman accomplished in the arts of music, conversation and sex.

• Athenian (Attic) red-figure fragment of a vase, terra-cotta, Agora Museum, Athens. The fragment depicts the upper part of a woman dressed in a chiton (tunic), himation (cloak) and headband.

APPENDIX 2
FUND RAISING

This appendix contains fund raising and solicitation guidelines, supplied by CPG Enterprises, Shaftsbury, VT, and sections of a self-study guide on fund raising written and supplied by the New York State Archives and Records Administration.

FUNDRAISING SUMMARY
VARIOUS WAYS TO RAISE MONEY . . .
IN VARIOUS CIRCUMSTANCES

Annual Fund Drive: When you need cash now, and expect to ask for it again next year. Traditionally this involves higher level requests on a personal basis, and lower level requests through the mail or on the phone.

Membership Drive: When you can offer tangible returns like magazines, free or reduced admissions, calendars, tee shirts, ID cards, etc.

Capital Campaign Drive: When you need support over a period of time (usually more than one year, but a finite time) for a specific purpose: building or major renovations, a very large purchase of equipment. Traditionally a structured, planned version of an annual drive geared toward the same people who give you your annual gifts.

Special Drives: When you need immediate cash for a very short time and very specific purpose; for instance, funds to repair the electrical system, or to purchase the xerox machine or to hire a short-term employee.

Phonothons: A telephone method used effectively for relatively small gifts in either an annual drive or capital drive, or even for special purpose drives. Has the added benefit of quasi-personal contact with your donors: gives them the opportunity to ask questions and gives you the opportunity to check their address and other information storage.

Special Events: When you have more volunteers than time; highly labor-intensive events that rely on many people working on a finite event, getting donated supplies, and raising money from the general public, who always get some THING in exchange for money spent. Includes raffles, fairs, dinners, balloon rides, flower sales, etc.

Grants: Written applications followed by personal meetings or communications with foundations, businesses and/or governmental units, to provide larger blocks of funds usually for specific, finite purposes.

Person-to-person fundraising: This is involved in all the above, though most people think you can manage without in phonothons, special events and special drives (where they often think an ad in the newspaper will do it). In fact, all fundraising is a person-to-person activity of one sort or another.

YOUR FUNDRAISING LETTER SHOULD BE SPECIAL . . .
BUT IT ALSO NEEDS CERTAIN KEY CHARACTERISTICS.

name address city, state, zip	as much personalization as you can afford
Dear (name)	if you can't personalize, at least make the salutation individual: "Dear Friend," "Dear Helper," "Dear Art Lover."

Why you are writing . . . you share an interest. Explain your connection with him or the cause. TELL HIM YOU WILL ASK FOR A GIFT.

How your group will be responsible in using the gift. Cost effectiveness, responsibility in reporting, low administrative expenses and a straightforward approach are valued by donors at any level.

Where they can see evidence of the gift's usefulness. Explain who the ultimate recipients are, let the donor share your pride in advanceing the cause.

What you want him to give, where to send it, that it is tax deductible. Don't pussyfoot about the request! The biggest mistake, and the most frequent, is that solicitors forget to ASK!

Express your gratefulness.

Signature (personal if possible)

P.S. Studies have proven that the postscript is the most frequently read portion of any letter. If you lose him above, you've still got a chance down here.

DO'S AND DON'TS FOR A SOLICITATION CALL

DO:

Be well-prepared
Make sure you are the right one for the assignment
Bring information with you
Know about the campaign
Be committed to the project
Make your own gift first
Be candid about your reasons for calling/meeting
Understand the possibilities for pledging
Get the gift or make a specific date to get it
Thank the prospect--for the gift and for their time

DON'T:

Squeeze your request in at an inopportune time
Ask for two organizations at once
Talk for too long
Say "We have you down for . . ."
Leave without some answer or commitment
Make a lunch or cocktail appointment for solicitation
Get discouraged!

* * * * *

Remember:

People need to know the goals
People like to feel part of a positive movement
Most people will only pay attention for a short time
People are flattered to be asked
Your confidence in the project will make the difference

Also:

Make your gift first . . . make sure it is meaningful in terms of the project and your ability to give.
Giving comes from the heart; rationalization comes later.
No one ever got richer by giving money away, nor do they expect to!
State the case first, ask for the gift second.
Aim high!
Listen, and encourage dialogue. Answer questions. Speak for yourself.

DON'T GET DISCOURAGED! LOTS OF GIFTS TAKE MORE THAN ONE REQUEST.

SUCCESSFUL SOLICATION WITHOUT FEAR

Ask for an appointment, and be frank about the purpose.

Plan in advance!
Know your cause and know your donor.
Stress your organization's importance to the community.

Focus your conversation.
Lead quickly to the campaign and its purpose.
Stick to the subject.
Be clear that you are asking for a contribution.

Explain the budget for the organization and the project, briefly.

Take only 20 minutes.

Ask for the gift!

Suggest an amount, and show how it fits in the giving range for the organization . . . charts, past giving, current pledges.

Tell about your own gift.

Listen to your friends' thoughts.

For major gifts, suggest a family discussion before the pledge.

Get the gift or pledge, or make a specific appointment to pick it up . . . don't have them "put the check in the mail."

Express your gratitude--for the gift, or if you don't get one, for their time and attention.

Self-Study Questions

Basic Issues to Consider Before Starting Fund-Raising

YES NO N/A

____ ____ ____ 1. Has the repository completed an evaluation of its programs, including the development of a mission statement and a plan for accomplishing that mission? (Use the elements in sect. 2 of this guide for such self-evaluation.)

____ ____ ____ 2. Is the leadership of the repository shared by a volunteer governing board and senior staff?

____ ____ ____ 3. Does the repository's governing board establish general policy?

____ ____ ____ 4. Are the administrative duties of the repository the responsibility of the executive director?

____ ____ ____ 5. Will the responsibilities of fund-raising be shared by both staff and governing board?

____ ____ ____ 6. Has the repository sought funds from any of the following types of sources?
   a. Federal (such as the National Endowment for the Humanities or the National Historical Publications and Records Commission)?
   b. State government (such as the Preservation/Conservation Program of the New York State Library's Division of Library Development)?
   c. Local government (such as city and county legislatures)?
   d. Foundations?
   e. Businesses or corporations?
   f. Individuals?

____ ____ ____ 7. Has the repository developed a financial plan that includes both private and public sources of income?

Emulating Successful Fund-Raising Programs

YES NO N/A

____ ____ ____ 8. Has the repository based any fund-raising effort on the merits of its historical records holdings?

____ ____ ____ 9. Does the repository know of any successful fund-raising campaigns that it can emulate?

____ ____ ____ 10. Does the repository share any similarities to the ones with successful fund-raising programs described above?

   a. Is there anyone involved with the institution who could provide a motivating challenge gift, as happened at the DeWitt Historical Society?

b. Does the repository have a board as committed as the YMCA's board to use its influence (write letters, make personal calls)?
c. Are there any individuals (or groups) with a self-interest in the preservation and maintenance of the repository's holdings who may make a financial contribution?

Considering the Public Sector as a Source of Financial Support

YES NO N/A

_____ _____ _____ 16. Has the repository identified projects that are likely candidates for grant applications to public funding agencies? Will these grant projects address an ongoing objective of the repository?

_____ _____ _____ 17. Has the repository considered the amount of staff time necessary for a successful grant application?

_____ _____ _____ 18. Has the historical records program approached its local government for financial support?

The Private Sector as a Source of Support: The Case Statement

YES NO N/A

_____ _____ _____ 19. Has the repository considered the private sector as a potential source of funds?

_____ _____ _____ 20. Has the repository developed a case statement it can use for fund-raising?

_____ _____ _____ 21. Has the repository completed a self-evaluation process that has enabled it to draft a long-range strategic plan that can be used to prepare a case statement?

_____ _____ _____ 22. Does the repository have information about uses of its historical records that have benefitted its community and society in general and that can be used in a case statement?

_____ _____ _____ 23. Has the repository considered how to best present the case statement to potential donors; i.e., length, format, design, and packaging?

_____ _____ _____ 24. Does the repository have a clear statement of mission that can be the basis of a case statement?

_____ _____ _____ 25. Were members of the governing board and repository staff involved in the process of developing the case statement?

Seeking Private-Sector Support: Identification of Prospective Donors

YES NO N/A

_____ _____ _____ 26. Is the repository aware that almost 90 percent of charitable contributions come from individuals?

_____ _____ _____ 27. Does the repository have a development committee that is able to identify potential donors?

______ ______ ______ 28. Has the historical records program effectively identified the potential donors in its community?
______ ______ ______ 29. Has the repository decided to conduct a development study?
______ ______ ______ 30. If the repository has decided to conduct a development study, has it carefully thought about the topics to be covered in the survey and promotional information it would like to use?
______ ______ ______ 31. Has the repository identified who will conduct the development study?

Seeking Private-Sector Funds: Corporations and Foundations

YES NO N/A
______ ______ ______ 38. Does the repository have access to a library that maintains a reference collection from the Foundation Center?
______ ______ ______ 39. Has the repository adequately identified foundations and corporations that may be likely sources of support?
______ ______ ______ 40. Does the repository governing board or staff have connections to area businesses and corporations that may consider financial donations?
______ ______ ______ 41. Has the repository sufficiently studied the needs and requirements of potential businesses and corporate donors?

The Role of Events in Fund-Raising

YES NO N/A
______ ______ ______ 42. Has the repository sponsored events in the past to raise funds for its programs?
______ ______ ______ 43. Has the repository evaluated the fund-raising effectiveness of these events?
______ ______ ______ 44. Can the repository's sponsorship of events be used to develop better public-awareness programs, increased membership, additional volunteers, and thereby assist its main fund-raising efforts?

Looking for Help: The Role of a Consultant

YES NO N/A
______ ______ ______ 45. Does the repository have a dedicated core of volunteers committed to fund-raising?
______ ______ ______ 46. Does the repository have enough time and staff to implement the consultant's recommendations?
______ ______ ______ 47. Does the repository contemplate hiring additional staff for a fund-raising effort?
______ ______ ______ 48. Has the repository compared the cost of hiring additional staff (if that is its intention) with hiring a consultant?
______ ______ ______ 49. Does the repository know of any other institutions in its area that have successfully used a fund-raising or development consultant?

APPENDIX 3
PLANNING SPECIAL EVENTS

This appendix contains a special events planning guide, planning checklist, contract form, event summary, timeline, budget planning guide and notes on planning a bicentennial project, supplied by Julie Bressor, Shelburne Farms, VT.

SPECIAL EVENTS

(A General Planning Guide)

Prepared by
Julie Bressor
Shelburne Farms, VT

Special Events and Public Relations

First, determine the **theme** and **focus** of your event. Refer back to the material from Workshop I to clarify this important step.

Next, identify the **audience** for your **event.** Is it for people in your community; is it primarily for visitors? Do you want to attract adults, children, families, school groups?

Remember to **plan, plan, plan,** then plan some more. Work as a team to accomplish your planning goals. Develop timelines, checklists, task assignments, and coordination as a committee; share the responsibility.

Identify the **staff, performers, volunteers,** and other people you'll need. Make sure everyone knows exactly what's expected of them when; write out the responsibilities. Have all performers sign contracts.

Determine your **technical needs.** Is your event a one day bash or a month-long show? Is it inside or out? Schedule your space, arrange for equipment, plan for parking, think of the public's needs (bathrooms, water, telephone).

Plan for **supplies.** Do you need paper, flyers, banners, tables, chairs, food?

Develop a realistic **budget.** What will all of this cost? Who will pay for it? If you seek grant funds or corporate contributions, know deadlines and procedures.

Prepare for the unthinkable: rain, missing volunteers or performers, accidents, loss of power, plumbing back-up. Know when and where to turn for help.

Plan your **public relations** strategy. Do you want press coverage? Do you want simple calendar announcements? Will you have a poster or flyer to publicize your event? How should you distribute information?

After the fact, **assess you event.** What was best, and worst? Use this assessment for future events planning.

And always, ask others for help, information, ideas. When you're asking for ideas, remember to ask what was the best, and the worst, experience associated with the event.

Shelburne Musem
Special Events Planning Checklist

4 Months in Advance:

Determine Program:
- Goals
- Audience
- Need
- Format
- Arrangements (AV, refreshments, accomodations, registration procedure, etc.. See list for others.)

Determine Program plans concerning:
- •Adminstrative Calendar
- •Collections Department
  - Exhibit support
  - Personnel support
  - Conservation support
  - Photography
  - Housekeeping
- •Education Department
  - Personnel support
- •Public Relations
  - Develop publicity plans
    - -national press
    - -local press
    - -newsletter
    - -poster/flyer
  - Determine deadlines
  - Personnel support
- •Buildings and Grounds
  - Major work requests
  - Personnel support
- •Protection Services
  - Operational procedures
  - Personnel support
- •Revenue
  - Determine fees
  - Personnel support

Notify, in writing, the cooperating departments, summarizing the reponsibilities of each, as determined in the planning process.

Feed deadlines and reponsibilities into the remaining months.

2 Months in Advance:

Program Announcement notice to Switchboard and Protection Services
Conduct appropriate meetings
Send appropriate memos and work requests

1 Month in Advance:

Once again, check all details with:
- Administration
- Protection Services
- Collections
- Buildings and grounds
- Revenues
- Public Relations
- Education

2 Weeks in Advance:

All work requests out
Requisition payments
Requisition purchase orders

After the program:

If necessary, conduct a debriefing meeting
Send any outstanding payments
Send necessary thank you letters
Compile and circulate Event Summary

Planning Tips:

- Plan early
- Remember details. Some may be:
    - Caterer
    - Deliveries
    - Audio-Visual needs
    - Contracts for outside personnel
    - Photography
    - Refreshments
    - Signage
    - Tents
    - Flowers
    - Tablecloths
    - Press coverage of the event
    - Volunteer assistance
    - Memos and work requests regarding tasks to be completed after the program
- Remember to use the appropriate forms:
    - Work Request
    - Program Announcement
    - Program Registration Form
    - Special Activities Memo
    - Special Events Summary

Shelburne Museum
CONTRACT

AGREEMENT between the Shelburne Museum and

____

This agreement is understood that ______________________________ will

provide ______________________________ (said services)

for Shelburne Museum, at Shelburne Museum

on ______________________________ (date)

at ______________________________ (time)

Shelburne Museum agrees to pay ______________________________ the sum

of ______________________ for said services. Payment will be on the date of

services or within 10 days following.

______________________ signed ______________________

for the Shelburne Museum for ______________________

Shelburne, VT 05482 address ______________________

(802) 985-3346 ______________________

phone ______________________

date ______________________ date ______________________

Shelburne Museum
Special Events Summary

Route to: Brian Alexander
Cathy Wood
Gail Rosenberg
Read File

Program Title:

Event Type:

Date: **Time:**

Location(s):

Weather:

Total Registration: **Total Attendance:**

Nature of Publicity: (attach clippings and press releases if applicable)

Description of Program:

Staffing: (include year-round, seasonal, contracted and volunteer assistance)

Comments: (problems, criticisms, and suggestions)

Expenses:

Income:

Submitted by:

Date:

PLANNING TIMELINE

Task	Plans Made	Task Completed
1. Develop planning triad	___	___
a. theme	___	___
b. audience	___	___
c. format	___	___
2. Assign responsibilities	___	___
3. Develop project timeline	___	___
4. Write budget	___	___
5. Develop funding plan	___	___
6. Raise money	___	___
7. Finalize project budget	___	___
8. Implement project timeline	___	___
a. determine location(s), date(s)	___	___
b. organize personnel	___	___
c. prepare publicity plan	___	___
d. have a successful project	___	___
e. cleanup	___	___
9. Evaluate project	___	___
10. Write thank-you notes	___	___

BUDGET PLANNING

	Cash Costs	In-kind
<u>Expenses</u>		
Personnel		
Wages (use local equivalents)		
Honoraria/Fees ($100/day, negotiable)		
Benefits (only for permanent employees)		
Supplies		
Office (paper, xeroxing, etc.)		
Project (ie. tapes for oral history, exhibit supplies)		
Postage		
Telephone		
Publicity & Promotion		
Posters, flyers (production and distribution)		
Radio/TV		
Newspaper Advertising		
Travel		
Mileage ($.24 per mile)		
Other ($25 per day for meals and hotel)		
Food		
Rentals		
Space		
Equipment		
Evaluation & Clean up		
Totals	$xxxx	$yyyy
Cash to be raised	$xxxx*	
Income Sources		
Matching grants		
Town contribution		
Local donations		
Fundraising events		
Other		
Total	$xxxx*	

*Cash income should equal cash expenses.

In-kind expenses are important when applying for matching grant funds.

Planning a Bicentennial Project

I. Four Basic Planning Questions

<u>1. Do you want to celebrate or educate?</u> A project can do one or the other, both, or--if you haven't planned well--neither.

<u>2. Who cares about this project?</u> Is it important for you, the planners? for your organization or institution? for your community? for your audience? Planning and presenting a program will take commitment. Part of your work will be creating and sustaining enthusiasm and commitment to the project.

<u>3. Is the program itself the final goal?</u> Some programs can have the goal of calling attention to an organization, ongoing program, or continuing need in the community. Programs can be fund-raisers. Projects can help organizations achieve their own goals. Programs can be entirely devoted to educating and/or entertaining the community and other audiences.

<u>4. What specific outcomes, if any, do you want from the project?</u> Let your audience and/or the people helping you present the program know what the anticipated outcomes are. Include ways to tell them in your plan and give them tools to move toward those outcomes or activities.

<u>Notes:</u>

II. Planning essentials: A planning triad

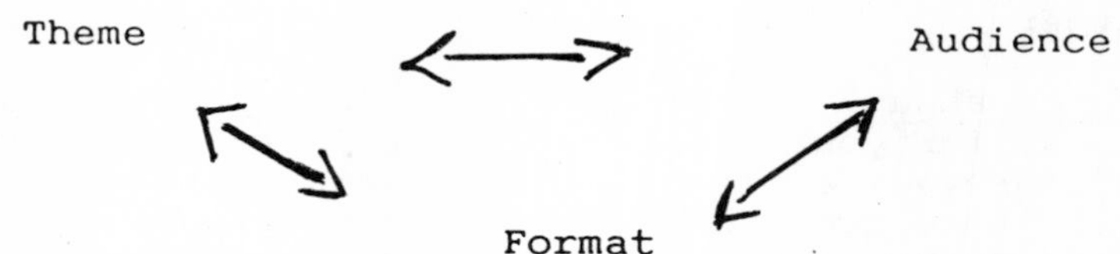

Theme or topic, audience, and format form a triad of central planning issues. They are interlocked and inseparable.

A. Theme and topic

A theme is a broad statement; topics are narrower points of interest within the theme.

Example:

Theme: "Making a Living in Henryville--Work and Enterprise in a Vermont Town"

Topics: "Agriculture in Henryville--Adapting to Change"
"The Henryville Blast Furnace and Forge--A History and Walkabout."

Try to write a clear statement of the theme in one sentence. If it has to be longer, make sure it is no longer than one short paragraph.

1. Significance
--What makes the theme significant or relevant to your community?
--Is this something new or a reworking of what is already fairly well known and widely known?
--Is it important that you present something new in the project or program?

2. How broad or deep is the theme?
--Is it really worth spending your time and effort and the audience's time on the theme?
--Can you identify some topics within the theme? List them.

3. What information related to your theme is available?
--Types of resources:
Manuscripts, articles, books
Speakers
Visual or artifactual items
People to do performances, demonstrations, tours
--Are the resources local? readily available?
--Are there enough resources to accomplish your goal?
--What will it cost to bring them to your community?
--Can you reasonably expect to get them in your community when you need them?

B. Audience
1. Who is your audience?
--Is there more than one audience? Identify each.
--Are you sure there is any audience?
2. Where is the audience? Local, regional, statewide, nationwide, international.
3. Do you know how to reach your potential audience?
Publicity: what kinds of publicity work best for this project?
Networks: who knows whom and how will that help you?
4. Can you reasonably expect that the potential audiences will show up, learn about and use your project?
--Do you expect the audience to come to you?
--Do you plan to bring or send the project to them?
5. Relationship of audience to theme. Which has the highest priority for you?

C. Format
1. What formats are appropriate for the theme and audience of your project. What opportunities, advantages, limitations, does each present?

A list of possible formats (not exhaustive)

-- Conference, lecture (one or series).
-- Forums and town-meeting style programs, debates.
-- Exhibits, demonstrations, "workshops" or other hands-on programs.
-- Media programs: slide/tape, radio, video, film.
-- Oral history collecting. Video history collecting.
-- Reading program, with or without discussions, one or a series.
-- Parades, festivals, fairs.
-- Tours--guided or self-guided: walking, bike, auto, bus, train, boat, air.
-- Publications.
-- Re-enactments, pageants, theatrical presentations, other performances.
-- Building or structure conservation, preservation, or beautification projects.
-- Photography--new photographs, old photographs.
-- Community arts projects--concerts, murals, sculptures, etc.
-- Time capsules and corner stones.
-- Book, document, or artwork conservation or preservation projects.

2. Is there a single best format for this project?
3. Is your project limited to one format? Would linking two or more work well? draw a larger audience? expand your ability to examine the theme?
4. What can you afford to do? (time, money, energy, expertise, community or group involvement). Do you have sufficnet resources of all of the above to produce a main program and satellite programs?

III. Time

GIVE YOURSELF PLENTY OF TIME TO PLAN, RAISE FUNDS, PUBLICIZE, COMPLETE, AND FOLLOW UP THE PROGRAM OR ACTIVITY.

A. Timing

1. When is the best time to present your program? This is related to format and audience choices.
   --Seasonal considerations, climate, and weather as factors for the program.
   --Indoor or outdoor programs.
   --Good travel season? A good program for a time when people stay close to home?
2. When is the best hour to start and end the program or presentation (applies to some kinds of projects only, e.g., lecture or discussion programs, parades, pageants, performances, potlucks and similar gatherings).
3. Marking an anniversary or a specific date. How important is it? How much flexibility can you allow yourself?
4. What other programs will compete with yours? What chances are there for overlap, piggy-backing on other programs in the community or area? Try to find out what else is happening in and around your community on the dates you want to present your program.

B. Planning time

1. Set a target date for the program, or completion of the project. Work backward from there. The more complicated, the more time you need. Think in terms of years when necessary.

2. Make a time-line or schedule of planning activities. Identify who does what, when, and for how long.

Notes:

C. Fund raising time

1. Develop a detailed, complete, and realistic budget for the project. Find out--don't guess--the costs of things, people, and services you need. This tells you how much you need and how much you have. The difference is what you have to get. How are you going to get it?
   - -- Fees
   - -- Sale of products, services related to the project
   - -- Subscriptions (helpful in major publication projects)
   - -- Raffles, auctions, other fund raising events
   - -- Voluntary contributions
   - -- Grants

TRY AS HARD AS YOU CAN TO STICK TO YOUR BUDGET.

2. Develop a plan for raising funds.
   - --strategies
   - --resources
   - --time lines, deadlines, and guidelines

IF YOU PLAN TO USE THE PROJECT TO RAISE FUNDS FOR YOUR ORGANIZATION, HAVE A FUND RAISING GOAL.

D. Publicity time

1. Prepare a publicity plan. What must you do to get the word out? Possible publicity media: newspaper articles and ads, mailings, brochures, posters, radio and TV announcements and media appearances (talk shows, news programs).

2. Work with professionals whenever possible. They know about format, design, timing, costs, lead time, production techniques. They know who to contact and how. Be prepared to pay for this expertise.

3. Ask daily and weekly newspapers about deadlines for news releases; ask radio and TV stations about public service and community calendar announcements.

4. Ask local printers and copy centers about services and turn around time.

5. If you use a bulk mailing permit, ask the post office about delivery. Depending on the time of the year, your bulk mailing can be delayed for days or weeks. It is the last thing to go in the mail carrier's sack. Holiday time--especially November through early January--is the worst time to send a bulk mailing.

GOOD PUBLICITY, CAREFULLY TIMED, IS A KEY ELEMENT IN GETTING A SATISFYINGLY LARGE AUDIENCE.

Notes:

E. Production or preparation time
How much time will it finally take to complete preparations? **LISTS HELP. WHAT HAPPENS WHERE AND WHEN?**

F. Program time
How long will the program or project last? Hours? days? months? a full year? more than that?

G. Followup time
What has to be done to cleanup or follow-up the project? This includes everything from picking up trash to paying the final bills, to publishing results, to completing final reports to co-sponsors and funding organizations, and writing thank you letters to participants and sponsors. Some projects have follow-up time that lasts longer than the program itself.

IV. Personnel
Who will do what?

A. Who is in charge? Someone has to oversee the whole project.

B. Make sure everyone involved in the project knows clearly his or her responsibilities and duties.

V. Evaluation

A. Try to evaluate audience reactions to your efforts. How many people came, used the project, participated in the ways you planned or expected? What did they think of the project?

1. Audience questionnaires, where appropriate and possible, are useful evaluation tools.

--KEEP EVALUATION QUESTIONNAIRES SIMPLE AND SHORT.
--QUANTIFIABLE RESPONSES ARE EASIEST ON THE AUDIENCE AND EASIEST TO USE TO STUDY RESULTS.

2. Interviews are the most effective evaluation tools, but hardest to do, most labor intensive, and require a good sample, enough time, and plenty of tact and persistence.

B. Try to evaluate your own response to your efforts? Was the project worth doing? Would you do it again?

Notes:

APPENDIX 4
VOLUNTEERS

This appendix contains the contents of a workshop handout prepared by Julie Bressor that aids the archivist in establishing a volunteer program, and a sample volunteer application form.

Getting and Keeping Good Volunteers

In our enthusiasm—and sometimes anxiety—about a project, it is easy to impose too much, too fast, on a volunteer, or be tempted to lure a good worker into our group without thoroughly explaining the assignments. In the long run, both approaches will backfire. There are ways to get terrific volunteers, despite everyone's fears. In fact, since the numbers of working women have increased dramatically in the past several years, the number of volunteers has also increased. You must learn new ways to think about volunteerism, seek your helpers from new groups, and learn a new flexibility in your methods of working with volunteers.

In seeking volunteers:

- consider retired people, college students, even high school students. These people have increased consciousness about community activity, and more time than the traditional volunteer groups
- give the prospective volunteer full information about numbers of meetings, times of meetings, whether they will be day or evening, etc.
- explain that fund raising is part of the job!
- don't always go for the proven volunteers...look for new people in town, people who have been showing interest in your organization's activities, friends of participants, people in different income brackets from your traditional volunteers
- tell the prospect *why* you want him or her on the board, and be honest about it!

Once you've got them:

- provide good board orientation
- stick to your work on assignments, meeting times, committee work, etc. Don't under- or over-do it.
- use the board member's expertise effectively
- conserve the volunteer's time
- allow board activities to provide some social pleasure without becoming gossip sessions
- if the board wants to socialize more, program it so that those who do not want to participate will not lose information or the opportunity to be involved in the board's work
- show appreciation
- make sure assignments are clear and manageable
- keep board members up-to-date
- send out minutes and other promised materials immediately after meetings
- make the working relationship between board and staff clear and do not circumvent it for convenience

- whenever possible, take the board member's advice or give it good consideration
- encourage planning
- stay flexible
- always keep the mission in mind!
- find a good balance between encouraging, and asking, a volunteer to take on a job, and graciously accepting a refusal.

Most importantly, keep good lines of communication open with all your board members. Know how they are working and feeling about the organization, be understanding about their temporary problems that may interfere with board work, accept resignations when necessary, and encourage growing commitment whenever possible.

Prepared by
Julie Bressor
Archives Consultant

Washington, DC 20408

DOCENT PROGRAM INFORMATION

Thank you for your interest in the National Archives Volunteer Program. At this time we are seeking volunteers who are interested in serving the National Archives as docents. Please complete and return the enclosed application and we will arrange an interview to answer any questions you may have.

I have enclosed information about the National Archives and a description of our docent program which prepares volunteers to be specialists in introducing visitors to the valuable holdings and activities at the National Archives. The success of our visitor orientation depends on the interest and enthusiasm of the volunteers.

The essential qualifications for an Archives docent are: 1) an interest in people, particularly children, since some of our tours are for school groups; 2) an interest in history and research; and 3) an interest in education. Enthusiasm for sharing these interests is equally important. Finally, the volunteer program requires a real commitment on the part of the volunteers. Although time commitments are only three to six hours a week, docents attend occasional extra workshops during the year. We have found that those who put the most time and effort into the program receive the greatest reward. We are looking for individuals who want this kind of challenge.

Since the training time is intensive and is conducted by the professional archival staff, we request an initial two-year commitment of 100 hours of service per year for two years. In addition, there is a monthly volunteer business/education meeting on the second Wednesday morning of each month. There are also optional field trips and other programs.

In return for your participation, we can offer you a very exciting, challenging and rewarding experience. I look forward to receiving your application in the near future. If you have any questions, please do not hesitate to call the office at (202)501-5205.

Sincerely,

Patricia Eames

PATRICIA EAMES, Coordinator
Volunteer and Tour Programs
Office of Public Programs
(202)501-5205

Position Description For A National Archives Docent

Dictionaries define the word *docent* as a teacher. It derives from the Latin verb, *docere*, to teach. Docents are an integral part of the National Archives Office of Public Programs' mission because it is their duty to inspire, develop and encourage in visitors an appreciation for America's documentary heritage. The purpose of this volunteer staff position is to conduct the Behind-the-Scenes tour and document workshops for the general public, students, community groups, and other visitors who may be accorded special status.

Duties

1. Presents tours and workshops as designed by the Volunteer and Tour Office and consistent with the program's goals and objectives.

2. Uses the inquiry method, as opposed to a strict lecture pose, to create a warm and inviting atmosphere for the visitor.

3. Records tour and workshop statistics as requested by the Volunteer and Tour Office.

4. Reads and re-reads their training manual and engages in independent research and relevant learning processes to augment their formal training.

5. Stays abreast of current information concerning the Volunteer Program and the National Archives.

6. Accepts all periodic evaluations of performance in a spirit of cooperation and flexibility.

7. Works under the direct supervision of the Education and Outreach Coordinator and overall supervision of the Volunteer Coordinator. An attitude of flexibility, respect, collegiality, and courtesy in all relationships with other volunteers and staff is required.

8. Functions at all times within the guidelines for the ethical standards of conduct for volunteers of the National Archives and Records Administration (NARA).

Qualifications

1. Ability to communicate with the general public.

2. A genuine interest in and enjoyment of public service.

3. Ability to attend all required training sessions.

Training Requirements

Upon acceptance in the docent program, docent-candidates must attend a training course for two days a week over a five-week period, followed by a period of on-the-job training which will culminate with a practice tour that must be completed before March 1st.

Docent Requirements

- **In-Service Training**

Upon completion of the docent practice tour, docents will be required throughout their tenure with the National Archives to attend 7 in-service training sessions each year. These training and informational sessions for docents are usually conducted by National Archives staff. In-service training months are September (*September begins the docent In-service year*), November, December, January, February, March, and May (*May ends the docent In-service year*). The docent has a choice of at least two possible dates to attend during the month.

- **100 Hour Yearly Service Requirement**

Anything associated with your role as a docent counts with regard to hours. Personal research not related to an approved docent function does not count. Coming in only to attend a performance or lecture in the theater does not count as well.

- **The Successful Completion Of Periodic Evaluation Tours.**

We believe evaluations work and are beneficial to volunteers and staff alike, and ultimately to the public we serve. What works for us is a confidential evaluation that recognizes your strengths and if necessary, offers constructive criticism in a manner that is encouraging in both tone and purpose.

NATIONAL ARCHIVES

Application for Volunteer Service

Thank you for your int⌐ ⌐st in the National Archives Volunteer Service Program. Please complete this form and .etu.n it to the address below. We will contact you later after the receipt of your completed application.

Namr ______________ Date ______________

Address ______________

____

Telephone (H) ______________ (W) ______________

Date of Birth ______________

Education ______________

____

Work Experience ______________

____

Volunteer Experience ______________

____

Special Interests ______________

What previous contact, if any, have you had with the National Archives?

____

____

Availability: Days per week ________ Hours per week ______________

Applicant Signature ______________

Please use the reverse side to tell us why you want to be a National Archives Volunteer and how you can make a positive contribution to the institution. Indicate the type of service you prefer, if you have a preference.

Also, please provide us with the names, addresses, and telephone numbers of two references who are not relatives.

Volunteer Office, NE-V
The National Archives
Washington, DC 20408
202-501-5205

About the Authors

MATT BLESSING ("Studies in Public Relations: Politicians and the Press in the Archives"). Now collections development archivist for the Mass Communications History Archives, State Historical Society of Wisconsin, Blessing previously worked as a public records and manuscript processing archivist. He holds undergraduate and master's degrees in history from, respectively, the University of Wisconsin-Stevens Point and the University of Montana, and a M.L.I.S. from the University of Wisconsin-Milwaukee.

JAMES and JULIE BRESSOR ("Troubleshooting"). James Bressor, a journalist, is policy analyst in the office of Howard Dean, Governor of Vermont. He holds a bachelor's degree in journalism from George Washington University. Now archivist at Shelburne Farms, Shelburne, Vermont, Julie Bressor was previously Vermont's Assistant State Archivist. Her professional activity includes service as education specialist for New England Archivists for whom she conducted workshops on public relations, president of the Vermont Museum and Gallery Alliance, and co-chair of the Society of American Archivists' Public Information Committee. She holds a bachelor's degree in history from the University of Vermont. The Bressor family lives in Montpelier, Vermont.

PAUL CONWAY (Co-author, "Talking to the Angel"). Conway, who holds a master's degree in history and a Ph.D. in information and library studies from the University of Michigan, conducted research at the National Archives from 1990 to 1992 on how researchers use the agency in Washington, D.C., and how government agencies use digital imaging and optical disk technology. During 1988 and 1989, he was Preservation Officer of the Society of American Archivists, carrying out a national survey of archival preservation programs. From 1977 to 1987, he was a staff archivist at the Gerald R. Ford Library (National Archives) in Ann Arbor, Michigan. He is now head of the Preservation Department at Yale University Library.

TIMOTHY L. ERICSON ("Anniversaries: A Framework for Planning Public Programs"). Beginning his career as university archivist and area research director for the University of Wisconsin-River Falls, in 1984 Ericson moved to the State Historical Society of Wisconsin, then became education officer for the Society of American Archivists in 1987. As director of the Milwaukee Urban Archives and adjunct instructor of the School of Library Information Science and Department of History at the University of Wisconsin-Milwaukee, Ericson has developed wide general use of his archives, ranging through faculty, alumni, public school, and community organizations, and has published in archival and historical journals in both the United States and Canada on the development of public programs. He has served on numerous SAA committees, including those on goals and priorities and education and professional development, nominating and program committees, and on significant Midwest Archives Conference committees. He is a Fellow of the Society of American Archivists and a member of the Academy of Certified Archivists. He holds an undergraduate degree in history and German and two master's degrees, the first in American history from the University of Wisconsin-River Falls, and the second in library science from the University of Wisconsin-Madison.

ELSIE FREEMAN FINCH (Editor and co-author of "Talking to the Angel"). Following stints as chief of the manuscript branch at Olin Library, Washington University, St. Louis, and assistant curator of manuscripts for the Archives of American Art, the Smithsonian Institution, in 1973 Freeman Finch moved to the National Archives, where as chief of the Education Branch she directed nationally delivered publication and teacher training programs for elementary through collegiate level instructors and students and adult learners, as well as conferences, workshops, lectures, demonstrations, and a theater program designed to encourage use of National Archives resources. She was co-founder and first chair of the Mid-Atlantic Regional Archives Conference and has been active for more than 25 years in the Society of American Archivists, serving on its Council, executive committee, as presidential nominee, and as chair of major committees. She is a Fellow of the Society and a member of the Academy of Certified Archivists. She has published and consulted widely on the use of historical resources. Before becoming an archivist-cum-educator, she taught in secondary school and university, was a freelance writer and editor, and worked for advertising and publishing firms. She holds an undergraduate degree in history and literature from the State University of New York-Albany and a master's degree from Boston University in literature and education. She is currently project editor for a series of case studies in electronic records and automated records management to be published by SAA under funding from the National Historical Publications and Records Commission.

JUDY P. HOHMANN ("Money Talk"). Coordinator of Public and Educational Programs for the New York State Archives and Records Administration, Judy Hohmann is author of the fund raising segment of *Strengthening New York's Historical Records Programs: A Self Study Guide,* funded by the National Historical Publications and Records Commission. Before joining NYSARA, she was an associate of The Development Consortium, a fund raising consulting firm, and was Executive Director of the Combined Health Appeal in Albany, N.Y. She holds a bachelor of arts degree from SUNY-Binghamton and a master of arts in political science from Stephen F. Austin University, Nacogdoches, Texas.

MICHAEL F. KOHL ("Studies in Public Relations: Once in a Hundred Years"). Now head of Special Collections for Clemson University Libraries, Clemson, South Carolina, Kohl's career has also included positions in Wisconsin, Rhode Island, and California, working with public, college, religious, and corporate archives as well as a wide range of manuscript collections. Active in the Society of American Archivists and a member of the Midwest Archives Conference since 1973, he is also active in numerous records management and library organizations. A Certified Records Manager and a member of the Academy of Certified Archivists, he holds masters' degrees in British history, library science, and business administration from the University of Wisconsin-Madison.

MEGAN SNIFFEN-MARINOFF ("In Print, On Air"). Before she became an archivist, Sniffen-Marinoff worked in public relations for the Boston Ballet and in the editorial, layout, and sales departments of a large chain of suburban Boston newspapers. She is now College Archivist for Simmons College and Director of Archives Management Programs for the Simmons College Graduate School of Library and Information Science. A founding member of the Boston City Archives Commission, she is an advisor to the WGBH-Boston Archives, a trustee of the New England Historic Society, and past president and board member of the New England Historic Genealogical Society and the New England Archivists. She earned a bachelor of arts in journalism from Boston University and a combined master of arts in history and certificate in archives management, historical editing, and the administration of historical societies from New York University.

PHILIP F. MOONEY ("Modest Proposals: Marketing Ideas"). Mooney is manager of the Archives Department, Coca-Cola Company, where he has worked since 1977. His programs have brought the historical component of Coca-Cola to national prominence, and he has recently been active in establishing Coca-Cola museums in Italy and Japan. He has chaired the Business Archives Committee of the Society of American Archivists, been a member of the Public Information Committee, and has led more than 10 SAA workshops on the management of business archives. Among his numerous publications are three chapters on business archives recently appearing in volumes of readings in the public history and library fields. He holds undergraduate and master's degrees in history from, respectively, Boston College and Syracuse University.

JAMES M. O'TOOLE ("Studies in Public Relations: The Pope and the Archives"). O'Toole is assistant professor of history at the University of Massachusetts-Boston, where he directs the master's degree program in history and archival methods. He had previously served as archivist of the Roman Catholic Archdiocese of Boston. He is the author of several books, including *Understanding Archives and Manuscripts*, and has been active in the Society of American Archivists since 1980. In 1993, he was made a Fellow of the Society. He holds a master's degree in history from The College of William and Mary and a Ph.D. in history from Boston College, where he also received his undergraduate degree.

AUDRAY BATEMAN RANDLE ("Volunteers and Friends"). Randle was curator of the Austin History Center, Austin Public Library, for 13 years. There she wrote a column on Austin history for the *Austin American-Statesman*, edited a pictorial history of Austin, co-authored several books, and appeared in numerous other publications. As a principal in obtaining funds for and directing the renovation the old library building, she received both local and state recognition. Active in the Society of American Archivists, she has been president of the Society of Southwest Archivists and was awarded their Certificate of Merit in 1983. Since her retirement in 1988, she has been a partner in David B. Gracy II & Associates, consultants in archival and records management. She holds a bachelor of science degree from Pennsylvania State University.

Index